THE SHEEP THAT GOT AWAY

THE SHEEP THAT GOT AWAY

Michael J. Fanstone

MARC
Tunbridge Wells

First published 1993

Unless otherwise indicated, biblical quotations are from
the New International Version.

ISBN 1 85424 181 8

British Library Cataloguing-in-Publication Data.
A catalogue record for this book is available
from the British Library.

Designed and Produced in England for
MONARCH PUBLICATIONS
P.O. Box 163, Tunbridge Wells, Kent TN3 0NZ by
Nuprint Ltd, Station Road, Harpenden, Herts AL5 4SE

*This book is dedicated
to those who have been closest to me...
My wife, Diane, and children,
Becky and Stephen,
my parents, Marjorie and Ron
Fanstone
and the two churches I have had
the privilege of serving as pastor,
Horley Baptist Church and
Emmanuel Baptist Church, Gravesend*

Contents

Chapter 2   Making Some Discoveries   49

Chapter 3   Identifying the Issues   65

SECTION 2   TACKLING THE ISSUES

Chapter 7   Problems of Irrelevance   159

Chapter 8   Problems of not Finding God   181

SECTION 3   RESPONDING TO THE TRUTH

Acknowledgements

WHILE I HAVE WRITTEN this material and take full responsibility for it, I could not possibly have done so without the support and encouragement I received from others. I express my deep appreciation to each one publicly. Their willingness and readiness to take an active part in this project means so much.

There are four main areas where I have received help.

a) Administration. My wife, Diane, and Church Office Secretary, Rosemary Green, have provided vital and valuable support.

b) Research. Many hard-pressed ministers and church leaders have directed questionnaires to those in their churches and others who have left. Other Christians in different parts of the country have actively secured completed questionnaires for me by taking to the streets and talking to people at random: my wife, Diane, Rev David Clarkson, Rev David Green, Dick Martin, Marlane Miller, John Palmer, Rev Stuart Petty, David Reynolds, Andy Roper and Liz and Alan Spooner. I also express my deep gratitude to all those who were willing to contribute the information contained in the three surveys referred to in this book.

c) Improvements to the text. A number of people have helped in different ways to make this book more accurate and clear: John Bowden, Valeria Brigden, Geoff Cook, Colin Crowhurst, Diane Fanstone, Rosemary Green, Rev Brian Snellgrove, Marion and David Thompson.

d) Illustrative material. Peter Phillips, a graphic artist, transformed numerical tables into imaginative and easy-to-follow diagrams. Peter Barkley, a former art teacher, provided the illustrations.

My last comments are reserved for two key people. The encouragement and help I have received from Peter Brierley, Director of The Christian Research Association, has been notable. His wisdom, skills and experience have been made available to me even when he had many other pressures. Finally, had it not been for Tony Collins, my publisher, this book would never have happened. I approached him with sketchy plans and very limited experience. For some reason he felt able to trust me with the project and his subsequent support and counsel has been invaluable.

All those I have referred to above are thoroughly committed Christians. This leads me to thank and praise the Lord for leading them to help me, and to him directly for the inspiration, motivation and energy he has given me to see this project through.

Michael J Fanstone

Foreword

MOST CHRISTIAN LEADERS are aware that Europe represents one of the most challenging mission fields in our world today. As a consequence of this recognition there has been a good deal of talk about the need for mission, for outreach, for evangelism. In my own writings I have argued strongly that the church needs to move from a purely pastoral model to restore an emphasis on those ministries, such as the apostolic, the prophetic and the evangelistic, which will help the church to become more missionary in its structures.

However, the concern for a broader missionary structure does not mean the abandonment of a concern for good pastoral practice. Michael Fanstone's work is a timely reminder of the need for an emerging missionary church to be just as concerned with what happens to those who are already in the church as it needs to be with strategies for bringing people into the life of the church. The author of this book paints a disturbing picture of the present pastoral situation of the church in Britain. It makes sobering reading.

Those who have engaged in evangelism, whether on a personal basis or as part of church-based initiatives, will know something of the reservoir of anger and hostility that is directed towards the church. Michael Fanstone's research goes some way towards understanding how that anger has developed. It is not just the case that those who have been directly hurt are angry with the church, but others in the community are perhaps more aware of the casualties of church life than we are ourselves. At the very least it needs to make us very careful in any evangelistic endeavour that suggests 'we have the answer' or 'we have something that you need'.

The author's actual encounters with those in pain have been important in producing some suggested solutions. A friendly word of caution points to the fact that although Michael's work is based on thorough research of a key problem, his helpful suggestions as to how we might tackle the problem are not necessarily themselves the result of the actual research itself. His reflections are based on much Godly wisdom and experience but the reader might want to use this book as a catalyst to extend the thinking of the church in offering additional solutions in a wide-ranging debate. Just such a debate seems to have emerged from the excellent research project which resulted in the book by John Finney, *Finding Faith Today*.

Every good piece of research inevitably raises further questions for others to investigate. This book is no exception. Michael has rightly concentrated his thinking on what we might do to improve the existing internal life of the church. But part of the problem also lies in the pressures on the church which come from the culture in which we operate. It is noticeable how age plays a significant part in defining the kind of problems which those who have left the church express. Those who are under the age of 35 seem to have a different emphasis in their experience of the church as compared with those who are older. This key finding is significant in that those who are younger are much more likely to reflect the concerns of our current culture with the church as compared to the poor pastoral practice of the church. This would seem to suggest that we need to think much more carefully about how we can evolve new forms of the church which will address much more directly the themes of relevance and direction.

The work of Lesslie Newbigin has highlighted the extent to which secular culture has attacked and undermined the apparent relevance of the Christian faith. The central claim of secularism is that the Christian faith is not credible as an explanation of the world in which we live. Any faith can only have value as a system of private beliefs which may provide some help to some individuals. The church by implication is seen as a private club for people who might like to share such beliefs. Newbigin has also pointed to the extent to which the church has colluded with this presentation.

Even apart from Newbigin's analysis we have to acknowledge that many inside the church as well as outside it use the model of 'club' as a way of understanding the church. Especially in nonconformist churches the way in which we organise is strongly reminiscent of club life. We appoint our chairman, our secretary and our treasurer and then create our club rules. While one understands that the church everywhere around the world draws to some extent on society for its organisation models—for example, the American church often feels like a business corporation—it is also true that we are called to be citizens of heaven as well as citizens on earth. The values of the Kingdom can never be the values of the club. Michael Fanstone's work is a contribution which helps us reach beyond the club to embrace the Kingdom.

Martin Robinson

Introduction

M ONDAY 4TH MARCH 1991 was not a good day for part of God's family on earth. On that day the findings of the English Church Census that had been conducted on Sunday 15th October 1989 were published. They told of a substantial and significant exodus of people from the churches over the previous decade.

In many countries around the world the 1990s have been designated 'The Decade of Evangelism'. In the UK as elsewhere fresh initiatives have been blossoming. Church planting is on the agenda of most Christian denominations and streams. There is a sense of expectation in many churches that God is going to work in new ways through his people as 2000 AD approaches.

Yet looking at the most recent statistical information we see the stark reality. Numerically the churches in Britain are in decline. People are dropping out of our churches. God's sheep, to use the picture language of Psalm 23 and John 10, are wandering away from the fold.

Two or three times after the results of the English Church Census were published, I attended sessions where MARC Europe's former European Director, Peter Brierley, mastermind of the whole operation, was interpreting the findings. Two things in particular struck me. The first was disconcerting. The number of people attending English churches had declined in the past decade from 11% to 10% of the population. This represents very many lost people. The second was amazing. It seemed to me that most of the churches and their leaders were not over-concerned about this decline.

I had a period of sabbatical leave to come and wanted to use it wisely. Increasingly I sensed that God was encouraging me to study the reasons why so many people are dropping out of the Christian church. Fairly early on I discovered that this is not just a phenomenon in British churches, but is a matter of concern in a number of other countries too. No recent research seemed available in the UK, so I committed myself to study the issues in the time available to me.

My first task, of course, was to find out why some people who used to go to church no longer go. With as many as 1000 people a week leaving English churches I assumed it would not be too hard to track down a number of them. I was wrong! Locating former church-goers proved a long, arduous task, but when I found some of them, what they said has been most illuminating.

I have uncovered a lot of pain, hurt and disillusionment. The Christian church, which should set an example of love and acceptance, seems to have the capacity to leave a trail of destruction in its wake. I am not suggesting that the churches and their leaders are wholly to blame. Regardless of who is at fault, a number of people are simply relieved to be out of the church. Some of them have no intention of returning; the pain and hurt has been too intense. Whether these people have rejected Christ too is not clear. My guess is that in most cases their relationship with him suffered when they left the church.

Having now had personal contact with a few hundred such people I feel in one sense as if I have a mission. They have given up on the church. Some of them, quite clearly, have given up on God too. Having read their responses in the questionnaires I feel I have a duty to represent these people. They were not in church last Sunday and they will not be there next Sunday. Rightly or wrongly they now have no means of having their voice heard. Their insights are lost to those of us still within the Christian church. It is not that *they* had an axe to grind and sought me out. Rather I needed *their* help and sought *them* out and received their cooperation. I am grateful to each of them because I believe they have tried to be open and honest. In my view they deserve to be taken seriously because if we fail to do so I fear they will be joined by others who at the moment are still with us.

We simply cannot allow this leakage to go on. We have lost too many sheep already. It must be breaking God's heart to see part of his family in this pattern of continuing decline. I hope this book will help us to recognize the areas of difficulty that provoke people to leave our churches so that we can then take whatever remedial steps are necessary to stop the flow. I trust we will act quickly and responsibly. As a minister myself I am attempting to implement the results of my research in my own church.

It may help if I expand just a little on my personal situation. I use the term 'born-again Christian' of myself and am happy to be classified also as an evangelical and a Baptist with charismatic tendencies. For most of my years as a pastor I have been an avid reader of church growth books and have no doubts at all that the Lord wants to see his church grow as many more people find new life by getting to know him personally. However in my pastorates I have not only had the joy of seeing many newcomers find the Lord—I have also seen far too many existing Christians slide out of church life. My wife and I and our leadership teams have found this painful and hard to handle. We still do.

I am a Christian praying for a mighty move of God in the next few years. Like General Booth, I intend working as if everything depended on work and praying as if everything depended on prayer. I trust that this book will be used by God in some way to help his church plug the gaps so that far fewer people are lost from his church than in recent decades. I would love us to reach the next millenium as part of a church that is alive, strong and effective.

Finally, I need to clarify two important points. First, this book is essentially about churches in the United Kingdom (with the exception of Northern Ireland). The Church Census conducted in October 1989 related to England only. However in the main Survey introduced in Chapter 2, I have gone beyond the boundaries of England for data in order to obtain a broader response. Secondly, this book is concerned only with people who used to go to church regularly and do not now. It takes no account of those who move from one church to another.

MICHAEL J FANSTONE
Gravesend, Kent
November 1992

SECTION 1

Facing The Facts

CHAPTER 1

Surveying the Changes

THERE WAS A TIME when half the British people went to church on Sundays. That was long ago. In those days health-care was basic, many people were poor and no-one had yet seen or heard of television. This was the era when renowned preachers like Charles Haddon Spurgeon at the Metropolitan Tabernacle in London attracted huge congregations of 5000 twice on Sunday. Victorian Britain was a very different place to the Britain of today.

Yet as life in Britain has changed over the decades, so church attendance has plummeted. This is tragic when we consider the purpose for which Jesus came into the world. He was sent so that sinners could see, understand and respond to God's grace and be 'no longer foreigners and aliens, but fellow-citizens with God's people and members of God's household' (Eph 2:19). Motivated solely by love, God wanted rebellious human beings to become part of his spiritual family.

More than that, he desired that once they had responded to his love, they should live as his representatives on earth. Jesus told his disciples, 'Go and make disciples of all nations' (Mt 28:19) and said that when the Holy Spirit came upon them they would be his 'witnesses in Jerusalem, and in all Judea and Samaria, and to the ends of the earth' (Acts 1:8). Christians are called by God to immerse themselves in the real world as his ambassadors, although Jesus was careful to clarify that 'they are not of the world any more than I am of the world' (Jn 17:14). Christians are to live distinctive lives for God in whichever era of history, culture or class of society they find themselves. As they do, God will work through them to win others to himself.

Two things are therefore important. First is the quality of their lives. What Christians *are* is fundamentally more important than what they do or say. They need to live by the words of Jesus, 'You are the salt of the earth' (Mt 5:13) and 'You are the light of the world' (Mt 5:14). Through their positive holy influence, God works to change the world for good. Secondly, the number of them is important. As in any sphere of life, sheer numbers have significance. God can obviously accomplish substantially more through one thousand committed Christians than he can through ten.

It is at this point that we see how tragic it is that church attendances have slumped in our land. We are not so naive as to believe that when half the population attended church every person was an active and committed Christian. What is clear, though, is that if fewer people go to church it must weaken the Christian influence within the nation as a whole. This has happened. A vast amount of ground has been lost and the erosion continues.

When we look at the statistics for England alone we notice how startling the rate of decline has been.

Table 1 Percentage of English population attending church[1]

Year	% of population in church
1851	39
1871	50
1900	30
1930	30
1952	15
1979	11
1989	10

Naturally we need to ask why this has happened. In due course we will examine internal issues related to the churches themselves, but first we will look at the society in which the churches are placed. The fact is that the British churches exist and function in a thoroughly different environment now compared to the days when Queen Victoria ruled the British Empire.

1. CHANGES IN SOCIETY

It may be that my memory is bad, but as I grew up in the 1950s I do not recall forever hearing about high levels of inflation, the breakdown of family life, homelessness or alcoholism. My perception is that the whole atmosphere in Britain has changed since those days. In no way am I lured into imagining that those post-war years were idyllic for our nation. I am aware of the austerity measures that were only gradually phased out after the Second World War ended. Life today is infinitely more comfortable and convenient in so many ways, and yet along with greater prosperity have come other social phenomena that are far less welcome.

Our impersonal society

David Winter makes an interesting observation about the way British people have altered. We are no longer a nation of joiners. Sociological changes have meant that people do not take part in group activities as much as they did. We have, instead, become a nation of receivers.[2] Television has undoubtedly made an enormous impact, and the proliferation of fast food and take-away restaurants seems indicative of a general swing of the population towards having whatever it wants served up quickly, efficiently and with the minimum of personal effort. If you want to play chess, why join a club when you can buy a computer game and try to outwit it from your armchair at home? If you want religion you can take advantage of services broadcast on radio or TV. As a consequence, football matches and cinema audiences as well as churches have suffered. Life is more impersonal than it was.

Our unemployed society

Sadly, unemployment and redundancies have become commonplace today. Because of technological advances unemployment is rising in previously labour-intensive industries. Young people today have a tough time finding work. One school leaver I know had to prove herself better than dozens of other candidates to be appointed to work for just six months in a building society branch. I know other youngsters who have been unemployed for some considerable time.

Our demoralized society

In one sense it is hardly surprising if demoralized, bored and frustrated young people unleash their feelings on society. It would be far more comfortable for the rest of us if they did not. Yet while many opportunities exist for some, others seem to have very few reasons for feeling optimistic about their future prospects. The main findings of a national survey of 509 youngsters between the ages of 16-24 conducted in September 1992 include:

* The fear of the dole queue blights their lives.
* One in three youngsters is staying on in education to brave the economic recession.
* Four out of every ten youngsters feel that state education has failed them.
* There is almost total distrust of politicians.
* Half those questioned are eager to take any job just to be in work; they are not work shy.[3]

Young people (and others) in Britain are having a hard time.

Our criminal society

The dramatic increase in crime is a major concern of many in Britain today. In 1893 burglary and robbery accounted for 9% of all crimes committed; by 1986 it was 25%.[4] In the spring of 1992 those who lived in London had cause to be worried. Statistics showed that property crime had risen to a higher level in the British capital than in all other European Community capital cities.[5] While figures showed that crime is rising rapidly throughout western Europe, the statistics for England and Wales are alarming. By 1990 the number of crimes increased by 69% over the previous ten years to 4.5 million. England and Wales experienced 79 crimes per 1,000 of the population and now

Londoners are more likely to be a victim of car crime or burglary than anywhere else in the EC. In crimes of violence only Berlin, among the larger cities, has a higher rate than London, says the report. It is not so long ago in Britain that it was thoroughly safe to go out and leave house windows open and doors unlocked; today a burglar alarm is almost mandatory.

Our multi-racial society

There have also been changes in the people who live in Britain over the past few decades. I do not recall any children in my primary or grammar school who were not white-skinned and Anglo-Saxon in origin. Our son, however, goes to a school where near to 50% of the children have Asian backgrounds. Many speak Punjabi at home. Since the 1950s Britain has opened its doors to vast numbers of immigrants. While having the freedom to settle where they chose, they have tended to congregate in areas close to others from their part of the world. There are, for instance, large numbers of Asians from India in the West Midlands, East Midlands, east and west London and along the Thames into Kent. Inevitably this means that the area changes. I pass many small Asian shops and businesses on my way to the office every day. Our church is located in the heart of the Asian community in Gravesend. To see people wearing saris or turbans is as natural and normal for me now as eating cornflakes for breakfast.

Our stressed society

Among the changes that Britain is having to cope with, though, is one that people particularly resent. Just recently we returned home from France where we had a family holiday in the Loire Valley. The pace of life seemed so slow and serene and while the children found it dull, my wife and I found it very relaxing. We appreciate occasional visits to the Channel Islands for the same reason. Life in Britain, however, seems so pressurized and tense. A survey published in 1991 revealed that 16% of Britons thought their lives were 'very stressful' and a further 36% saw theirs as 'fairly stressful'.[6] The four most popular answers to the question, 'Which of the following causes the most stress in your life?' were:

	Male	Female
Money	36%	29%
Work	33%	20%
Not having enough hours in the day	15%	19%
Children	8%	18%

For over five years I have been responsible for producing and presenting *Open Line*, a live phone-in counselling programme broadcast every Sunday night on Kent's Independent radio station, Invicta Radio. This is essentially a music station, yet this programme has been maintained because of the high level of demand from listeners for counselling help. Since May 1987 over 5000 people have phoned or written to us because of their worry or concern about an area of their lives. There is a proliferation of counselling agencies springing up across the country as caring people make themselves available to help those who suffer stress and anxiety. Stress can and does, it seems, affect us all.

2. CHANGES IN FAMILY LIFE

Not only has society in general altered over the years, so has life within many of the individual homes that make up our communities. The description of marriage in Genesis 1 and 2 has always seemed adequate to me as indicating the structure for the family units God intends in his world:

1. God creates male and female (Gen 1:27).
2. A man leaves his parents and is united to his wife (Gen 2:24).
3. They become one flesh (Gen 2:24) signifying both the sexual relationship that is now open for them to enjoy and the permanence of this relationship.
4. This couple is now to 'Be fruitful and increase in number' (Gen 1:28). It is into this secure and stable environment of love that children are to be brought into the world.

None of this is to suggest of course that every person (and certainly every Christian) will get married. As Julia Duin reminds us eloquently, both the Founder of Christianity and many of those who worked closely with him were single.[7] It does however provide us with God's general pattern for society that is later endorsed by Jesus (Mt 19:4-6).

Yet how the climate in Britain has changed. Back in 1966 no more than 5% of people cohabited before marrying whereas by 1987 it was 60%.[8] Maybe it is no wonder when we see that the average wedding in Britain now costs £7,640. A recent survey of newly-weds shows that the price of a top wedding, paying the most for everything, is £47,600. The smallest possible bill would be £311 if the bride were prepared to make do with an outfit that cost a mere £50.[9]

Not unexpectedly in the circumstances, the number of births outside marriage in the UK has rocketed from 81,000 in 1981 to 220,000 in 1990, an increase of 147%.[10] Of all children born to women under 20, 80% are now born out of wedlock. It seems that having children outside marriage is increasingly socially respectable. Also significant is that in a survey of engaged couples in the UK for *Wedding and Home* magazine, 40% accepted that their marriage would not last. As many as 5% of brides and 4% of grooms admitted to having been unfaithful to their partner even before their wedding day.[11]

It is no wonder there are so many divorces—up from 35,000 in 1966 to 180,000 in 1986.[12] One in three marriages fails and the proportion is rising. Sadly among the eminent casualties are members of the British Royal Family. It seems most unfortunate that the breakdown of celebrity marriages provokes enormous public interest whereas strong, stable and genuinely happy marriages rarely gain any media attention at all. There are plenty of these left, yet the typical British family with a married mum and dad and 2.2 children is much rarer than it used to be. In October 1992 the Office of Population Censuses and Surveys released figures showing that 42% of marriages where the couple are first-timers and have lived apart before the wedding now fail. When partners have been divorced or co-habit before marriage (or both), the failure rate rises still further.[13] Britain now has a million one-parent families, and some feel that things are made no easier with homosexuality being recognized as an acceptable sexual orientation and practice.[14]

3. CHANGES IN THE MORAL CLIMATE

We live in an era when many of the moral standards that were taken for granted just a few decades ago are regarded as thoroughly prudish and narrow. Now, 50% of girls lose their virginity by the age of sixteen and an estimate suggests that only 8% of women are virgins on their wedding day.[15] In the light of this it is no surprise that the number of abortions in the UK has trebled since 1969. In 1989 the number carried out in England, Scotland and Wales totalled 194,133 with fewer than 2% undertaken because the baby would be handicapped. Since David Steele introduced the 1968 Abortion Act those abortions carried out to save the mother's life or to prevent grave damage to her health amounted to just 427—a mere 0.013%. Professor Shebut Campbell, Emeritus Professor of Medical Statistics at the University of Wales and former World Health Organisation Statistician for Britain, has reported that by the end of 1989 three million children had been aborted since the Act came into effect.[16] This leaves, he says, 'three million bereaved, three million occasions on which a gynaecologist has betrayed the Hippocratic Oath'.

Things are no better in the United States of America. There it is calculated that every day...

> 8,441 teens become sexually active
> 2,756 teens become pregnant
> 1,340 babies are born to teen mothers
> 2,754 babies are born out of wedlock.[17]

The abuse of children has been featured heavily in news stories in the past few years. Spurgeon's Child Care estimates that 40,000 children a year are currently at risk of abuse.[18] It appears from stories such as that from *Dynasty* actress, Catherine Oxenberg,[19] that while children have been being sexually abused for years, it is only now that the moral climate has changed sufficiently for this to be brought out into the open. Mercifully the sexual abuse of children is still perceived as thoroughly perverted, but crimes against innocent minors continue to be committed.

Pornography and the deliberate use of sexuality for commercial ends is on the increase too in Britain. Three national daily papers now regularly display naked or near-naked girls. The top shelves of most newsagencies are filled with printed material that many recognize as pornography. It is not just for male consumption either as equivalent publications for women are also on sale. Britain's moral standards are certainly deteriorating. Compared to the godly moral codes taught strongly in Scripture, Britain is thoroughly decadent in certain aspects of its national life.

4. CHANGES IN THE ECONOMIC SITUATION

As a child there was a time when I received 1/- (one shilling, now 5p) pocket money. Even then it did not go very far. Today more than half Britain's 11-16 year olds own at least one of these items: a television, a camera and a hi-fi.[20] Many own a computer too. Children between five and eleven, as well as teenagers, are becoming increasingly sophisticated in their ability to influence their parents' spending, a recent report says. There is, it seems, more money in the average person's pocket or bank account to spend these days. By 1990 it was estimated that there were nineteen million television sets in Britain,[21] and it is reckoned that by 1995 one in three British homes will have satellite TV and one in twelve cable TV.

Yet despite these indications of wealth there is also a higher level of personal debt than maybe ever before. While eight million credit cards have been issued in Germany and two million in France, a massive twenty-nine million have been dispersed by banks in the UK.[22] Easy-to-come-by credit facilities are highly convenient for those who have no financial worries and who have the discipline to use them responsibly. For those, however, who have insufficient income to pay back the amounts borrowed in order to enjoy an enhanced lifestyle there can only be pain and torment as creditors close in. One of the subjects that often draws the greatest number of calls on Invicta Radio's *Open Line* counselling programme is 'Debt'. Our regular specialist is kept busy trying to help the many people who have got out of their depth financially.

An interesting survey comes from New Zealand. A selection of people, some who believe in God and some who do not, were asked their most important goal in life. People in *both* categories indicated highly that a prosperous life was for them the most important goal of all. No wonder that a letter received from Jim Veitch, a member of the Faculty of Arts at Victoria University of Wellington, said that he reckoned it to be the most secular country in the world.

Figure 1: NEW ZEALANDERS' MOST IMPORTANT GOAL IN LIFE

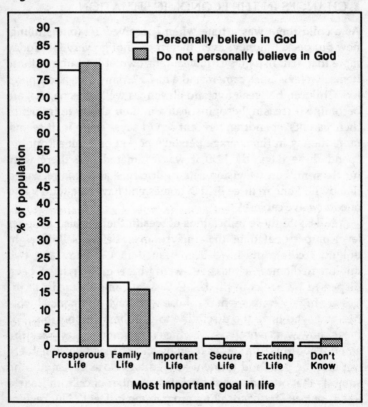

A sobering note on the western world's obsession with money and the things it can buy comes from Nicky Cruz. In his book, *The Final Warning* he expresses his deep conviction, based particularly on the prophet Nahum's ministry, that God will judge the USA and allow its economy to collapse. He foresees a time when other nations will withdraw the money they have invested in banks, and the country will be unable to finance its massive debt. At that time, says Nicky Cruz, 'it will all tumble and fall'.[24]

Many nations, including Britain, may have a price to pay in the long-term. It is the materialistic attitudes and lack of contentment and satisfaction in people despite all the privileges and possessions they have that is worrying. In a series, 'Idols for Today' in *LandMARC*, 'newness' is identified as a concept that shapes the behaviour and values of many Western Europeans. 'Newness', it says, 'is the fad of saying, "We must have something new"'.[25] This presents both a challenge and an opportunity to the churches.

5. CHANGES IN OUR LEISURE PATTERNS

My father has a very elderly 9.5mm cine projector on which he shows equally elderly movies that he made in his younger days. While I have visual evidence that he drove a comparatively well-equipped Lanchester car with pre-selector gearbox before the Second World War, I also sense that outings were less common than they are today for some.

Saturday is my day away from church responsibilities and often, to get away from the phone, we have a family day out unless we are visiting friends or entertaining at home. It is not always exhilarating, but more often than not it includes a visit to a well-known fast food restaurant. That tends to keep the children happy if nothing else! On average it appears that Britons now have a shorter working week and a higher percentage of income to spend on leisure. There are certain times and ways in which people use their free time.

Holidays

In the past twenty or thirty years it seems as if a whole mammoth leisure industry has blossomed around us. True, Thomas Cook's was always there to sell us holidays, but both the style and amount of advertising that is devoted to how we spend our leisure time now appears increasingly intense. Holidays for many are longer these days and trips abroad, usually to find the sun, are a major source of spending.

Table 2 Destinations, holidays abroad by UK holidaymakers[26]

	1970	1976	1980	1985	1989
Spain*	30	27	23	31	29
France/Monaco	11	11	14	12	12
Greece	2	6	7	8	8
Italy	10	8	8	5	5
Rep Ireland	8	4	3	2	4
Austria	8	3	3	4	3
Portugal	1	0.5	2	4	3
Malta	1	3	5	1	2
Yugoslavia	2	3	2	3	2
W Germany	5	5	4	4	2
Netherlands	2	2	2	2	2
Switzerland	4	2	2	2	1
All in Europe	88	82	80	84	79
USA	2	3	7	2	6
Canada	2	3	3	1	2
Rest of World	10	11	13	9	15

Notes: The figures above are by percentage of all UK holiday-takers visiting that location.
* Including Ibiza, Minorca, Majorca, Canaries (not Canaries prior to 1985).

These figures show the clear popularity of Spain, even over its nearest rival, France. Fewer UK holidaymakers now travel to the Republic of Ireland, Italy, Austria, Germany and Switzerland; more visit Greece, Portugal, Malta and the USA.

Back home the leisure industry is hard at work trying to encourage people to spend time and money here. While most paid-for attractions saw a fall in the number of visitors in 1991, an amazing number of people still took advantage of these very varied attractions.

Table 3 Top ten admission-charging attractions in 1991[27]

	1991	1990
Madame Tussaud's	2.2m	2.5m
Alton Towers	1.9m	2.0m
Tower of London	1.9m	2.2m
Natural History Museum	1.5m	1.5m
St Paul's	1.5m	- *
Chessington World of		
Adventure	1.4m	1.5m
Science Museum	1.3m	1.3m
Blackpool Tower	1.3m	1.4m
London Zoo	1.1m	1.2m
Flamingo Land, N Yorks.	1.0m	1.1m

* St Paul's did not charge in 1990.

Apart from St Paul's Cathedral (open for worship rather than as a tourist attraction), the top ten paid-for attractions are open on Sundays—which brings us to consider how this day has changed.

Use of Sunday

For many people Sunday will always remain a day for pottering around at home; others continue to use Sunday primarily for worshipping God. We are under pressure, however, to use Sundays more creatively. Why not go shopping at a supermarket that is open illegally, and pay a visit to a car boot sale? One Sunday I was preaching in Thanet, Kent and passed a school on the way to the church. There was a major traffic jam outside as cars and vans fought to get into the school grounds to park for a boot sale. The writer of a newspaper article estimates that about one million people buy and sell unwanted household goods in around 20,000 fields and car parks every weekend.[28]

There have already been many changes to the way British people spend their Sundays, and more are likely. In a rather cynical newspaper article, *The Other Side of America*, by Bernard Cornwell, he suggests that 'American religion is...more user-friendly than its British counterpart'. He observes that 'most (of the churches) are crammed every Sunday'. The church car parks are massive, he says, but while very many people go to church they do not 'perceive church attendance as an exclusionary activity. It is perfectly normal to attend church in the morning, a football match in the afternoon and a theatre in the evening, and any bishop who tried to anathematise the last two occupations would very soon find himself queuing up at a job centre.' [29]

Increasing alcohol-abuse

Many people do not only use their leisure time going on holidays, visiting attractions or cramming as much into a Sunday as possible. They like to socialise and they like to drink. Pubs have always been popular meeting-places for those who like the informal atmosphere and the chance to unwind with friends and a pint. However, recent figures show those in the 16-24 age group spending on average £14 per week on alcohol. Not surprisingly, they also spend a lot of time in pubs and clubs.[30]

Figure 2: AVERAGE HOURS SPENT IN PUB/CLUB

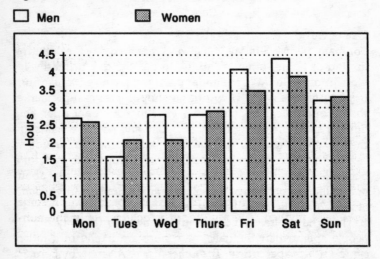

The Health Education Authority has compiled alarming statistics about the way that alcohol affects people's lives...

* Under-age drinking starts young: 89% of boys and girls in England have had their first 'proper drink' by the age of 13.[31]
* One thousand children aged under 15 are admitted to hospital each year with acute alcohol intoxication. All need emergency treatment, many in intensive care.[32]
* Young people's tolerance to alcohol is generally lower than adults and begins to affect their judgement long before they reach the legal limit to drive. At the legal limit an experienced adult driver is twice as likely to have an accident, while for a young driver the risk can be five times as great.[33]
* In a year an average adult in the UK drinks about 240 pints of beer or lager (136 litres), about 20 bottles of wine (14 litres), 8 litres (1.3 gallons) of cider *and* about 5 litres of spirits.[34]

Today we are led to believe that it is not natural or sensible to relax by either sitting quietly in the garden or going out for a gentle stroll in the country. The mass of advertising material that bursts into our homes gives the impression that there is so much more enjoyment to be found when we spend money. We are told that our lives will be enriched if we go there, buy this or try drinking that. No wonder we find stress and anxiety levels rising as people rush here and there trying to discover what they sense is missing in their lives. Some of us could tell them...

6. THE RELIGIOUS BALANCE HAS CHANGED

It is also true that there have been major changes in the general religious and spiritual life of the nation. Back in 1871 when 50% of the population went to church there was little other spiritual activity apart from that generated by the Protestant and Catholic churches. In a changing country, however, many new religious ideas and groups have emerged and older ones have in some cases been revived. The number of people active in the non-trinitarian churches (particularly the Jehovah's Witnesses and the Mormons) increased from 7% of the population of the UK to 8% between 1980 and 1990,[35] and Muslims now account for 3% of the national population.

While visitors from the cults may greet us in the streets or on our doorsteps, however, they are at least fairly easy to spot. Less readily discernible is the wide range of philosophies and beliefs that merged to create what is often called the New Age Movement. Three main strands have combined to form it:

Visitors from the cults...are fairly easy to spot

1. Belief that this is the Age of Aquarius
2. Eastern religion and belief
3. The world of the occult.[36]

At the heart of New Age belief is the understanding that god is everything and everything is god. If people just become conscious of god within them and tap into their divine potential they will move towards the 'higher self'.

In the 1992 British General Election the Natural Law Party emerged from nowhere to fight many constituencies. The Party took vast amounts of newspaper space to promote itself and to reveal (if you read enough of the small print) that 'the ultimate goal of the Natural Law Party is for everyone to enjoy Heaven on Earth through the implementation of Maharishi's Master Plan to Create Heaven on Earth'. Add to this the number of psychics who get exposure in the media and one realises the extent to which the New Age Movement has so quickly infiltrated the life of Britain. Many in the nation, aware of their spiritual needs, are finding what they perceive to be help from psychics and quasi-occult sources. Why are they not coming to the churches instead?

7. THE CHRISTIAN CLIMATE HAS CHANGED

It is in this situation of change and (some would say) decay that the Church of Jesus Christ seeks to minister and grow. As we established earlier, God's purpose is for Christians to live out their faith as his ambassadors in the thick of this world and its problems. This is no easy task in an environment that is changing as fast as ours. Things would possibly be easier to contend with if all the changes were *outside* the church. Even then there would be enough variables to make life tough, but the fact is that there are changes and movements going on *inside* the churches too. We will touch on some of them.

The charismatic movement
The pentecostal movement was first seen in Britain around the turn of the century. It was not until the 1960s, however, that what is now known as the charismatic movement began to affect churches in mainstream denominations. This, together with a revolution in Christian worship music, has altered the style of services in some churches almost beyond recognition. Worship

has become more informal, relaxed and fluid with a greater focus on the person of Jesus Christ, his victory, triumph and the ministry of the Holy Spirit. Many congregations now use contemporary worship songs as the predominant means of bringing their praise and worship to God.

Fewer paid ministers

Paid ministers in British churches have become less common, especially in the Church of England where numbers virtually halved between 1900 and 1990.[37] Since 1970 the number of Methodist ministers has been declining sharply too. In many sectors of the church, however, this has provided the opportunity for members of the fellowship to take a more active role in leading worship. It was back in 1964 that Mark Gibbs and Ralph Martin wrote *God's Frozen People* in which they argued that ordinary Christians ought to be encouraged to use their gifts more in God's service.

This is now happening. In the Diocese of Rochester, to take just one example, lay readers now outnumber ordained clergy. The situation is likely to continue to change rapidly as the Church of England starts to ordain women to the priesthood.

In many churches there seems to be a greater openness for God to work through more people in the congregation than previously. This is particularly the case in some of the independent churches in Britain, especially those that have only been founded within the last twenty years or so. Here members seem particularly to sense that they are valued and that they have something unique to contribute. According to the 1989 English Church Census, the House Church Movement is also the fastest-growing segment in the Christian church in the country today. Between 1979 and 1989 its growth amounted to 144%.[38] This contrasts sharply with the numerical decline or static attendance of most other denominations and streams.

Fewer nominal Christians

Maybe one of the most striking changes in British churches, although one of the hardest to detect, is the decline in nominal

Christianity. Broadly speaking there are three categories of those who call themselves Christians:

1. Notional Christians—people who say they are Christian but are neither church members nor regular church-goers.
2. Nominal Christians—people who say they are Christian and are church members but who do not regularly attend church.
3. Active and practising Christians—people who say they are Christian and are church members who regularly attend church.

Some fascinating research into what nominal Christians believe has been undertaken in Leeds.[39] Some 72% of respondents believed in God, of which number 91% saw him as love, 88% as Creator, 79% as Protector, 75% as Father, 73% as Redeemer and 59% as Sustainer. While 89% believed Jesus Christ to be 'someone special', only 43% thought he was the Son of God. Of the people surveyed 76% had thought about whether there is life after death, but only 40% of this number believed in it, with 44% not believing and 16% saying that they did not know.

Recently Professor Eddie Gibbs undertook research on people in Australia, Scotland and the USA who had stopped attending church for more than a year. Having learned of their reasons for doing so he presented his understanding of why people become nominal Christians:

1. They are ignorant of Christ's claims upon their life.
2. They are resistant to Christ's claims upon their life.
3. They are overly dependent on the spiritual experience of other Christians.
4. They are atrophied—their gifts were never identified and they were not encouraged to get involved in ministry.
5. They are burned-out as a consequence of over-commitment.[40]

Whatever the causes for any individual case of nominality, statistical evidence exists to show that from 1979 to 1989 the number of nominal Christians dropped from 9% of the English population to 8%.[41] This amounts to over half a million people.

Peter Brierley estimates that this is because two-thirds of them had died. His conclusion is that 'in Protestant churches in Great Britain people are, as it were, sitting less and less on the religious fence. Either one is religious or Christian or one is not. If one is, then there is a behavioural pattern which is part of one's Christianity, namely attendance at church'.[42]

Having described these changes both in society and within the churches, we are ready to look more deeply at the churches of Britain. We will do so largely using information given us by those who used to be a part of them but no longer are.

Notes

1   Monica Hill, 'Countering Decline', *Church Growth Digest*, Year 12, Issue 4, Summer 1991, p 1-2,7.

2   David Winter, *The Battered Bride* (Monarch: Eastbourne, 1988), p 185.

3   Survey by Audience Selection of young people throughout Great Britain on September 27-28, 1992 published in *The People*, Sunday 4 October 1992.

4   Home Office figures quoted in *Statistical News*, (HMSO, London, 1987).

5   Survey conducted for *The Independent on Sunday*, published 19 April 1992.

6   Gallup Survey reported in *Daily Telegraph*, 5 July 1991.

7   Julia Duin, *Sex and the Single Christian* (Marshall Pickering, London).

8   Peter Brierley, *Change in Europe* (MARC Europe: London, 1991), p 9.

9   Statistics from *Wedding and Home* magazine, reported in *Ashford Citizen*, 8 April 1992.

10   Statistics from 'Population Trends 67', Spring 1992.

11   Statistics from *Wedding and Home* magazine, October 1990, reported in LandMARC, New Year 1991.

12   Peter Brierley, *Vision Building* (Hodder & Stoughton: London, 1989), p 47.

13   Office of Population Censuses and Surveys figures from *Daily Mail*, 3 October 1992, p 31.

14   Peter Brierley, *Change in Europe*, p 9.

15   Quoted in *LandMARC*, Easter 1988, from a Conference on Reaching the Nation's Children conducted by the Evangelical Alliance, January 1988.

16   *Life Link*, Issue 1, February 1992, Firgrove Family Trust, Southampton.

[17] *International Urban Associates Magazine*, Chicago, Winter 1991, quoting from material supplied by Children's Defense Fund, Washington DC.

[18] *Open House*, Issue 21, Spurgeon's Child Care, Bedford, p 4.

[19] Article in the *Sunday Mirror*, 7 June 1992, p 4.

[20] Mintel survey, "Children—The Influencing Factor' reported in the *Daily Telegraph*, 25 October 1991, and quoted in *LandMARC*, MARC Europe, London (Spring 1992), p 3.

[21] Michael Shoesmith, EMA Conference, November 1990, quoted in *Change in Europe*, MARC Europe: London, 1991.

[22] Peter Brierley, *Change in Europe*, p 6-7.

[23] Extracted from A.C. Webster and P.E. Parry, *The Religious Factor in New Zealand Society*, 1989.

[24] Nicky Cruz, *A Final Warning* (Kingsway: Eastbourne, 1992), p 123-127.

[25] From *LandMARC*, MARC Europe: London (Summer 1992), p 3.

[26] Statistics from BTA Digest of Tourist Statistics No.14, quoted in *The Berlitz Guide to the British Traveller*, 1970-1991.

[27] Statistics from BTA Poll published in the *Daily Telegraph*, 23 May 1992, p 10.

[28] Article in the *Daily Mail*, 12 October 1991, p 24.

[29] 'The Other Side of America', Bernard Cornwell, *Daily Mail*, 5 February 1992, p 8.

[30] Statistics from 'Young Britain: a Survey of Youth Culture in transition', Euromonitor & Carrick James Market Research, quoted in *LandMARC*, MARC Europe, London (New Year 1991), p 5.

[31] HEA/Young People's Health & Lifestyles 1989.

[32] *BMJ*, Vol 292, 22 February 1986.

[33] *The Facts about Drinking and Driving*, Transport and Road Research Laboratory, 1986.

[34] Brewers' Society, 1991.

[35] Peter Brierley, *'Christian' England* (MARC Europe: London, 1991) p 205.

[36] Michael Cole, Jim Graham, Tony Higton, David Lewis, *What is The New Age?* (Hodder & Stoughton: London, 1990), p 9-11.

[37] Peter Brierley, *A Century of British Christianity* (MARC Europe: London, 1989), p 54.

[38] Peter Brierley, *'Christian' England*, p 45.

[39] The Leeds Common Religion Project, Dr Robert Towler.

[40] Eddie Gibbs, 'Nominality—The Challenge of the 1990s', *LandMARC*, MARC Europe, London (Summer 1992), p 1.

[41] Peter Brierley, *'Christian' England*, p 204.

[42] Peter Brierley, *Church Nominalism*, p 12.

CHAPTER 2

Making Some Discoveries

WHEN JESUS SAID 'I will build my church' (Mt 16:18), he had very high expectations for its future. This was of course utterly reasonable since he, the Son of God, was to be the builder. The fact that he said these words to Simon Peter made it plain that he intended to use imperfect human instruments to fulfil this work. When Jesus continued by declaring that 'the gates of Hades will not overcome it' he was making clear that no sinister power would eradicate his workmanship on earth. Even at this stage in his ministry, Jesus could foresee that his church would be a formidable force for bringing men and women into the Kingdom of God.

In the Acts of the Apostles, Luke records how the Holy Spirit came upon some one hundred and twenty believers. He goes on to tell how, from that Day of Pentecost onwards, the Gospel of Jesus was proclaimed throughout an increasingly large area of the world. Progress was not always easy and the personal cost to some evangelists and church planters was high. Yet more and more people heard about Jesus and responded to the message of salvation. Jesus' hopes were being realized! As the Apostle Paul says, 'God was reconciling the world to himself in Christ, not counting men's sins against them' (2 Cor 5:19).

When Christianity first came to Britain is uncertain. Gerald Coates wonders if it was by AD 40.[1] We know that the Good News of Jesus came with Augustine in 597 and that by 1851 39% of the English population attended church.[2] Yet by 1989 it had dramatically dived to 10%,[3] with nothing to suggest that the decline has been halted by now. It can be argued of course that church attendance does not give a thoroughly accurate indication of those who have personally responded to the Good News of Jesus. This is true and yet there is undoubtedly a major correlation. Since the first days of the Early Church, believers in Jesus have both wanted and needed to be together to share, encourage one another, worship and pray (Acts 2:42-44). While life in the nation has undoubtedly changed radically, the decline of church attendance suggests some serious problems in the spiritual life of the churches too.

It also suggests to me at least that God may have something vitally important to say to his people at this time. In Amos 1:2 the prophet introduces his message to the people of God with the words, 'the pastures of the shepherds dry up, and the top of Carmel withers'. Haggai was given the hard task of convincing the returned exiles that they should heed God's call to rebuild the temple in Jerusalem. He suggested that they 'give careful thought' to their ways (Hag 1:5). He also reminded them that although they 'planted much' they 'harvested little'; they 'earn wages, only to put them in a purse with holes in it' (1:6). In both cases it is in times of *loss* and *decline* as opposed to growth and prosperity that the prophets suggest that God has something to tell his people if they will listen.

What then is God saying to his church in countries like Britain where there is a decline in church attendance? Believing that the Lord reveals himself and his truth through a variety of means, I set out to explore what is causing ordinary men and women to abandon going to church. The decline from 11% to 10% from 1979 to 1989 amounts to a substantial average drop-out rate of a thousand people a week. The churches can only be compared to a rusting bucket that allows water to escape from the bottom while constantly being topped-up.

To keep things in perspective, however, we need to note that there are signs of life and encouragement in parts of the British church. The Anglicans, for instance, logged 60,000 confirmations in 1991,[4] while from 1975-1989 the Independent churches grew by over 75%. The Afro-Caribbean and Pentecostal churches notched up increased Sunday attendances too.[5] None of this was

The churches are like a rusting bucket...

enough, though, to offset the decline in Church of England, Salvation Army, Methodist, Roman Catholic and United Reformed churches. Here the leakage in places was alarming.

To understand this leakage I needed some contemporary research data and devised a survey of a sample of those who no longer attend church to explore their reasons for leaving. I then began to work at the problem of how to get it to the people who could furnish the information I needed. It is one thing knowing that a thousand people a week are leaving the churches—but who are they? Where are they? After consultation it seemed that

I might discover who some of the most recent non-attenders are by contacting ministers and clergy from all the main Christian denominations and streams. I created a list of 300 Christian leaders by random selection from denominational directories.

I then wrote to ask these ministerial colleagues if they would help me by giving me up to five names of people who used to go to their church but do not now. I told them that I would then write to these people explaining the research and enclosing a questionnaire to be completed and returned. I received only 135 completed questionnaires (out of a potential of over 1500). Now I understand why the Consumers' Association *Which* magazine sometimes says when reviewing consumer articles, 'Too few members reporting for reliable information'. I knew I had inadequate data.

Action was called for! Armed with a clipboard I took to the streets in an attempt to find people who used to go to church and no longer do so. I have been careful to avoid interviewing in the town where I live as I could not afford my objectivity to be threatened. I excluded anyone who has moved from one church to another—only those who used to attend but do not go to church regularly now come within the parameters of this study. Aided by others I gained a further 338 completed questionnaires by this means. These with a further thirty-six from miscellaneous sources brought the total to 509. Now I could start work!

The sample of people who participated in my Survey has been analysed and compared with the national average.

Table 4 Sex of people taking part in the survey

	Male	Female
National average %	49	51
Survey participants %	50	50

It is also important to see how the ages of the people surveyed compare to the average across Britain.

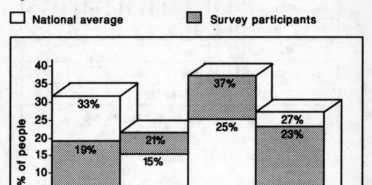

Figure 3: PROPORTION OF AGES OF SURVEY PARTICIPANTS

☐ National average   ▨ Survey participants

It is true that those interviewed for my survey have tended to be older rather than younger. Yet these are the people who in the past years and decades have experienced the Christian churches in this country and who, in many cases, have rejected them. It is *precisely* these people whom I set out to locate. We need to hear what impressions and past recollections of churches and the Christian faith they have.

I analysed the data from these 509 people to see who they are and what background they had in the church. Each questionnaire asks 'Which denomination were you associated with most recently?'

While responsible attempts were made to elicit sufficient data from denominations grouped as 'Others' that would allow them to be analysed separately, inadequate numbers were received. Consequently these other streams have been grouped together for analysis although they are very varied. This is evident from a breakdown.

Figure 4: DENOMINATIONAL BREAKDOWN OF PEOPLE SURVEYED

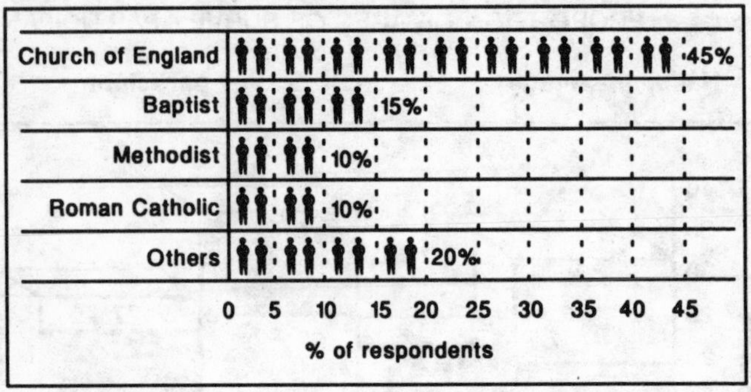

Table 5 Denominations combining to create 'Others'

Denomination/stream	Number of respondents %
Mainline churches	12
Pentecostal churches	3
Independent churches	3
Others	2
Total (= 100%)	509 respondents

It is also important to see the spread of the ages and denominational background of the people surveyed.

Naturally, an attempt was made in the Survey to collect balanced information from which to work. Where we see unexpectedly low or high figures in Figure 5, interesting questions are raised. Do the comparatively low percentages of Anglican and Methodist under 25s, for instance, suggest that these denominations attract fewer young people? Does the lower proportion of 25-34 year-old Baptists surveyed suggest there are fewer of this age-group in Baptist churches? Does the lower percentage of 55 and overs in Roman Catholic and the 'Other' denominations suggest that older people leave these churches more quickly if unhappy? Also, is the high percentage of older (55+) Methodists

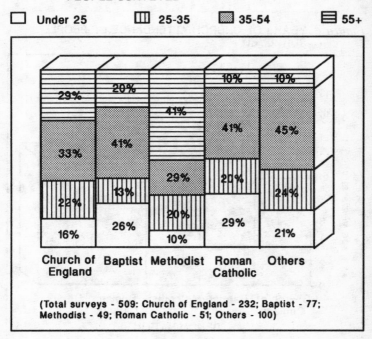

Figure 5: AGE AND DENOMINATIONAL BREAKDOWN OF
PEOPLE SURVEYED

☐ Under 25   ▥ 25-35   ▨ 35-54   ☰ 55+

	Church of England	Baptist	Methodist	Roman Catholic	Others
55+	29%	20%	41%	10%	10%
35-54	33%	41%	29%	41%	45%
25-35	22%	13%	20%	20%	24%
Under 25	16%	26%	10%	29%	21%

(Total surveys - 509: Church of England - 232; Baptist - 77;
Methodist - 49; Roman Catholic - 51; Others - 100)

answering the Survey a pointer to the fact that this denomination is a particular haven for the elderly?

Looking at the Figure overall, we need to recognize that it is
these people who have had contact with Christianity and
churches and who have now chosen to stay away. This was
clearly, for most, not a snap decision or one taken lightly. It is
not unusual to come across a questionnaire that tells of a person,
now a non-church-goer, who attended for thirty or forty years.
People are prepared to change the habits of a lifetime to escape
from something it appears that they can tolerate no more.

Desperate measures are being taken by some. Not everyone who completed a questionnaire indicated for how many years they went to church, but many did.

Figure 6: YEARS OF CHURCH ATTENDANCE OF PEOPLE
              SURVEYED

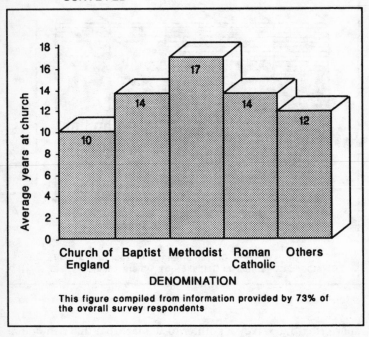

This figure compiled from information provided by 73% of the overall survey respondents

What we see is that the people who completed the Survey have given years of their lives to being at church regularly each Sunday. Some 54% of surveys show that the respondent used to attend church once a Sunday, while a further 31% said they attended more than once a Sunday. We can calculate that the average person surveyed has probably sat through a minimum of 650 services and sermons over 13 years before deciding not to go regularly any more. This figure is based on going to church once a Sunday for fifty weeks of the year.

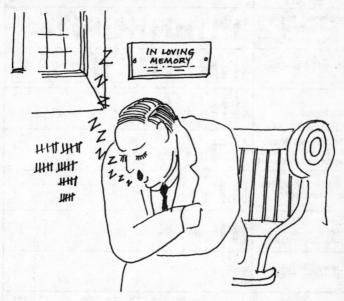

...sat through 650 sermons...

Yet what happened in those years when they went to church regularly? Those completing surveys were asked about the extent to which they or their parents had been committed to a church.

Many of those surveyed, therefore, are from families where there was at least some kind of religious acceptance even if their parents were not themselves church-goers. Over three-quarters of those surveyed were taken to a church for a special service as a baby and just under this number were taken or sent to Sunday School. They grew up with at least some kind of God-awareness even if the Christian faith as such never became very real to them.

The confirmation figures are interesting, especially as the Survey showed that children as young as nine are confirmed in

Figure 7: CHRISTIAN BACKGROUND OF THOSE COMPLETING
SURVEYS

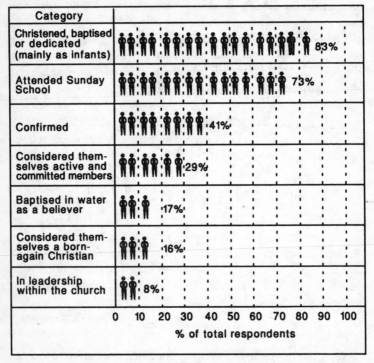

Category			
Christened, baptised or dedicated (mainly as infants)	83%		
Attended Sunday School	73%		
Confirmed	41%		
Considered themselves active and committed members	29%		
Baptised in water as a believer	17%		
Considered themselves a born-again Christian	16%		
In leadership within the church	8%		

0   10   20   30   40   50   60   70   80   90   100

% of total respondents

the Roman Catholic Church and that confirmation seems almost expected in many Church of England parishes at around the age of fourteen. As we shall see presently, Anglican and Roman Catholic confirmation services can provide a wonderful opportunity for a person to dedicate themselves to God. However, unless the person is ready spiritually for such a step of dedication, it seems to have little long-term effect on their life. That so many who have been confirmed drop out of churches must surely raise questions about the readiness of children to make such a deep commitment with sincerity.

Believers' Baptism takes place in certain denominations when a Christian is immersed in water following a profession of faith. Candidates are often encouraged to give a personal testimony to the congregation of their relationship with God through faith in Jesus before being baptized. This greatly reduces the likelihood of people being baptized who have not had a personal encounter with Jesus Christ.

That over a quarter of those surveyed should claim to have been active and committed members of their church provokes two comments. First, that in this sector we have those who have taken a serious share of the load in church life in the past. They have been the doers, those dedicated enough to accept at least a measure of responsibility. Maybe it was singing in the choir, taking a Sunday School class or running a meeting. It is this group that was missed most from their church when they stopped attending; they left gaps behind.

A second comment is provoked by the conclusion that if 29% were active and committed, 71% never were. In all their years in church they never took the opportunity to become involved—or maybe were never invited to do so. This is a high proportion to have on board in any church as inactive pew-warmers, but appears perfectly normal. Experience suggests though that it is often left to 20-30% of the attenders in many churches to take the full responsibility for maintaining and running them.

It is sad that 8% of the non-attending respondents were once leaders. They have been where the action was, where notable and maybe bold decisions had to be taken. Often they had responsibility not only for activities and programmes but for people too. Others with needs perhaps leaned on them for support, encouragement, prayer ministry and guidance. Now, for whatever reasons, they are not just out of church leadership, but out of the church. They seem to have no opportunity for ministry in God's service any more within the church that Jesus founded.

These surveys, then, come from a mixed group of people, but they have one thing in common if nothing else. Whereas they once went to church usually at least once a Sunday, now they do not. How then do they spend their Sundays? Those completing the Survey had the freedom to tick as many categories as was appropriate.

Figure 8: USE OF TIME ON SUNDAYS

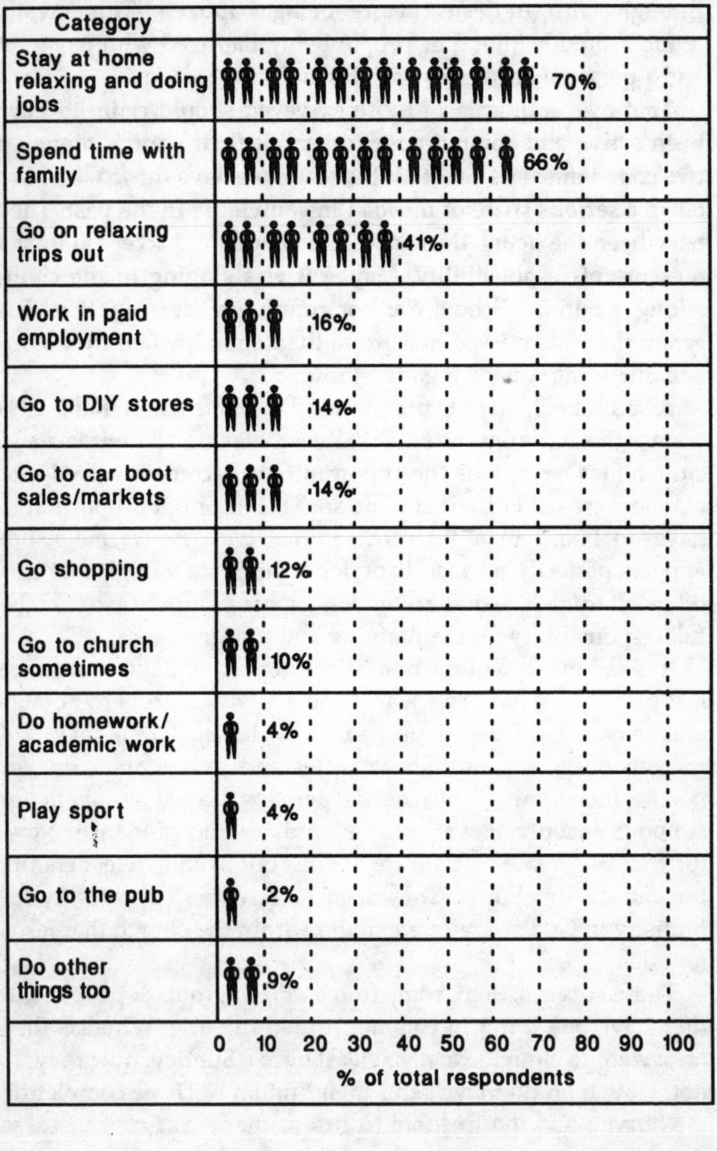

Category	
Stay at home relaxing and doing jobs	70%
Spend time with family	66%
Go on relaxing trips out	41%
Work in paid employment	16%
Go to DIY stores	14%
Go to car boot sales/markets	14%
Go shopping	12%
Go to church sometimes	10%
Do homework/ academic work	4%
Play sport	4%
Go to the pub	2%
Do other things too	9%

0 10 20 30 40 50 60 70 80 90 100
% of total respondents

Former church-goers seem to use Sunday primarily as a day to relax. They take advantage of time to engage in other activities and invest time in relationships that cannot be enjoyed during the rest of the week. Within this group there seems to be a desire and determination to 'Keep Sunday Special' and different, although regular committed church-going is not now part of their weekend programme. Those who said that they 'do other things' listed many diverse activities. These included attending orchestral concerts, writing letters, staying in bed, working on local hospital radio, serving as a Special police constable, baby-sitting, undertaking St John's Ambulance Brigade duties and serving as a volunteer at the local zoo.

Having understood something about these people whose personal circumstances have been revealed on their question-naires, we need now to look carefully at their answers to the key question. We must discover why we lost them, and what it was about the churches they attended that provoked them to stop going. They had the opportunity to answer 'Yes', 'Maybe' or 'No' to a series of possible reasons. We can therefore distinguish between what they perceived to be the key issues and those that were secondary. Those who completed surveys were told that they could answer as many categories as was appropriate (see Figure 9).

That such a diverse catalogue of complaints should be hurled at British churches by those who have the credibility to bring them is alarming. However these are not the only issues raised by those who completed the Survey. Respondents also had the opportunity to add other reasons why they no longer attend church.

A few people said that the lack of transport stopped them going to church. Three admitted that another human relation-ship had got in the way, four spoke of their feelings of guilt that kept them away while two admitted to not being able to make a full commitment. A number referred to their confusion over some theological issues. Two said that they did not like what they had become since going to church, and one adamantly objected to the constant references to money and the need for church-goers to give more. Five reported that the easiest way

Figure 9: REASONS WHY PEOPLE DON'T GO TO CHURCH ANY LONGER

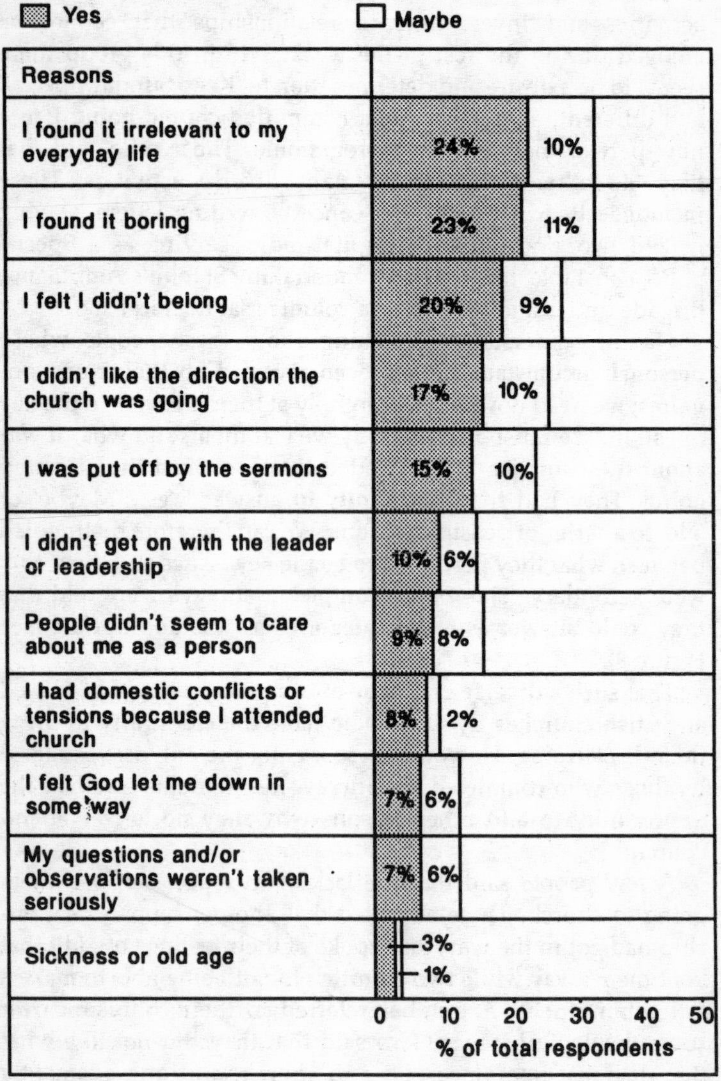

▨ Yes   ☐ Maybe

Reasons	Yes	Maybe
I found it irrelevant to my everyday life	24%	10%
I found it boring	23%	11%
I felt I didn't belong	20%	9%
I didn't like the direction the church was going	17%	10%
I was put off by the sermons	15%	10%
I didn't get on with the leader or leadership	10%	6%
People didn't seem to care about me as a person	9%	8%
I had domestic conflicts or tensions because I attended church	8%	2%
I felt God let me down in some way	7%	6%
My questions and/or observations weren't taken seriously	7%	6%
Sickness or old age	3%	1%

0   10   20   30   40   50

% of total respondents

Table 6 Other reasons given for not going to church now

Reason	% of total respondents
I'm too busy	5
I moved home and didn't find another church in my new area to go to	4
I can't cope with the hypocrisy and falseness that I see in churchgoers	4
I've lost my faith and don't believe now	3
I have to work on Sundays	3
I opt to spend time with my family on Sundays	3
I was made to go to church when I was younger and it put me off	3
I have just got out of the habit	2
I have a serious problem with the leadership	2
I can't cope with the current style of worship in the church	2

out of the difficulties caused when a Protestant marries a Catholic is for at least one, if not both, to abandon their church-going. Just four (I expected more) said that in their view you do not need to go to church to be a Christian.

In Luke 15 Jesus tells three stories. He was surrounded by 'tax collectors and sinners' with the Pharisees within earshot muttering and complaining about the company he kept (v1-2). He spoke of a lost sheep, a lost coin and a lost son. In each case the loss was a dreadful tragedy for the person to whom it belonged, but each story has a happy ending. The shepherd finds his sheep, the woman her coin and the father renews his relationship with his son. Each story tells of a party to celebrate the good news.

Our concern is with the reasons why people are leaving churches—because each one who goes causes sadness and grief in the heart of God. If the shepherd cannot rest until he finds his lost sheep, we know that God is anxious about those who are leaving the fold of his church.

We have begun to understand why people drop out. Our task now is to understand what the problem areas of British churches are so that we gain a fuller picture of the difficulties that exist. Ultimately, though, as in Jesus' three stories, we are looking towards the time when some lost sheep return to the fold in the arms of the shepherd.

Notes

[1] Gerald Coates, *An Intelligent Fire* (Kingsway: Eastbourne, 1991) p 82.

[2] Horace Mann, *Religious Worship in England and Wales*, the Report of the 1851 Census, George Routledge: London 1854.

[3] Peter Brierley, *'Christian' England* (MARC Europe: London, 1991), p 30.

[4] *1991 Church Statistics*, The Central Board of Finance of the Church of England: London 1992.

[5] Peter Brierley, *op cit*, p 38.

[6] Source: Office of Population Censuses and Surveys, amended due to differing age categories.

CHAPTER 3

Identifying The Issues

BRITISH PEOPLE ARE RENOWNED for their respect for tradition. Maybe the popular pageantry at the Trooping the Colour or the Lord Mayor's Show in London shows how deeply ingrained tradition is in British culture. We respond with enthusiasm and admiration when entrepreneurs like Richard Branson or Anita Roddick emerge into the limelight. However the truth is that we are a nation of people with a degree of conservatism who appreciate structures that have some shape to them. We find it hard to understand a more relaxed approach to time-keeping in countries where, for instance, an appointment at a fixed time may take place an hour or so later. We like to know where we are and if something is part of our regular routine it makes life easier to cope with.

Once we have become habitual church-goers, therefore, it is not a simple matter to stop. Yes, of course, we are free to decide not to go any more. However when we have attended for many years this requires a drastic change of habit unless we feel we have been so severely alienated or insulted that it is impossible to return. Mercifully, this is fairly rare. As we know, people do decide to stop going to church, but usually by means of a gradual decline in attendance.

The other group is those who, after being there every Sunday for many years, are suddenly missing. This is totally out of character. The people who sit near them regularly assume that they must have been taken ill or an emergency cropped up just as they were leaving home. Their absence may become a talking point for a few moments. For the person who is missing, how-ever, this was a painful, courageous and bold step. Today they have broken out of a routine that they have been locked into for a long time. Probably they will be in church again next Sunday, but it will not be as hard to absent themselves a few more times in the next few months if they want to.

What are the underlying issues that seem to encourage a person to leave church? Looking both at the matters highlighted in the first two chapters and other insights from my experience as a pastor, I propose to deal with the wide range of problem areas that I have found. They all have a bearing on why people leave churches. For convenience we will examine them alpha-betically.

1. BOREDOM

When asked whether they found church boring before they left, 23% of those answering the Survey said that they did, with another 11% giving a 'maybe' response. Over a third of our participants are saying definitely that the churches they attended were uninspiring and boring. This is part of the reason for their non-attendance now.

Quite how Christianity can be made so bland would be a complete puzzle to the New Testament writers. When Paul wrote to the churches in Galatia, Ephesus and Colossae he was full of joy and incredulity at God's love and grace. He reminds his readers in Galatia that they 'are all sons of God through faith in Christ Jesus' (Gal 3:26). He tells believers in Ephesus that although they used to be dead in their 'transgressions and sins', they are now 'alive with Christ' (Eph 2:1-5). He teaches the Colossians that God has 'rescued us from the dominion of dark-ness and brought us into the kingdom of the Son he loves' (Col 1:13). How can a faith that is based on truths like these be boring?

Our survey respondents, however, are quite certain that many church services are boring. Almost a quarter of them said that they were put off to some extent by sermons. Eddie Gibbs suggests that the problem is sometimes wholly the fault of the

preacher. 'The word of God proclaimed in a cold, abrasive manner can often alienate people', he says.[1] In today's world people
are used both to seeing and hearing messages that are pro-
fessionally prepared to secure and hold their attention. Only
when Christian preaching is not just Bible-based and God-
centred but also well prepared and clearly presented in a lively
manner will it command the attention of a congregation. Christians have many years experience of being able to switch off
mentally during church services.

2. BURN OUT

None of the people who responded to the Survey identified this
as a reason for stopping going to church. Yet I know some
people from my own church experience who have reached the
point of feeling that they can take no more. They are simply
worn out, or feel that too much was expected of them. Moreover,
in his research, Eddie Gibbs reports that 43% of his Australian,
Scottish and American respondents said that they were expected
to make 'too many commitments', while 42% said that 'the
church was demanding too much from me'.[2]

It is true, of course, that churches often ask a lot of their
members. Rightly or wrongly, churches have ministry programmes that operate each week for children, young people and
adults from both within the church community and the wider
population. The ideal might be that the only programmes run at
any given time are those for which willing, gifted and committed Christian people are available. The truth is that sometimes churches overstretch themselves and rapid recruitment of
'volunteers' is necessary. It is very easy in such circumstances
for well-meaning Christians to become overloaded and to agree
to help 'just for a little while' only to discover three years or
more later that they have become virtually indispensable. All
sorts of circumstances lead to caring and committed people
burying themselves in work to do with God's Kingdom. It does
them no good and they lose their vital relationship with the
King.

...well-meaning Christians...become virtually indispensable

While recognizing the utter validity of Christians saying that they are burned out, we have to understand that serious commitment is what Christianity is all about. This does not necessarily mean relentless activity, of course. Some Christians are called to an in-depth ministry of intercession, for instance. The prime example of dedication to God's will is displayed by Jesus Christ himself. We are told how he 'made himself nothing, taking the very nature of a servant...he humbled himself and became obedient to death—even death on a cross!' (Phil 2:7-8).

As he trained his disciples in public ministry, Jesus gave them instructions that showed that an easy-going lifestyle was not his intention for them. 'Take nothing for the journey except a staff—no bread, no bag, no money in your belts. Wear sandals but not an extra tunic', he told them (Mk 6:8-9). A little while later he took the opportunity to spell out more clearly the cost of being one of his true disciples. 'If anyone would come after me, he must deny himself and take up his cross and follow me' (Mk 8:34).

It seems that the possibility of disciples in any era becoming burned out in Jesus' service will always be there. By virtue of the very nature of Jesus' example and calling, there will be some who find that they have fully stretched themselves and now need to rest. Jesus recognized this when he called his disciples to be alone with him (Mk 6:31). A serious problem arises when people find that their church does not or will not understand this so that the only way out is to extricate themselves from the church altogether.

3. CONFUSION

This is an apt description of the intellectual state of some who leave our churches. They themselves will not necessarily describe it in these terms because they may be some of the most academically gifted people who used to come to worship on Sundays. Some of my Survey responses, however, show the dilemma that some of them have. 'Roman Catholic teaching, in some areas, now contradicts what I was taught in my youth. Church teaching is also contradicted by modern scientific knowledge'. This man also says that for the last twenty years or so he has regarded himself as a humanist.

Another man answered, 'I do not sense God's love and cannot square the Christian view of him with my experience of life in the world'. One young lady admits, 'The more questions I asked and the more I found out, the more scared and confused I became so that in the end I preferred to be ignorant'. She continues by saying, 'There are too many questions with illogical or impossible answers and my faith will not extend that far'. One man interviewed in Scotland reckoned that 'Religion became a funny concept; it aroused as many questions as it answered'.

Many of us find it hard to discuss points of view like these with those who hold them. Often we feel that their unbelief and scepticism is so strong that nothing can make any impact at all. On the shelf in my office is that notable book, *Who Moved the Stone?* As an unbelieving lawyer, its author set out to prove that Jesus Christ did not rise from the dead. During his work he was soundly converted to the Christian faith.[3] Maybe the intellectually confused are leaving or have left the church claiming that they cannot cope with all this stuff about a 'God'.

4. GUILT

In the last chapter we noted that a few Survey respondents reported that guilt feelings contributed to their leaving church. For some this guilt will be real and it exists as part of God's mechanism to bring us to repentance. God is by nature truth, love, just, holy, righteous and, because of sin, separated from people who have rebelled against him. When we sin, a sense of guilt before God is natural and utterly appropriate.

Not all guilt feelings, however, are legitimate. Some people seem prone to feel guilty when there is really no justification for it—such as the moment the name of God is mentioned. It is not really these that I have in mind here, but what may be worth saying is that the Devil (more about him in Chapter 9) is a past-master at making people feel condemned. They do not know why they feel condemned, but they just do. This is undoubtedly one of his tactics for demotivating and paralysing Christians who could otherwise be of great value in the service of God.

Here we are considering primarily Christians who stop going to church because something from their past or present keeps coming to the forefront of their minds. When in a church service, they feel grossly uncomfortable about it before God. Maybe they sense God's unhappiness about their cohabitation arrangement, abortion, theft, adultery, sex outside marriage or obsession with pornography. 2 Samuel 12 tells how God confronted King David following his adulterous affair with Bathsheba. God continues to speak to confront people today about sin in their lives. It is certainly not comfortable at the time and I understand why people stop going to church as a result. They are, I think, under the same misapprehension as Jonah, concluding that if you run away from the place where God speaks to you, you will cease to hear him. The story of Jonah suggests that it is not always as easy or final as that!

5. HYPOCRISY

Sufficient people surveyed said that they were put off church by the hypocrisy that they saw within it that at times I wondered if I should have included it in my list of reasons for people to tick. On reflection I am glad I avoided it because while some have gruesome stories to tell, others might have jumped on the bandwagon and identified this as a factor without much thought. That I have received comments like 'Church-goers are two-faced and evil' and 'Christians are prejudiced, bigoted and hypocritical' does give cause for concern. I well understood the charge of hypocrisy put forward forcibly by one woman. Having started to go to an Anglican church when she was fifteen, she visited Rome and claims nearly to have been raped by a priest in the Catacombs. Not surprisingly, her attendance at church ceased after this at the age of twenty. She has not been back since.

Maybe any religion is particularly prone to accusations of hypocrisy. Wherever there are normally accepted codes of behaviour that are usually carefully adhered to, it is easy for motives other than those originally intended to creep in. In Amos 5:21-24 for instance, God through his prophet condemns the Jews for perpetuating their religious festivals and symbols of personal devotion to him while at the same time allowing their land to be characterized by terrible injustices. Jesus is disparaging about those who specifically choose to utter their wordy prayers in public places. Prayer, he teaches, was always intended to be personal communication between an individual and their Father in heaven (Mt 6:5-8).

I feel sure that no-one would be foolhardy enough to say that hypocrisy is not a problem in our churches. That is bad enough in itself. Far worse is the consequence of that. There are those who do not and will not go to any church regularly today because of what they have seen and heard about churches in the past. The problems would probably not be as severe if Christians did not claim to be different from others because of their faith. The difficulties start when those who claim to be Christians and to follow Jesus fail to live up to his standards in their own lives. It is more serious still when preachers disregard the attitudes and standards of behaviour that they teach from the

pulpit. It is when these failures and omissions are apparent
without even the merest hint of regret or apology by the per-
petrator that some in our churches just cannot take it any more.

6. IGNORED

Another group of people who leave churches up and down the
country are those who feel that they have nothing of value to
contribute. Even if they have, no-one has ever asked them to
take any active part in the church. This group is often made up
of the more shy and retiring members. They are lovely people,
but it takes longer than average to get to know them. They can
be wonderfully kind and generous, but will never push themselves forward or allow others to do so for them. Consequently
they tend to stay in the background within the church. They
may have some friends in the fellowship, but often tend to be
loners. They may feel an awakening inside if they hear that the
next sermon series will be on the spiritual gifts that God has
given his church. They may rush home to read 1 Corinthians 12
before the studies. They may tell the Lord in private that they
are more than willing to be used within his church, although
they may be uncertain as to the particular gifts that he has given
them.

There is often a sad outcome for these people when the
sermon series on the gifts ends. Yes, they may have heard every
sermon, but still have no clue as to the contribution that God has
given them to make to the overall ministry of the church. Addi-
tionally, they find it hard to go to the leader and ask for help
with this. Consequently they find themselves drifting back into
the background but now with less hope than ever of becoming
involved in frontline ministry. These people need help! God has
given them gifts and ministries. They truly are a valued part of
the Body of Christ. Their problems come because of their natural
reluctance to draw attention to themselves, and because church
leaders find too much of their time and attention is taken up
with people who are not backward in coming forward.

Being ignored, though, is a painful and isolating feeling and
goes on only as long as the person feels that they can stand it.

Jesus had a wonderful capacity with Simon to foresee what he could and would become in the future—the 'rock' on which Jesus' church would be built (Mt 16:18). The churches need leaders with this vision and the time to invest in people such as we have described, but in the meantime some will undoubtedly depart silently and without fuss through the church's back door.

7. INTROSPECTION

Monica Hill, having examined the results of the 1989 English Church Census and writing in *Church Growth Digest*, considers introspection a substantial problem in some churches.[4] Whereas 'growing churches usually look outward...declining churches look inward!', she says. Peter Lloyd, Parish Ministry Consultant in the Anglican Diocese of Auckland, New Zealand, wrote that he sees 'the basic philosophy/mindset of Anglicanism which is pastoral rather than evangelistic' as one reason why people leave churches. In other words it gets too intense for people to cope with. They find that Sunday after Sunday they are forced into spiritual navel-gazing exercises. The church's prayers are

SPOT THE DIFFERENCE COMPETITION

RING THE SEVEN DIFFERENCES

SEND YOUR ENTRY FORM TO

...forced into spiritual navel-gazing exercises

primarily based on the needs of their existing fellowship, and their social events are for those who come each week. After a while some can no longer tolerate it and decide to opt out.

For Christians to spend time together in prayer, Bible study and fellowship is to follow the pattern of the early church in Acts 2:42. Jesus himself made time specifically for his twelve disciples (eg Mk 4:10; 35-36; 6:30-31). However if this introspective environment is all our church life consists of, it is narrow, restrictive and grossly inadequate. While some churches persist, maybe for the purest of motives, to focus primarily on themselves, some people will inevitably call it a day.

8. IRRELEVANCE

With 24% of the people surveyed declaring that they found church irrelevant to their everyday life, we find ourselves confronting the chief reason people stopped going to church. Church seemed a million miles away from the real world that occupies their attention for the rest of the week. A further 10% gave a 'maybe' answer to the same question. All the evidence from the Survey suggests that many churches are isolated little enclaves that do not impinge on the real world—or allow the real world to impinge on them.

This seems in stark contrast to the picture of Christianity in the Bible where those who trust the Lord find their lives thoroughly enriched despite difficulties and hardships they have to face. The Psalmist's testimony is that 'even though I walk through the valley of the shadow of death, I will fear no evil, for you are with me, your rod and your staff, they comfort me' (Ps 23:4). True Christianity brings God to people at their point of need. In Nazareth Jesus explained that God had sent him to 'preach good news to the poor. He has sent me to proclaim freedom for the prisoners and recovery of sight for the blind' (Lk 4:18). The Christian church in any generation has a very serious problem if it does not relate to ordinary people; I have no doubt that it has this problem today.

9. ISOLATION

Of the respondents to the Survey, 29% said that their leaving the church was to some extent related to the fact that they did not feel that they belonged. There are many possible explanations for this. When people answer surveys it is hard to determine their own emotional health. Some people are more emotionally needy and vulnerable than others. While some have the self-esteem not to need constant reassurance and encouragement from people around them, others need it all the time. Otherwise they seriously doubt they are liked and appreciated—indeed, they conclude positively they are not! I would sleep more easily at night if I thought that all 29% of my respondents came into this latter category and that therefore the problem was *theirs*. I cannot believe this, though. Eddie Gibbs reveals that 46% of the people who helped him with his research said 'the congregation was not welcoming'.[5] I had to report to my Church Meeting a conversation I had with a young woman who visited our church. She was unimpressed by the lack of genuine welcome she received. I trust we are doing better now.

People who come for the first time as well as those who have been coming for years *need to know* that they are welcome. They need to sense that not only is God glad that they have come to worship him, but that the people around them are glad too. To have the cold feeling that you are isolated and separate from others sitting close to you is not good. It seems to be a common problem in some of our churches.

That Christianity is a faith based on love and acceptance is undisputed. John's first letter majors on love, stating the truth that 'God is love' (1 Jn 4:16) and showing how God demonstrates this practically. 'How great is the love the Father has lavished on us, that we should be called children of God', he says (3:1). Because we have been loved so greatly by God, it is imperative, he argues, that we 'love one another' (4:7). How then within Christian churches today can there be such a lack of love and acceptance that people leave because they feel they do not belong?

10. LACK OF COMMITMENT

One day a young man approached Jesus. He arrived in a hurry and asked Jesus the most important question of all, 'What must I do to inherit eternal life?' They had a discussion before the young man went away. Mark tells us that he was 'sad, because he had great wealth' (Mk 10:17-31). This man discovered the truth that Jesus looks for 100% commitment from those who become his disciples. When inviting Simon, Andrew, James, John and Matthew to join him, he used the simple words, 'Follow me', to call them. This meant that four of Jesus' followers had to relinquish their fishing careers, the fifth his work collecting taxes for the Roman overlords in Judea. True Christian discipleship necessarily involves self-denial and putting Jesus first.

It seems easy, I know, for a minister who has been spared many of the normal pressures of life to talk about putting Jesus first. Having read the 509 Survey forms returned to me, I noted that 5% of respondents have said that they do not go to church now because they are too busy. I believe that number would have been higher had this been included as one of the listed options. In a later question (the results of which I have not yet given), 21% of all the people surveyed say that they would like to go back to church but life is too busy. Doing homework (4%), spending time with the family (3%), having to work on Sundays (3%) and involvement in sporting activities (less than 1%) were all reasons given for stopping going.

The last thing we must suggest is that any of these things is wrong or sinful. None of them is, and yet people give them as reasons for not going to church any more. I cannot help but compare this list with that given in the Parable of the Great Banquet where some guests are invited to a meal. The Bible says, 'But they all alike began to make excuses' (Lk 14:18). The first had bought a field, the second a yoke of oxen, the third has just married. These too are valid reasons for not attending. In his story, though, Jesus reports that the host 'became angry' when he heard that his invitations had been spurned. Jesus is not teaching here about attending church, but about responding to God's invitation to enter his Kingdom. However, the point should not go unnoticed in this context.

It is very easy for us to fail to see what the priorities really are and so allow all sorts of apparently valid and worthwhile pursuits to take our time and attention. Jesus warns us to take care to get our priorities right in the light of eternity. 'Seek first his (God's) kingdom and his righteousness', he teaches in the Sermon on the Mount (Mt 6:33). This is easier said than done.

One questionnaire deserves particular comment at this point. Giving her reason why she does not go to church any more a lady simply and honestly says, 'I was unable to make a full commitment'. This is the same honesty as was recorded by John when he records that 'many of his (Jesus') disciples turned back and no longer followed him' (Jn 6:66). We can easily criticize them, but we have to respect their integrity. They faced the fact that they may not be able to handle the level of dedication that Jesus was asking of them. I sometimes remember a letter from my former college principal, Dr Raymond Brown, in the early stages of planning this book. I had explained my intention to use a survey method to discover why people stop going to church, and he commented:

> I imagine that your greatest problem...is of arriving at the *real* reason why they no longer attend. In other words, isn't your main difficulty that very few of your people are going to say that in the end of the day money came to matter more than God, or that they had enjoyably adopted a lifestyle which was constantly challenged by Christian values or that they had established a relationship with someone who was not a Christian who was luring them away from church?

This is valid. I would be the first to admit that people's initial responses to questions about non-attendance at church may not reveal the deepest possible answer. I do not doubt that there were others who answered my Survey but who did not have the insight or honesty of the lady we mentioned. She brings to our attention the truth that to follow Christ with integrity demands total commitment. Some leave the church because they know that they will not be able to give it.

11. LEADERSHIP FAILINGS

With 16% of those surveyed saying that they did not get on with the leadership to some extent, it is clear that here we have a further area of difficulty that affects church-going. It is those things ministers and leaders do and fail to do, say and do not say and the attitudes they exhibit that makes their congregations warm to them—or not as the case may be.

I wanna be loved by you

It is, of course, impossible at a distance to make pronouncements about the churches, ministers and issues involved, but undoubtedly there is a major problem area to be tackled here. Differences of opinion and difficulties in personal relationships between leaders and people in their congregations should not be driving people away from church.

Yet they are. 'I found little compassion among some Elders and little guidance, advice or commiseration when I had problems with my daughter', one says. Another said that since the arrival of a new minister she felt there was a lack of caring support in the church in times of personal crisis. I met one lady in her forties in the street in South East London who told me what happened when she was eleven. Her mother had an

Anglican background and her father was a Roman Catholic. She herself was the youngest of five daughters. The local Catholic priest visited the home and in front of the children called them 'bastards'. Her father, she said, nearly killed the priest and threw him out of the house. None of the family went near a church after that. From the other side of the world comes a true story of a churchwarden whose feminist vicar accused him of being a male chauvinist. He resigned, left the area and no longer worships anywhere. Yes, problems concerning leadership can be very real.

12. LOSS OF FAITH

I was surprised to find that only 7% of respondents to the Survey said that they felt that God had let them down in some way. Naturally it is sad for these thirty-four people, but I was encouraged that the number was not larger. Another 6% answered the same question with a 'maybe' response. Further down the form are answers like 'I no longer believe in God', 'I was bereaved and lost my faith', 'I believe in Jesus but not in God' and 'I was hurt in the past for which I blame God, but I still believe in him'. One man interviewed in the street in Southern England had been a prisoner of war. He had, he said, 'seen a lot of suffering and did not see how there could be a God'. There are people with whom we rub shoulders every day who once accepted that there is a God and who maybe personally trusted in him, but who have now largely written him off.

Eddie Gibbs' 1991 research revealed that 65% of his respondents 'had serious doubts about the Christian religion' when they left their churches.[6] Jesus, of course, taught that there would be some who would initially follow him who would not remain loyal to him. It can be argued that 'The Parable of the Sower' is better called 'The Parable of the Soils'. Here the focus of Jesus' words is very much on the variety of soils into which the sower's seed falls. Some, he said, 'fell on rocky places, where it did not have much soil. It sprang up quickly, because the soil was shallow. But when the sun came up, the plants were scorched, and they withered because they had no root' (Mt

13:5-6). In his interpretation Jesus explains that such a person, 'since he has no root, he lasts only a short time. When trouble or persecution comes because of the word, he quickly falls away' (Mt 13:21).

Writing from Ngongotaha, New Zealand, where he is both a vicar and co-ordinator of Anglican Renewal Ministries, Dr Don Battley says that he believes the area of faith crisis and failure '...is bigger than we acknowledge. The corrosion of unbelief and the difficulties of believing today are claiming many, especially amongst those raised young in the church but not serviced with suitable apologetics and interpretation of belief in the modern world after age 18'. When people find their faith crumbling, it is no surprise that their pattern of church attendance alters radically too.

13. MEDIA PUBLICITY

Previous sections have focused on internal problems in churches experienced by those who attend. In this section, however, we look at the image of the church that the public at large gains from the media (especially the Press) and the way this affects church attendance. I suspect it is sometimes a factor.

For some months I have been collecting newspaper articles that mention Christianity or the church. Examples I have found include 'Testing time for gay clergy', a report 'on the controversy in the Roman Catholic Church about Aids and chastity'.[7] *The Daily Mirror* reported on David Icke: 'I'm not the son of God any more...I'm a snowplough'.[8] 'Sent home! Schoolgirl who was not baptised' was another *Daily Mirror* headline that told the story of Nicola McDowell who was banned from her Catholic school by the local priest because she was not baptized.[9] Not to be left out, the *Daily Star* reported, 'Oh Baby! Rotter Rev plays Mary hell over name' and told of the Anglican vicar who refused to baptize baby Jaymie Marie Mary Hayes until her name is changed because, he reckons, the names Marie and Mary are the same.[10] More seriously, *The Observer* sent its Science Correspondent to a debate at which a geneticist took on the Archbishop of York. 'God comes a poor second before the majesty of

...the image of the church in the Press

science' was his summary of what took place.[11] The examples could go on...and on.

Having read the full stories in those newspapers I confess that had I not been collecting them for a specific purpose I would have turned over the page and forgotten about them. When we consider what Christianity is really all about we have to agree how unfortunate it is that this sort of thing gets exposed to the public in this way. An active and committed Christian may not be in the least affected by these stories or may even find them amusing. We wonder, though, what effect they have on a vulnerable Christian who finds these stories being talked about at work? I guess they are embarrassed, and wish one of two things; either that the ground would open up or that they were not a church-goer. This would enable them to identify with the ridicule without fear of being called hypocritical.

In no way am I calling on the press to report more sympathetically on stories to do with Christianity or the church. I believe that no Christian should expect any special treatment. If others in society are mocked for petty and stupid decisions, for instance, Christians must expect the same. I just express concern, though, that media treatment that ridicules anything to do with Christianity can have a detrimental effect on those already on the slippery slope out of the church.

14. PASTORAL FAILING

My wife was clearly upset when I met her again in a town centre where she had been approaching people in the street to complete surveys. She had just met a man who had been an active and committed Christian some years before. He was a regular lay preacher and sounded as if he had truly sought to put God and his work first in his life. He then had a personal crisis in his own life that he could not handle alone. Yet when he turned to his church for help there was no support forthcoming. 'There was no love', he said. Now, for some three decades, he has been away from any church and no longer believes that Jesus was God—just a great man. Pastoral neglect undoubtedly costs churches some of their members and attenders. To be honest I am not surprised and feel that people have some right to be unforgiving when the church founded and supposedly sustained by Jesus deserts them in their hour of need. In a fascinating paper from Canada, *Understanding the Church Dropout*, is the following paragraph.

> Three families became church dropouts around the times of family bereavement. A pastor who took a funeral and then never came back to deal with them in their grief and bewilderment! Repeated in all three family cases, it forced these people outside the church to do their questioning and crying. All the time they stood outside the church looking in. They blamed others for these deaths, and then

themselves, and finally God. Neither pastor nor people shared that journey.[12]

Having sought to share this objectively I need to make an observation as one entrusted with pastoral caring. God has not given me the gift of mind-reading. I do not always know when people are unwell, in hospital, depressed or dying. I need to be told. On balance, though, I have to take the point thrust at me by Luke 15:4. How did the shepherd in Jesus' story of the lost sheep know that he had lost one? It can only be because he took the initiative to count them. Some of us will have to accept that we can make excuses that we 'didn't know of a need' only occasionally.

15. PRESUPPOSED REJECTION

In Chapter 1 we considered a range of social and moral issues that are uppermost in Britain today. Couples cohabiting, children born outside marriage, divorce, abortion, child abuse, homosexuality, pornography and single parent families were all mentioned. Two things are true about the varied contents of this list. First, they are all comparatively common-place and becoming more 'normal' and socially accepted whether we like it or not. Secondly, they are all in one way or another contrary to God's ideals for mankind. Some are clearly sinful according to the teaching of the Bible. I remember one person whose door I knocked on during my surveying work. 'I feel too sinful to go to church', she said. Another lady told me, 'I've spent the last two years trying to get rid of the guilt of not agreeing with the church'. A few people told me that their feelings of guilt were now a blockage for them.

Whether these particular people were alluding to a sense of guilt that hindered them from relating to God or his church—or both, I am not sure. I am aware, though, that some people stay away from church because they feel sensitive about something that has happened to them or that they have done. One lady told me on a questionnaire, 'After being divorced I felt it was not the done thing.' People are very sensitive about the charge of hypocrisy. If they think that a moral lapse (such as an adulterous relationship, sexual experience before marriage or obsession with pornography) might become known within the church, they may stay away instead of taking the risk of becoming embarrassed and put on the spot.

Where those issues are examples of a growing trend in this country (like increasing divorce rates), some may feel that to have had a broken marriage makes them a second-class Christian. In all these cases the deeply-held personal feeling is this: 'I'm certain that people in the church would reject me if they *really knew* everything about me.' Victims of sexual abuse and rape feel this too sometimes because the thought goes round in their minds, 'What happened must have been partly my fault'. What we are calling 'presupposed rejection' here is sad, but it is very real for some. They feel in some way they are just not good enough to go to church, and they stay away rather than face the possibility of someone at church rejecting them once their story comes out.

16. SOUR RELATIONSHIPS

It is sad but true: Christians sometimes fall out with one another. Sometimes they disagree over a point of doctrine, at other times they completely misunderstand each other. Often they can get over it quickly and comparatively easily. Sometimes they cannot and will not. As a pastor I sometimes hear members of our fellowship griping about each other. I suppose in a situation where people of all sorts, shapes, backgrounds and types are thrown together in close quarters, some abrasion and conflict is inevitable. I just wish it were not so.

I find two passages in Mark's Gospel are encouraging in this respect. Mark 9:33-35 tells of a squabble among Jesus' disciples. Apparently they had been arguing during a journey and, presumably because they were embarrassed about it, tried to keep this from Jesus. They failed. He knew that their conflict was over which of them was 'the greatest', by which they presumably meant the most valued by him. I am sure that they never forgot his words, 'If anyone wants to be first, he must be the very last, and the servant of all'. Possibly not long afterwards James and

John approached Jesus to ask that they each sit one side of him in his glory (Mk 10:37). Not surprisingly, the other ten disciples were 'indignant' at this (10:41).

Jesus is well aware of the weaknesses and failings of human beings, even those who have made a serious commitment to follow him. At times bad relationships can become so uncomfortable for those involved that they feel they cannot stay near those with whom they have fallen out. Sad though it is, our churches lose people because unhappy relationships are not resolved.

We have covered, then, a number of problem areas in churches and individuals. We clearly need to find workable solutions to these and will turn our attention to remedies in Section 2. Before that, however, there is more information from the Survey that we need to absorb.

Notes

1 Eddie Gibbs, 'Nominality—The Challenge of the 1990s', *LandMARC*, MARC Europe: London (Summer 1992): p 1.

2 Gibbs, *op cit.*, p 1.

3 Frank Morrison, *Who Moved the Stone?* (Faber & Faber: London, 1958).

4 Monica Hill, 'Countering Decline', *Church Growth Digest*, Year 12, Issue 4 (Summer 1991): p 1-2,7.

5 Gibbs, *op cit.*, p 1.

6 Gibbs, *op cit.*, p 1.

7 Article in *The Independent on Sunday*, 15 March 1992, p 8.

8 Article in the *Daily Mirror*, 14 February 1992, p 19.

9 Article in the *Daily Mirror*, 11 February 1992, p 15.

10 Article in the *Daily Star*, 28 March 1992, p 11.

11 Article in *The Observer*, 19 April 1992, p 9.

12 From a Working Paper, 'Understanding the Church Dropout', source unknown.

CHAPTER 4

Comparing The Responses

THIS CHAPTER PRIMARILY analyses and compares further information from the Survey beginning with clarification of the four main categories into which the responses fall. Readers who find this demanding are advised to turn to Chapter 5. Figure 9 (Chapter 2) showed the reasons why the respondents no longer go to church. From this we see that they have problems with themselves, with church leaders, with relevance and with God.

A. PERSONAL ISSUES

Definition: problems in *me* that make me feel that either I cannot or do not want to go to church any more.

Reasons: I felt I didn't belong
People didn't seem to care about me as a person
I had domestic conflicts and tensions because I attended church
My questions and/or observations weren't taken seriously

B. LEADERSHIP ISSUES

Definition: problems concerning *church leaders* that make it either hard or impossible for me to go to church.

Reasons: I didn't like the direction the church was going
                   I didn't get on with the leader or leadership

C. RELEVANCE ISSUES

Definition: problems I have about the *way things happen* at
                   church and the fact that I do not necessarily find any
                   correlation between the content of the service, how
                   it is presented and my own life and needs.

Reasons: I found church irrelevant to my everyday life
                   I found church boring
                   I was put off by the sermons

D. GOD ISSUES

Definition: problems I have with *God*'s existence, character,
                   actions or lack of them and whether or not I feel I
                   can trust and believe in him.

Reasons: I felt God let me down in some way

We will examine these issues in greater depth in Chapters 5-8,
but first need to look at further information highlighted by the
Survey. Various comparisons between different results will help
us discover more about Britain's churches today.
First, let us focus on five areas where we see the differences in
response between...

1. ...Males and females
2. ...The various age-groups surveyed
3. ...The various denominations surveyed
4. ...The various areas of the United Kingdom from which
   surveys have emanated
5. ...Those surveys sent by people nominated by a minister as
   opposed to those obtained elsewhere (mainly 'cold' on the
   streets)

In each area Part A will show us the different ways in which
commitment to the church or God has been expressed by the

people interviewed or, when they were children, by their family. In Part B we shall learn why these people have left their church. This information is in summary form; the complete Tables are in the Appendix where it is also made clear which responses have been combined to provide the Part A figures. The notes following each Figure include comments only on matters of any significance.

Imbalances between the sexes

Figure 10: COMPARISON OF RESPONSES BETWEEN MALES AND FEMALES

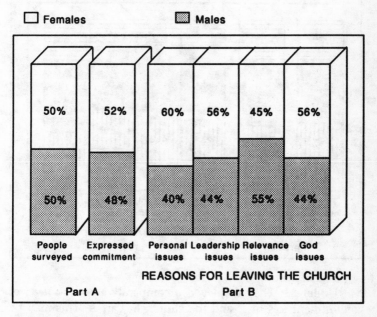

☐ Females   ▨ Males

	People surveyed	Expressed commitment	Personal issues	Leadership issues	Relevance issues	God issues
Females	50%	52%	60%	56%	45%	56%
Males	50%	48%	40%	44%	55%	44%

REASONS FOR LEAVING THE CHURCH

Part A   Part B

What we learn:

* **Women** were more heavily committed than men to God's work in the churches. They had more problems than men with Personal, Leadership and God issues. The Personal issues figure of 60% is high because of the larger number of women who had problems at home because of their church-going.

* **Men** seemed less likely to leave a church for Personal reasons. They were more concerned that church and Christianity was relevant and meant something in their lives. They were less tolerant than women about the way the church presents the Christian Faith.

Imbalances between the age groups

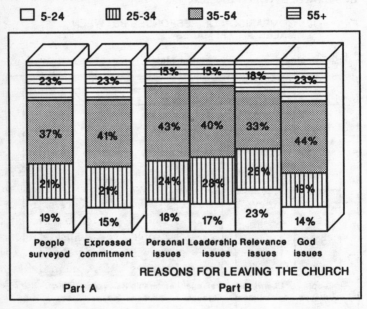

Figure 11: COMPARISON OF RESPONSES BETWEEN AGE GROUPS

□ 5-24   ▥ 25-34   ▦ 35-54   ☰ 55+

REASONS FOR LEAVING THE CHURCH

Part A   Part B

What we learn:

* **Under 25.** They displayed a comparatively weak level of commitment to Christ and the church in Part A. This may be because they have had less time in which to express their Christian dedication. On the other hand, in Part B, they expressed fewer complaints. It was a lack of relevance that they complained of most vehemently.

* **25-34s.** They register high levels of complaint against the church although, notably, not against God. There was a strong reaction here to the leadership of the church and in particular to

the direction in which their churches were going. This age-group seems least likely to get on with the leadership and some felt disenchanted at the seeming irrelevance of the church. In the area of Personal issues we found that a number of these people felt that they did not belong. These responses need to be taken seriously. They give strong clues as to the vulnerability of other young adults who are still with us.

* **35-54s.** They have expressed strong Christian commitment during their time at church. Some have been in leadership and a good proportion has expressed its dedication to Christ and his church in other tangible ways. However Part B shows that while they did not seem to find church as irrelevant as those who are younger, they were less happy about the level of caring and love. They had a tendency not to get on with the leadership, and (notably) were the age-group that felt most let down by God. This could be because of mid-life crisis, marital disintegration or job disillusionment traumas that cause the faith of some to be severely tested.

* **55 and over.** What is significant with this group is the much lower level of complaints about the church. Maybe it is because they have grown used to the church and its foibles after all these years or that they have grown in personal patience and tolerance. Perhaps they recognize that for the church to survive for succeeding generations, younger people's needs must be understood and accommodated. Certainly this age-group had the capacity to make waves at changes being introduced into church life today, yet appears to have displayed a remarkable level of acceptance.

Imbalances between the denominations
What we learn:

* **Church of England.** It appears to have drawn out a low level of commitment from those who attended, but this is balanced by a lower level of complaints about the Personal issues raised. Anglicans, though, seem more likely to find the church irrelevant and not to get on with the leadership.

* **Baptist churches** are where, of all the denominations, the highest level of commitment to Christ and the church was

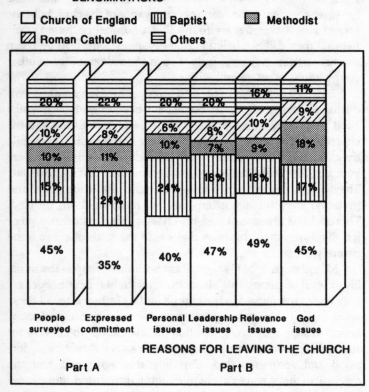

Figure 12: COMPARISON OF RESPONSES BETWEEN THE DENOMINATIONS

☐ Church of England   ⊞ Baptist   ▦ Methodist
▨ Roman Catholic   ⊟ Others

REASONS FOR LEAVING THE CHURCH

Part A   Part B

expressed. Baptists, however, do not come out of this Survey well in terms of the level of problems that cause people to leave. Problems in the area of Personal issues seem excessive; they sensed a lack of care and not belonging, and their questions and observations were not taken seriously.

A fairly high level of Baptists did not get on with the leadership, and here we find a number of people who felt that God had let them down. Frankly, of all the named denominations, it was in Baptist churches where we found the highest levels of complaint. Is it that they have most to complain about or does the

Baptist system, which encourages active participation in church government by its members, promote this?

* **Methodist churches** are also where a fairly strong level of commitment to Christ and the church was to be found. We appear far less likely to find problems between church members and their leaders in Methodism, but considerably more likely to find those who feel that God has let them down in some way. Fewer Methodists found church boring or irrelevant.

* **Roman Catholic churches.** They come out well as having fewer problems across the areas surveyed. They shone particularly in the area of the Personal issues of loving and caring. They also had fewer problems over leadership, and fewer felt that God had let them down. Of all the named denominational groupings it is here that we found least people with complaints and dissatisfaction. This may be related to notions of infallibility and obedience to church leaders. Part A of the Table reveals, though, that the level of active dedication to the Lord and church was comparatively meagre.

* **Others.** It is hard to comment on such a diverse group of churches as makes up 'Others'. We observed a strong level of expressed commitment in the members and a low level of complaints about irrelevance. Comparatively few in this group sensed that God let them down. The level of complaints here was less than in the named denominations.

There are undoubtedly some lessons to be learned from a comparison such as this. What we need to recognize, though, is the variety of backgrounds and therefore expectations in the people who supplied the data. Some may have experienced only one denomination or type of church. Therefore they may be oblivious to the many other ways in which Christian worship, fellowship, support and encouragement are expressed elsewhere within the Body of Christ. Unless and until we have an objective means of measuring very different churches we can only treat conclusions such as these as interesting. It is possible that there are hints here for individual churches and denominations to take seriously.

Imbalances between the geographical areas surveyed

Our Survey results represent the views of people from many parts of Britain which we now compare. Appendix B gives this information in full. South East England includes London, Essex, Kent, Surrey, East Sussex and West Sussex. The rest of the United Kingdom covers Wales, Scotland and the Channel Islands. Figure 13 below now reports on imbalances that are revealed.

Figure 13: COMPARISON OF RESPONSES BETWEEN THE REGIONS OF THE U.K. SURVEYED

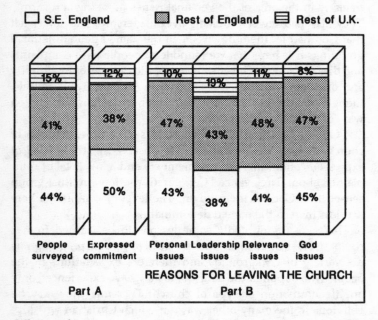

☐ S.E. England   ▨ Rest of England   ⊟ Rest of U.K.

People surveyed	Expressed commitment	Personal issues	Leadership issues	Relevance issues	God issues
15%	12%	10%	19%	11%	8%
41%	38%	47%	43%	48%	47%
44%	50%	43%	38%	41%	45%

Part A   REASONS FOR LEAVING THE CHURCH   Part B

What we learn:

* **South East England** had an enviably high level of church commitment compared to the rest of the UK. More children went to Sunday School and quite a lot more were christened, baptized or dedicated. A comparatively high number express their Christian commitment in confirmation or Believers' Baptism. Far more than average were born-again Christians, and there were many active, committed members in the churches. Part B continues to provide good news for the South East. There were comparatively few problems over leadership and the churches of South East England were not seen as irrelevant to the same extent as others.

* **The rest of England.** In contrast to the South East we found a lower level of commitment here, but a higher level of complaints against the churches. This could relate to social class distribution. Many found their church irrelevant, and the figures reflecting both Personal issues and feelings that God had let them down were comparatively high too. It is in this geographical area that most dissatisfaction with the church existed.

* **The rest of the United Kingdom** displayed a level of Christian commitment in the churches that seems comparatively meagre. Fewer children were christened, fewer were confirmed, there were fewer born-again Christians and fewer active, committed members. There were also far fewer who have been in leadership within the churches. A very different picture emerges, however, in Part B of the Table. While the commitment may be shallow, complaints generally were far fewer. Difficulties with leadership were comparatively high, but far fewer found church irrelevant and the same is true of the Personal issues. A remarkably small number spoke of feelings that God had let them down in some way. In short, this is a geographical area with lower levels of commitment, but equally lower levels of complaint.

If these figures reflect the tendencies of those who remain in the churches, then clearly the South East is where the greatest density of active and committed church members is to be found. It is in the rest of England, however, that there is the greatest cause for concern. Here the level of expressed commitment is lower, and the problems and complaints of those who have left the churches are highest. The vibes emanating from this area are alarming.

Imbalances between the surveys obtained via church leaders and others

As reported earlier the number of completed surveys that was returned from minister colleagues was grossly inadequate for serious research. These had to be supplemented by other means.

I undertook a small amount of random door-knocking and some twenty-five came from my Invicta Radio listeners. The vast majority, however, were from random contact with people on the streets. I was so grateful to get the cooperation of others in this mammoth task. One friend in the West Country told me, 'It was harder than expected'. Another, who took to the streets of Edinburgh, reported, 'It was a *very* difficult exercise although thoroughly worthwhile'. My own experiences showed me how many delightful and helpful people there are in this country, but also how many there are who have a capacity to be rude and obnoxious for no good reason. I found that on average one person in ten of those approached was willing to complete a questionnaire. No wonder interviewing took so long! Finally, however, a further 374 surveys became available by this means.

There is a reason why a comparison of the surveys from these two different sources is important. It is probably fair to assume that those people contacted via ministers have recent experience of a church. It is likely that they have only fairly recently stopped attending and were known to the minister. Therefore we can presume that they had some reasonable level of contact with the church while they were there. Those approached in the street who said that they used to go to church, though, may have had a very different background. Their days of attending church were often a while ago and they may never have become very involved. In short, some contacted on the street may never have got beyond notional or nominal Christianity.

What we learn:

* **Contacts via churches.** Those contacted through their former church exhibited a far higher level of dedication than those contacted at random. On examination of the figures that make up Part A we see a most interesting phenomenon (see Appendix C). The questions that cover the population more widely (like christening, Sunday School attendance and confirmation) get average response. However, when steps of personal spiritual commitment are scrutinized we see a major difference. Here we find that those contacted through their former churches displayed a much higher level of dedication. There is a far greater likelihood that they were active and committed, have been

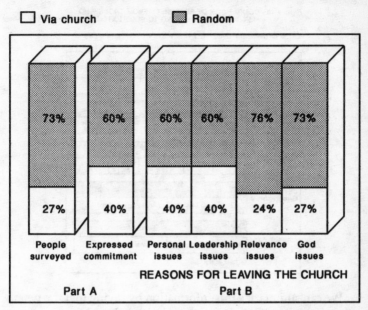

Figure 14: COMPARISON OF RESPONSES BETWEEN SURVEYS RECEIVED FROM CHURCH CONTACTS AND OTHERS

☐ Via church   ▨ Random

73%	60%	60%	60%	76%	73%
27%	40%	40%	40%	24%	27%
People surveyed	Expressed commitment	Personal issues	Leadership issues	Relevance issues	God issues

REASONS FOR LEAVING THE CHURCH

Part A   Part B

baptized by immersion, and have been leaders in their churches. In Part B we find that those whom we contacted via their former church tended to have problems about Personal and Leadership issues but they did not seem to find church irrelevant.

    * **Those contacted at random.** The levels of commitment expressed by this group are low. When saying why they left church, they predominantly express a reaction against the church's irrelevance. They suggested that Personal and Leadership issues did not generally cause them to leave. This is probably not only because of their lesser involvement, but also because of the time-lag since they were at church. It does not necessarily mean that the issues that provoked their departure are any different to the other group. It may be that any pain has had time either to be buried or dissipated.

Those feeling they don't belong at church

Figure 15: COMPARISON OF RESPONSES FROM THOSE WHO FELT THEY DIDN'T BELONG TO SOME EXTENT

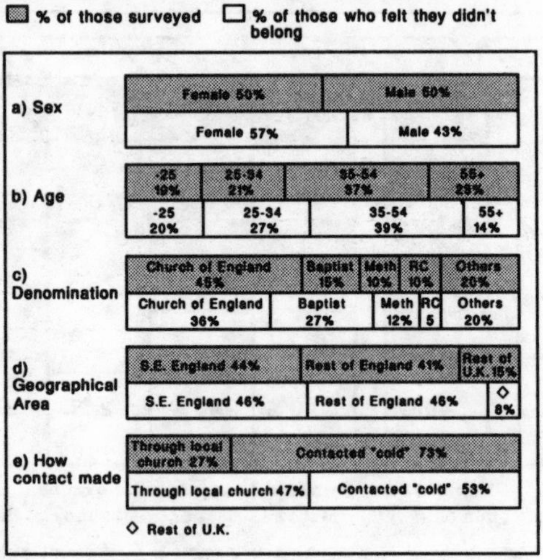

▓ % of those surveyed   ☐ % of those who felt they didn't belong

a) Sex	Female 50%		Male 50%	
	Female 57%		Male 43%	
b) Age	-25 10% / 26-34 21%		35-54 37% / 55+ 29%	
	-25 20%	25-34 27%	35-54 39%	55+ 14%
c) Denomination	Church of England 45%	Baptist 15% / Meth 10% / RC 10%	Others 20%	
	Church of England 36%	Baptist 27%	Meth 12% / RC 5	Others 20%
d) Geographical Area	S.E. England 44%	Rest of England 41%	Rest of U.K. 15%	
	S.E. England 46%	Rest of England 46%	◇ 8%	
e) How contact made	Through local church 27%	Contacted "cold" 73%		
	Through local church 47%	Contacted "cold" 53%		

◇ Rest of U.K.

We can summarize this information by saying that the people who seem more likely to feel they do not belong in a church are:

* Women more than men (Figure 15a).
* Younger people (especially those aged 25-34) more than older people. Those aged 55 and over seem to feel positively that they do belong (Figure 15b).
* Baptist Christians (and to a lesser extent Methodists) more than Anglicans or Roman Catholics (Figure 15c).
* Former church-goers in England more than those living in the rest of the UK (Figure 15d).

Those not being cared for at church
We can summarize this information by saying that the people who seem likely to feel that others do not appear to care about them as a person are:

* Women more than men (Figure 16a).

Figure 16: COMPARISON OF RESPONSES FROM THOSE WHO
HAD SOME FEELING THAT PEOPLE DIDN'T SEEM TO
CARE ABOUT THEM AS A PERSON

▨ % of those surveyed   ☐ % of those who felt people didn't
seem to care

a) Sex	Female 50%	Male 50%
	Female 57%	Male 43%

b) Age	-25 19%	25-34 21%	35-54 37%	55+ 23%
	-25 18%	25-34 22%	35-54 45%	55+ 15%

c) Denomination	Church of England 45%	Baptist 15%	Meth 10%	RC 10%	Others 20%
	Church of England 37%	Baptist 23%	Meth 8%	RC 7%	Others 25%

d) Geographical Area	S.E. England 44%	Rest of England 41%	Rest of U.K.15%
	S.E. England 31%	Rest of England 51%	Rest of U.K. 18%

e) How contact made	Through local church 27%	Contacted "cold" 73%
	Through local church 41%	Contacted "cold" 59%

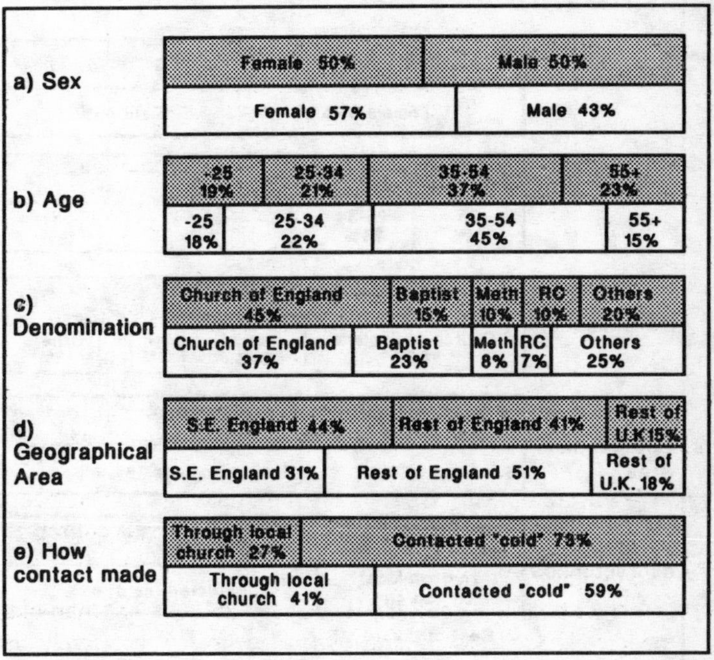

* Middle-aged people (35-54) more than people aged 55 and over (Figure 16b).
* Baptists and those in the 'Others' category more than Anglicans, Methodists and Catholics (Figure 16c).
* Those who went to churches in the rest of England more than those from churches in South East England (Figure 16d).

Those whose questions and observations were not taken seriously

We can summarize this information by saying that the people who seem likely to feel that their questions and observations are not taken seriously at church are:

Figure 17: COMPARISON OF RESPONSES FROM THOSE WHO FELT THAT TO SOME EXTENT THEIR QUESTIONS AND OBSERVATIONS WEREN'T TAKEN SERIOUSLY

▨ % of those surveyed ☐ % of those who felt their questions weren't taken seriously

a) Sex	Female 50%	Male 50%
	Female 55%	Male 45%

a) Sex	Female 50%			Male 50%	

b) Age

-25 19%	25-34 21%	35-54 37%	55+ 23%
-25 21%	25-34 24%	35-54 37%	55+ 18%

c) Denomination

Church of England 45%	Baptist 15%	Meth 10%	RC 10%	Others 20%
Church of England 42%	Baptist 24%	Meth 10%	RC 6%	Others 18%

d) Geographical Area

S.E. England 44%	Rest of England 41%	Rest of U.K.15%
S.E. England 37%	Rest of England 56%	◇ 7%

e) How contact made

Through local church 27%	Contacted "cold" 73%
Through local church 40%	Contacted "cold" 60%

◇ Rest of U.K.

* Women more than men (Figure 17a).
* Younger people (up to the age of 34) more than older people of 55 and above (Figure 17b).
* Baptist Christians far more than Roman Catholics (Figure 17c).
* Those in churches in the rest of England more than those from South East England and the rest of the UK (Figure 17d).

Those who encountered domestic conflicts or tensions
We can summarize this information by saying that the people who seem likely to leave church because of domestic conflicts and tensions are:

Figure 18: COMPARISON OF RESPONSES FROM THOSE WHO LEFT CHURCH BECAUSE OF SOME DOMESTIC CONFLICTS OR TENSIONS

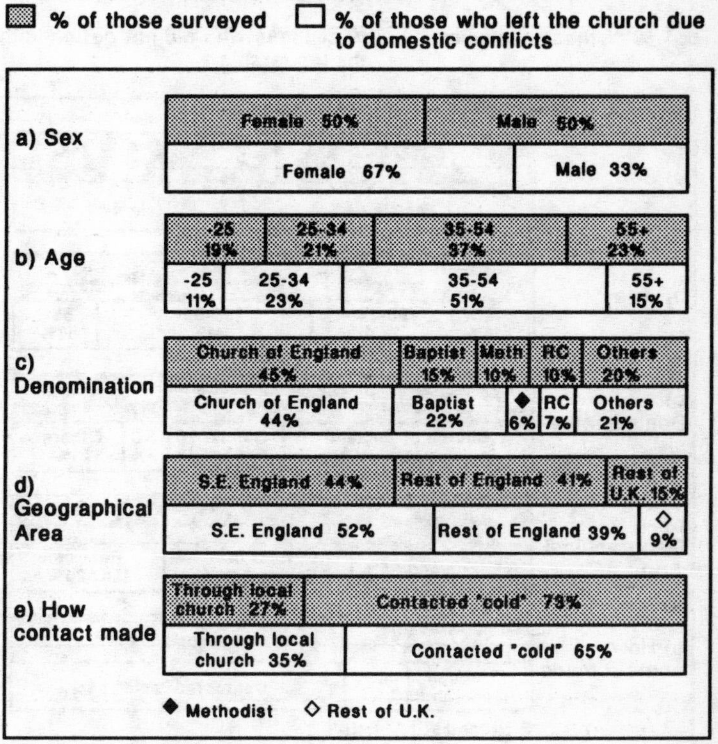

▓ % of those surveyed   ☐ % of those who left the church due to domestic conflicts

a) Sex	Female 50%	Male 50%
	Female 67%	Male 33%

b) Age	-25 19%	25-34 21%	35-54 37%	55+ 23%
	-25 11%	25-34 23%	35-54 51%	55+ 15%

c) Denomination	Church of England 45%	Baptist 15%	Meth 10%	RC 10%	Others 20%
	Church of England 44%	Baptist 22%	◆ 6%	RC 7%	Others 21%

d) Geographical Area	S.E. England 44%	Rest of England 41%	Rest of U.K. 15%
	S.E. England 52%	Rest of England 39%	◇ 9%

e) How contact made	Through local church 27%	Contacted "cold" 73%
	Through local church 35%	Contacted "cold" 65%

◆ Methodist   ◇ Rest of U.K.

* Women far more than men (Figure 18a).
* Middle-aged people (35-54) more than those 24 and under and those 55 and over (Figure 18b).
* Baptist Christians more than Methodist Christians or Roman Catholics (Figure 18c).
* Those in churches in the South East England more than those in churches in the rest of England or other parts of the UK (Figure 18d).

Those not getting on with the leadership

Figure 19: COMPARISON OF RESPONSES FROM THOSE WHO DID
NOT GET ON WITH THE LEADERSHIP IN SOME WAY

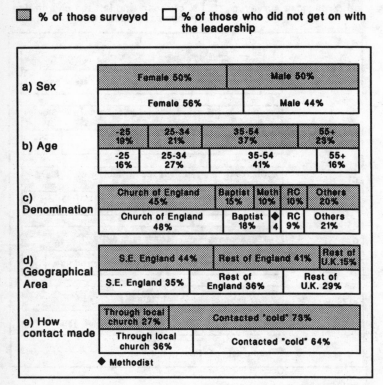

We can summarize this information by saying that the people who seem likely to leave church because they do not get on with the leadership are:

* Women more than men (Figure 19a).
* Those aged from 25 to 54 more than younger and older people (Figure 19b).
* Anglicans and Baptists more than Methodists (Figure 19c).

* Former church-goers in the rest of the UK more than those in England (Figure 19d).

Those unhappy about the direction of the church

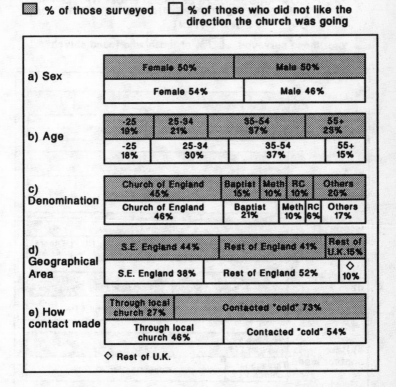

Figure 20: COMPARISON OF RESPONSES FROM THOSE WHO DID NOT LIKE THE DIRECTION THE CHURCH WAS GOING IN TO SOME EXTENT

▓ % of those surveyed   ☐ % of those who did not like the direction the church was going

a) Sex
| Female 50% | Male 50% |
| Female 54% | Male 46% |

b) Age
| -25 10% | 25-34 21% | 35-54 37% | 55+ 23% |
| -25 18% | 25-34 30% | 35-54 37% | 55+ 15% |

c) Denomination
| Church of England 45% | Baptist 15% | Meth 10% | RC 10% | Others 20% |
| Church of England 46% | Baptist 21% | Meth 10% | RC 6% | Others 17% |

d) Geographical Area
| S.E. England 44% | Rest of England 41% | Rest of U.K. 15% |
| S.E. England 38% | Rest of England 52% | ◇ 10% |

e) How contact made
| Through local church 27% | Contacted "cold" 73% |
| Through local church 46% | Contacted "cold" 54% |

◇ Rest of U.K.

We can summarize this information by saying that the people who seem likely to leave church because they do not like the direction in which it is going are:

* Women more than men (Figure 20a).
* Those aged 25-34 more than people aged 55 and over (Figure 20b).

* Baptists more than Roman Catholics or those in the 'Other' denominations (Figure 20c).
* Church-goers in the rest of England more than those in South East England or the rest of the UK (Figure 20d).

Those unhappy at the church's irrelevance

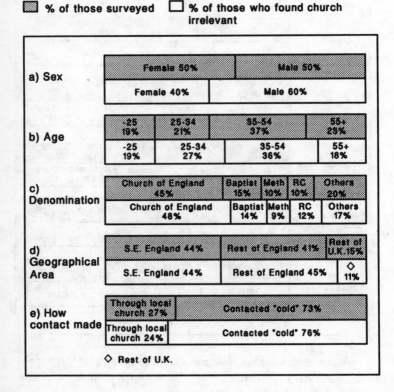

Figure 21: COMPARISON OF RESPONSES FROM THOSE WHO FOUND CHURCH IRRELEVANT TO THEIR EVERYDAY LIVES TO SOME EXTENT

▨ % of those surveyed   ☐ % of those who found church irrelevant

a) Sex

Female 50%	Male 50%
Female 40%	Male 60%

b) Age

-25 19%	25-34 21%	35-54 37%	55+ 23%
-25 19%	25-34 27%	35-54 36%	55+ 18%

c) Denomination

Church of England 45%	Baptist 15%	Meth 10%	RC 10%	Others 20%
Church of England 48%	Baptist 14%	Meth 9%	RC 12%	Others 17%

d) Geographical Area

S.E. England 44%	Rest of England 41%	Rest of U.K. 15%
S.E. England 44%	Rest of England 45%	◇ 11%

e) How contact made

Through local church 27%	Contacted "cold" 73%
Through local church 24%	Contacted "cold" 76%

◇ Rest of U.K.

We can summarize this information by saying that the people who seem likely to leave church because it appears irrelevant to their everyday lives are:

* Men more than women (Figure 21a).
* Younger people (25-34) more than those aged 55 and over (Figure 21b).
* Church of England and Roman Catholic church-goers more than those in the 'Other' denominations (Figure 21c).
* People in England (but not the South East) more than those in parts of the UK outside England (Figure 21d).

Those unhappy that church seems boring

Figure 22: COMPARISON OF RESPONSES FROM THOSE WHO AT LEAST PARTLY FOUND CHURCH BORING

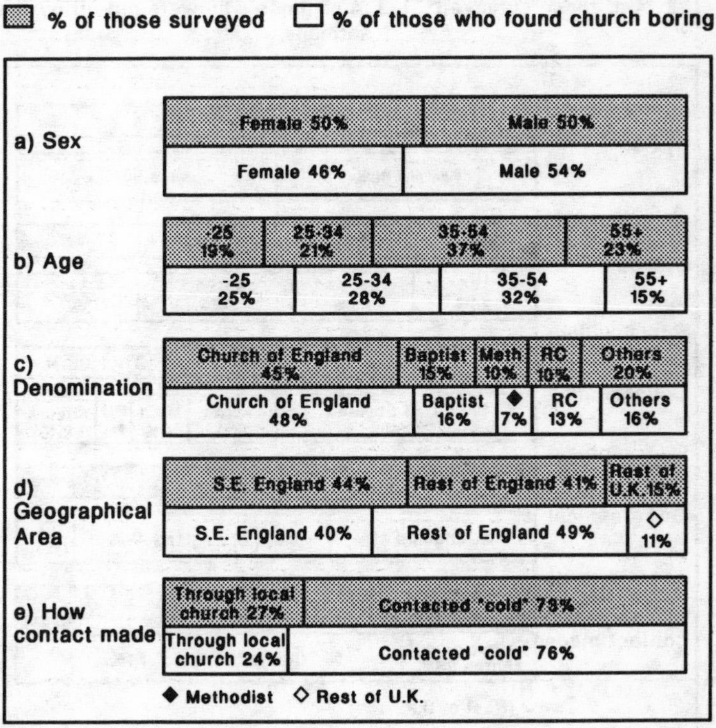

▨ % of those surveyed   ☐ % of those who found church boring

a) Sex	Female 50%		Male 50%	
	Female 46%		Male 54%	

b) Age	-25 19%	25-34 21%	35-54 37%	55+ 23%
	-25 25%	25-34 28%	35-54 32%	55+ 15%

c) Denomination	Church of England 45%	Baptist 15%	Meth 10%	RC 10%	Others 20%
	Church of England 48%	Baptist 16%	◆ 7%	RC 13%	Others 16%

d) Geographical Area	S.E. England 44%	Rest of England 41%	Rest of U.K. 15%
	S.E. England 40%	Rest of England 49%	◇ 11%

e) How contact made	Through local church 27%	Contacted "cold" 73%
	Through local church 24%	Contacted "cold" 76%

◆ Methodist   ◇ Rest of U.K.

We can summarize this information by saying that the people who leave church because they find it boring are:

* Men more than women (Figure 22a).
* Those aged up to 34 far more than those aged 35 and over (Figure 22b).
* Anglicans and Catholics more than Methodists and those in the 'Other' denominations (Figure 22c).
* People in the rest of England more than those in South East England and the rest of the UK (Figure 22d).

Those put off by the sermons

Figure 23: COMPARISON OF RESPONSES FROM THOSE WHO TO SOME EXTENT WERE PUT OFF BY THE SERMONS

▨ % of those surveyed   ☐ % of those who were put off by the sermons

a) Sex	Female 50%		Male 50%	
	Female 50%		Male 50%	

b) Age	-25 19%	25-34 21%	35-54 37%	55+ 23%
	-25 24%	25-34 23%	35-54 30%	55+ 23%

c) Denomination	Church of England 45%	Baptist 15%	Meth 10%	RC 10%	Others 20%
	Church of England 50%	Baptist 17%	Meth 11%	RC 7%	Others 15%

d) Geographical Area	S.E. England 44%	Rest of England 41%	Rest of U.K. 15%
	S.E. England 40%	Rest of England 49%	◇ 11%

e) How contact made	Through local church 27%	Contacted "cold" 73%
	Through local church 26%	Contacted "cold" 74%

◇ Rest of U.K.

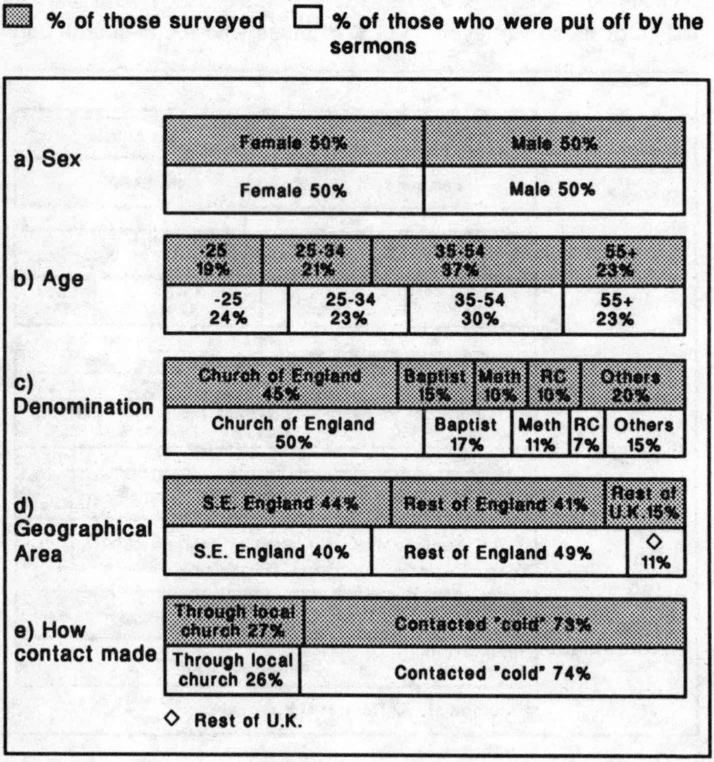

We can summarize this information by saying that the people who seem likely to leave church because they are put off by the sermons are:

* Those aged 34 and under more than those aged 35-54 (Figure 23b).
* Anglican, Baptist and Methodist Christians more than Roman Catholics and those in the 'Other' denominations (Figure 23c).
* Those from the rest of England more than those in South East England or the rest of the UK (Figure 23d).

Those feeling that God let them down

Figure 24: COMPARISON OF RESPONSES FROM THOSE WHO FELT GOD LET THEM DOWN IN SOME WAY

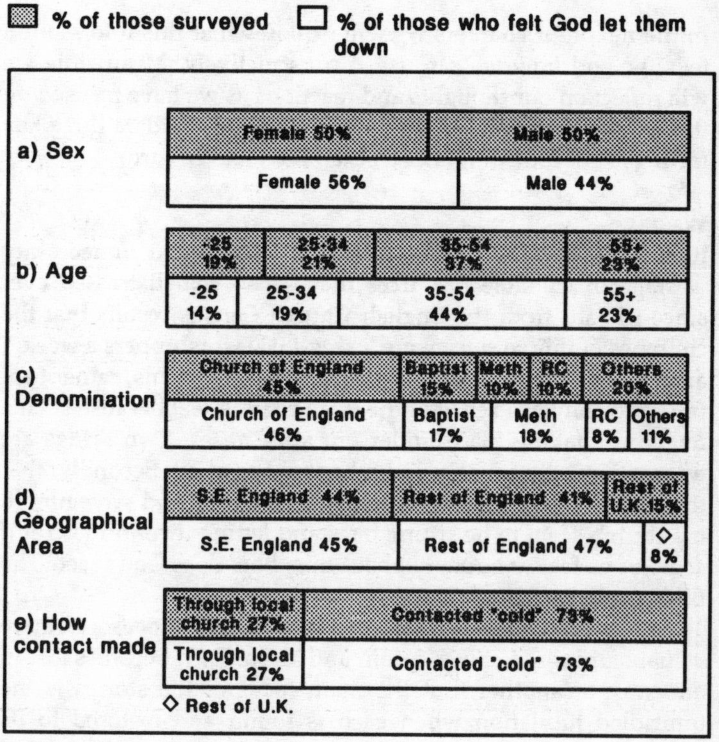

▓ % of those surveyed   □ % of those who felt God let them down

a) Sex	Female 50%		Male 50%	
	Female 56%		Male 44%	

	-25 19%	25-34 21%	35-54 37%	55+ 23%
b) Age	-25 14%	25-34 19%	35-54 44%	55+ 23%

	Church of England 45%	Baptist 15%	Meth 10%	RC 10%	Others 20%
c) Denomination	Church of England 46%	Baptist 17%	Meth 18%	RC 8%	Others 11%

	S.E. England 44%	Rest of England 41%	Rest of U.K. 15%
d) Geographical Area	S.E. England 45%	Rest of England 47%	◇ 8%

	Through local church 27%	Contacted "cold" 73%
e) How contact made	Through local church 27%	Contacted "cold" 73%

◇ Rest of U.K.

We can summarize this information by saying that the people who seem likely to leave church because they feel that God has let them down in some way are:

* Women more than men (Figure 24a).
* Those aged 35-54 more than those aged 34 and under (Figure 24b).
* Methodists, and to a lesser extent Baptists, more than those in the 'Other' denominations (Figure 24c).
* Those in England (but not so much those in the South East) more than those living in the rest of the UK (Figure 24d).

OVERALL IMPRESSIONS

In the next four chapters we will explore what this information tells us, and how we can use it constructively. Meanwhile we will reflect on our thoughts and reactions as we have focused on these many and varied issues. As I analysed the data three key feelings kept returning. Let us examine them in turn.

Wastage

It may be because I have a natural aversion to unnecessary wastage of valuable resources that I have felt distressed ever since I heard from the English Church Census results that the churches of this country were losing 1,000 worshippers a week. I am not trying to be dramatic or emotional about this; rather I am trying to convey a sense of the deep regret I feel because such a tragedy is taking place under our very noses. Two things are wrong. First, that it should be happening at all. Secondly, that those of us who are continuing to follow Christ and serve him in his church seem to be sitting back and letting it continue. Yet if some of us feel so strongly about this, how does God react? The Bible gives us clues.

As we have already seen, in Luke 15 Jesus speaks of three valuable things: a sheep, a coin and a son. Each becomes lost in one way or another, but the main focus of the stories is the unbridled jubilation when each is found and restored to its rightful place. This reveals how much value God puts on what he has made. Later in his ministry, Jesus told the Parable of the

Talents. Three servants are entrusted with resources of differing values to use wisely in their master's absence. When he returns they have to account for their stewardship decisions. The people honoured are those who have made wise and responsible use of their resources while he was away. The servant who is condemned acted in a lax and irresponsible way (Mt 25:14-30).

In the light of this, how must God feel when he sees one thousand people fewer in church worship services this weekend as compared to last? I can only believe that a God who takes such care of the resources he has made despairs to see such wastage as people continue to flow out of his church. Maybe they did not all have a personal relationship with him. Maybe they were not all dedicated to the work of his church, but at least they took time each week to spend an hour in his presence. They were at least in the environment where he can speak clearly and definitively to those who will listen. Now they are not there any more it is likely that the distance between him and them will increase. Here, then, are people who are by no means beyond God's ability to touch in the future, but whose decision to stay away from church makes it less likely that they will have a fresh encounter with him soon. This sense of loss and futile wastage must, whatever the background causes, invoke great pain in the heart of God.

Broken vows

In Figure 7 we examined the Christian background of the people who contributed to the Survey. Among the areas highlighted are those where a degree of response and commitment is necessary. In this category are infant christening, baptism and dedication, together with confirmation and Believers' Baptism. Let us briefly survey the promises and responses that have to be made.

When young children are taken to the Church of England for christening the parents and godparents are told:

> Those who bring children to be baptized must affirm their allegiance to Christ and their rejection of all that is evil. It is your duty to bring up these children to fight against evil and to follow Christ. Therefore I ask these questions which

you must answer for yourselves and for these children. Do
you turn to Christ?
Response: I turn to Christ
Do you repent of your sins?
Response: I repent of my sins
Do you renounce evil?
Response: I renounce evil
Later... Do you believe and trust in God the Father, who
made the world?
Response: I believe and trust in him
Do you believe and trust in his Son Jesus Christ, who
redeemed mankind?
Response: I believe and trust in him
Do you believe and trust in his Holy Spirit, who gives life
to the people of God?
Response: I believe and trust in him.[1]

These are not easy words to say with meaning. Those who
speak them make a declaration of faith as well as speaking on
behalf of the child being baptized. In the Anglican Confirmation
Service the same form of words is used. The bishop addresses
the person who now says that these convictions have become
personal.

A massive 84% of the Survey respondents had been christened, baptized or dedicated; 41% had been confirmed. 17% had
been baptized by immersion in water as believers. This represents a great amount of commitment. Across the country millions
of people have stood in church and have spoken words of
declaration and promise in the presence of God. Most of them
are now not to be found in our churches. How does God respond?

The God revealed in the Bible is a God of honour and integrity who keeps his word as a matter of principle. He is a God
who makes covenants with people who love and respect him.
These are firm promises which he declares he will keep. After
the devastation of the flood he made a covenant with Noah (Gen
9:8-17). He unconditionally promised never to destroy all earthly
life again with any natural catastrophe. He made two covenants
with Abraham (Gen 15:9-21; 17:1-27), and later the memorable
covenant with Israel at Sinai in which he promised to protect his

people (Ex 19:1—24:18). It is noteworthy that God has never broken any of his promises. This includes the New Covenant, the covenant of pure grace, which makes access to God through Christ possible for those in sin and rebellion (Jer 31:31-34).

In the light of God's character, what do we imagine to be his response to the seemingly flippant way that vows are made before him in churches and then apparently taken very lightly? Again we can only surmise how strong his sense of sadness and despair must be. Maybe he is angry too.

Pain

What we must realize at this point is that when a person stops going to church, there is pain generated at both a human and divine level. I was sent these paragraphs from New Zealand— they came originally from Canada:

> One interesting facet of the church dropout to note...is that they are 'pain-filled' persons. Research consistently indicates that they leave the church for painful reasons. They did not go easily. They left with a great deal of heartache and/or turmoil. This may well have been unrelated to their life in the church community. The church or its people may not have been at fault. It may have been the 'deck of cards' life was dealing out to them at that time. One thing is certain: they left in pain. And another thing is certain. We who were fellow members with them did nothing about that pain. We were oblivious to their cries for help—the agony that was oozing from their humanity. Hence they left to lick their wounds elsewhere.[2]

In his teaching about the shepherd and his flock Jesus described the sheep pen as a place of safety and security (Jn 10:1-21). Here his flock could find peace and refreshment. Jesus must feel pain when he sees his church hurting people so much that they have to leave it. After all, his church is where people should be able to go to find acceptance, love and support. He must frequently despair of his earthly children. It is a mercy that God is patient and loving with us.

In this Section we have identified and described the problem facing the British churches. People are leaving in significant numbers for a variety of reasons. We need now to discuss what action can be taken by the churches to stop this erosion.

Notes

1 *The Alternative Service Book 1980* (Clowes, SPCK, Cambridge University Press: Cambridge, 1980) p 245-247.

2 From a Working Paper, 'Understanding the Church Dropout', source unknown.

SECTION 2

Tackling The Issues

CHAPTER 5

Problems of Personal Pai...

I N LISTENING TO our Survey respondents, we have heard their reasons for ceasing to attend church. In Chapter 4 we identified four main categories that between them encompass these reasons. In this and the next three chapters we will look at these categories in more depth.

Our first is quite subjective and comes from the intuitive side of our human nature. It is what is in me that makes me feel that either I cannot or I do not want to go to church any more.

Let us recognize at the outset that feelings have enormous power over us. The more subjective a person's temperament the more he or she will be deeply influenced by their feelings. Our feelings can, of course, lead us to make mistakes. However we can never be all God intends us to be if we dismiss our feelings as intrusive. When they arise within us they need investigation to see if they are valid and realistic. The Survey shows that, rightly or wrongly, many people have left churches largely because of their feelings. Let us begin, then, to consider some of the personal issues their responses raise.

1. 'SHOULD I STOP GOING TO CHURCH IF I FEEL I DON'T BELONG?'

Because of the way God made us, a feeling of acceptance and belonging is a vital ingredient in our lives. In the past people in the West lived in smaller communities where they were known and accepted. Today life has become so impersonal for many.

The church has the capacity to help people feel accepted, and it is God's intention that it should.

In Ephesians 2:8-10 Paul refers to the fact that all who are true believers have come to Christ the same way. Whether or not an individual meets Jesus on the road to Damascus is not the point. What matters is whether a person has come to Christ as Saviour by simple trust and faith. Paul reminded the Galatian Christians that they 'are all sons of God through faith in Christ Jesus...you are all one in Christ Jesus' (Gal 3:26-28). The message is plain: there is a spiritual glue that should bond Christians together because they have a deep experience in common—they have all had their lives changed by Jesus. They were in the 'slimy pit'; now they have their 'feet on a rock' (Ps 40:2). A sense of belonging should therefore permeate every Christian church.

...a sense of belonging

The sad thing is that it is often not like this and our Survey results confirm it. One fifth of the respondents said that they felt that they did not belong and that this was part of the reason they stopped attending church. A further 9% gave a 'maybe' answer to the same question.

We have already seen a breakdown of this group of 29% of

the Survey participants in Figure 15 (Chapter 4). We know that they are:

...women more than men
...younger more than older people
...Baptists more than Anglicans and Roman Catholics
...English people more than those from the rest of the UK

Their feelings of not belonging, not surprisingly, helped hasten their departure from church.

What explanations are there for these conclusions? Perhaps women are more in tune with their feelings and so may leave before men if they feel negative vibes. Younger people have not had the same amount of time to get established in the church as those older than themselves. They may leave if they feel they are outsiders or intruders. As for the denominational and geographical differences, explanations are not easy to find.

The sociological part of the problem

What are the people who ticked this box on the survey forms saying? They did not feel a part of the church they left. They went regularly and yet felt isolated even when surrounded by the other people present. They may have been aware of Paul's teaching about the church as the Body of Christ, but it did not help them feel an integral part of it. There are a number of reasons why this may have been so:

* It seemed too big a group to relate to so that they felt lost in it.
* It felt too small a group so they felt intimidated by the closeness of other people around them.
* There appeared to be no appropriate time or place in the life of the church when relationships could be made with others whom they saw at a distance at church services.
* It felt as if the type or class of people who went to the church were very different from them in terms of lifestyle and life-values.

All these feelings are very real and can cause a person to consider leaving, even if they have been going to the church for some years. James Sire helps us understand the increased likelihood of this happening in the West when he contrasts this individualism with the greater immediate and extended family bonds regarded as normal in Eastern society.[1]

Figure 25:   **CONTRASTING VIEW OF WESTERN AND EASTERN SOCIETY**

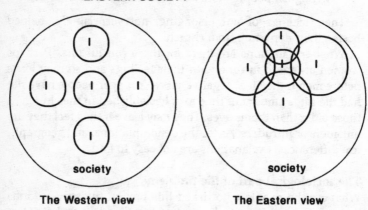

The Western view   **The Eastern view**

Monica Hill has concluded that:

> the whole of western society is founded upon a belief in the ultimate value of the individual and therefore emphasises individual freedom and individual rights. This has been a major force in the break-up of the extended family, and consequently of community life.[2]

A little later she makes observations about the effect of this on the churches.

> The breakdown of family life in society has had a major effect on church life throughout the western nations. Whereas at the beginning of the twentieth century most church congregations included whole families of three or four generations, often very large families, today by contrast there are few congregations where there are families of more than one generation. The largest group is very

often that of singles...Thus many people in the western churches suffer from loneliness and isolation.[3]

It is not surprising that some of them find this too painful and leave.

The psychological part of the problem

People who feel they do not belong sometimes have inner feelings of insecurity. H. Norman Wright, in his book, *Overcoming your Hidden Fears*, says, 'All of us are afraid sometimes. That's normal. But some of us are fearful most of the time. That's *not* normal'.[4] Further on he introduces Judy whose problem is both extreme and serious. She seemed sure that others would always reject her. If people around her seemed genuinely friendly she was suspicious. He concludes, 'Judy's fear of rejection was consuming her'.[5] For a variety of reasons that go back to their past, people like Judy never feel they belong anywhere. Until they receive the appropriate help and begin to accept love they will not be able to be integrated fully in any community—even a caring, loving Christ-centred church.

Most people do not suffer as much as Judy, but many of us feel or have felt insecure with others at times. It takes love, friendship and acceptance to help us through. There is a great need for our churches to become places where those who feel a lack of acceptance begin to feel truly accepted—not only by God, but by his people too.

The spiritual part of the problem

There is a strong emphasis on community in Scripture. God wants people to experience his love and full acceptance. This comes in two ways. First, as they meet him in a personal encounter at the cross of Jesus, they enter into relationship with him and become part of his family. Secondly, they make relationships with his people in the church. Our research shows that the second part does not always happen as intended. We need to see why some Christians fail to become integrated into the Body of Christ.

* They do not become a part of a small group. John Savage's research into church drop-outs in the USA shows that people

integrated in small groups are far less likely to leave a church.[6] The flourishing Willow Creek Community Church in Chicago states,

> It is the goal of the leadership...to have everyone who is involved...become a member of a small group...The goal of the small group is to help each person mature in Christ through the process of discipleship. The group provides accountability, instruction, encouragement and support for each of its members.[7]

Michael Green argues strongly for the same thing.

> It is a notable fact throughout the world that the churches which are growing fastest are those where there are natural meeting-places for small sections of the congregations— normally meeting in homes. It is in this way that relation- ships can be forged, problems talked over, personal and maybe financial needs addressed, and individuals can feel that they matter and are loved.[8]

* They are not actively nurtured as new Christians. Lynne, a regular caller to my late-night radio show, told me one week that she was caring for some new-born hedgehogs that had been abandoned by their mother. To survive they required round- the-clock attention and help. New converts to Christ need spir- itual food, encouragement, support and love from those who are established in their faith. Otherwise they become very vulner- able and almost certainly begin to feel isolated from others in the church because of their comparative lack of experience.

* They are not encouraged to discover and use their spiritual gifts. We have already referred to Paul's teaching in 1 Cor- inthians 12 on the gifts God has given to people in the Body of Christ. He makes it clear that every Christian has at least one gift to use for God (v7), that there is a great variety of gifts (v8-10) and that it is important that all these gifts are used in the church (v21-26). Where no attempt is made to identify the God-given gifts of a Christian while others around are clearly using theirs, that person will inevitably feel isolated, estranged and unvalued.

* They do not make real friends in the church. Ajith Fernando shows us that Scripture identifies two types of friend. He refers to Proverbs 18:24, which says 'A man of many companions may come to ruin, but there is a friend who sticks closer than a brother'. We can have acquaintances who are not real friends or those who show us 'affection and loyalty'.[9] When people experience real friendship at church they are far less likely to leave.

The way ahead

At this point we need to ask an important question. With 29% of those surveyed feeling that they did not belong in their church to some extent, what action can churches take to rectify this problem? God's heart must be sad because many people are finding the church of Christ a cold and unwelcoming place. The answer is in the points that we have already considered. To reduce this problem, we need to engage in both prayer and positive action. This action is the antithesis of the points made above:

* Encourage the church to provide times for social events and relaxing fellowship.
* Provide the environment where God's healing love can radiate to those with feelings of rejection.
* Strongly encourage everyone into small groups.
* Actively nurture new Christians.
* Encourage the discovery of the spiritual gifts within the church and their subsequent development and use for God.
* Encourage those in the church to make real and deep friendships with each other.

2. 'SHOULD I STOP GOING TO CHURCH IF I FEEL THAT I AM NOT CARED FOR?'

We deal here with the extent to which those attending church feel real love, concern and understanding for them as a person. Whether part of a church with twenty-five or 2000 regular attenders, they need to know that any problems they have will be taken seriously. In the Survey 9% of the respondents said they left church at least partly because the church did not seem to care about them as a person. A further 8% gave a 'maybe' answer here.

This is serious, especially as the Bible insists that love and caring within the church is mandatory. The New Testament is littered with 'one another' references that describe different aspects of corporate life. In John 13:34 Jesus shares his new command: 'Love one another. As I have loved you, so you must love one another.' 1 Corinthians 13 teaches that in a church of many parts, the rich and selfless love of God needs to flow to keep the fellowship bonded together. Clearly this is not happening in some British churches as God intends.

In Figure 16 (Chapter 4) we gained a deeper insight into the 17% of Survey respondents who sensed a lack of care in their church. We know that they are:

> ...middle-aged more than older people
> ...Baptists and those in the 'Other' denominations more than Anglicans
> ...those from the rest of England more than those in the South East

What explanations are there for these points? Older people may be more hardened and able to cope without a sense of caring, but reasons are again hard to find for the denominational and geographical findings. We note a trend, though, in both sections dealing with feelings of acceptance and care in churches that we have covered so far in this chapter. The Anglicans fare better than average while Baptist churches are portrayed as less loving, accepting and caring.

The Problem

The question we need to face is this—are the people who come to our churches uncaring, insensitive and unsympathetic? Are they unable to show genuine concern to others, even if their lack of spiritual maturity means they experience Christ's love in only a limited way? This is of course impossible to answer. There may be some churches where many who attend are self-centred. Generally, Christian people seem to have a capacity to be fairly caring and compassionate. What is going wrong?

Maybe Alice Fryling has the answer. She tells what happens when she attends social gatherings.

> After spending two or three hours with friends, I some-times leave with a sense of sadness. Many times I relate this sadness to the fact that no one asked me anything about myself. No one seemed to want to know about me, my interests and activities. No one reached out to touch me with a personal word of encouragement or a loving question. I do not think this is because people really do not want to reach out. I think it is because they do not know how...I sometimes think that if our society were to be pictured symbolically on film, we might choose millions of dots, each with many fast-moving, concentric circles sur-rounding it. They bump into each other, to be sure, but they rarely penetrate each other's spheres.[10]

Problems are exacerbated for church-goers whose churches do not provide them with care and support when crises occur in their lives. It is then that they feel very isolated and unsure of where to turn for help. From his extensive research in the USA, Dr John Savage sees a pattern of behaviour in the lives of church-goers when a 'cluster' of problems in their life outside church occurs. Many people will not openly talk about them at church, he says, but may well drop a broad hint to the pastor that they are under pressure when they meet him on the steps outside church on their way home.

The church becomes part of their problem if and when these hints are ignored or go unnoticed. They begin to think, 'My church doesn't care about me'. These sentiments may turn to anger and bitterness in due course and a major problem between the individual and the church then exists.[11] The person may be even more reticent to talk about their problems at this stage if someone from the church makes contact with them. They will not be sure that their motives are thoroughly pure. 'Maybe they're just contacting me to keep me coming to church so that I continue to give financially', they may surmise.

What then are the main problems? Restricting it to three these are:

* Some Christians share their problems within the church but fail to receive adequate support from fellow church-goers.
* Others fail to share their problems openly but drop clues as to the levels of stress or trauma they are experiencing. They hope that someone will pick this up and make personal contact with them.
* Others feel unable to come close to people around them and so restrict conversations to impersonal topics.

Sometimes, however, problems are more superficial initially. In response to my letter to ask for help with my Survey, one minister gave me the brief case history of a teenage girl who left church. She had been brought up in a Christian family but felt slighted when the new minister consistently failed to remember her name correctly. Consequently she missed church once or twice and when there was no follow-up she ceased attending altogether. The extreme sensitivity of some can make simple errors appear like grave offences.

The way out

Recognizing that Christians rightly perceive it vitally important that their church cares for them, we consider three remedies to the problems we have uncovered.

* Churches need a shared pastoral ministry. It is now more common for full-time church leaders to delegate some pastoral work to others, while retaining overall responsibility. However, there are still many churches where this is not so. 1 Peter 5:2 advocates a plurality of carers in a church. God has gifted more than just the main leader of a church with pastoral gifts. Those other identical gifts, maybe as yet undiscerned and untrained, need releasing into the service of God and his people.

The other factor to consider at this point is the unrealistic expectation of some Christians. They much prefer their pastoral caring to be from the church's pivotal leader, the vicar, rector, minister or pastor. While such leaders often provide as much personal care as they can, pressure of time means they are severely limited if the church is larger than twenty or thirty people. Shared pastoral caring is the only option.

* Churches need structured pastoral caring. It is surely a

devious ploy of Satan to suggest that it is either unnecessary or unspiritual to formalize pastoral caring in a church. The bigger the gaps, the greater number of people can slide through them. We need to ensure that everyone who is considered part of the church is properly encompassed by a workable system of caring. This can be through the Deacons, PCC or (as is the case in the church where I am Minister) by appointing Pastoral Carers who are each allocated a group of the congregation. People need to be visited in their homes regularly and assured that someone is available at any time if a need arises. This is the only way that we can take Peter's words seriously. 'Be shepherds of God's flock that is under your care' (1 Pet 5:2).

* We need to be more sensitive to people's problems. Everyone who accepts pastoral responsibility becomes frustrated at times to discover that someone in their care had a need but did not talk about it with them. The reluctance of people to share their problems openly is a reality whether we like it or not. This is why senior church leaders in particular need training to recognize the signs and clues that people give them that all is not well in their lives. John Savage tells how he used to get his secretary to stand beside him at the church door. She would note down the name of anyone who gave even the slightest hint that they were under some kind of internal pressure. He then ensured that a trained team member from the church phoned these people within hours to make themselves available to help. He estimates that by taking this action he reduced the drop-out rate from his church by 95%.[12]

3. 'SHOULD I STOP GOING TO CHURCH IF MY QUESTIONS AND OBSERVATIONS AREN'T TAKEN SERIOUSLY?'

This is another area that reflects the extent to which a church values its congregation—or not as the case may be. Just as people become upset if they sense a lack of belonging or care in the church, they also become resentful if their views or questions are ignored, rejected or sidelined. They feel they are not important and that their opinions are of no account. Clearly this can be a contributory factor to their leaving the church.

In our research 7% of those surveyed said that their questions and observations were not taken seriously. A further 6% responded with a 'maybe' answer to the question. This is sad. While there are undoubtedly some stirrers and troublemakers in our churches, most people who have been in a church for some years have its interests at heart. They care about it now and they care about its future.

Therefore it is no surprise that they raise points for consideration by the church or leadership. This seems perfectly natural and healthy, but leaders can be highly sensitive and defensive. I know—I am one! Even innocent questions can appear threatening and challenging at times. Yet we notice that in his ministry, Jesus was prepared to answer any questions put to him, however tough they were. He was obviously totally secure in his knowledge that he both had and was God's Truth (Jn 14:6).

In Figure 17 (Chapter 4) we learned more about the 13% of our Survey respondents who left church partly because they felt their questions or observations were not taken seriously. We know that they are:

    ...Women more than men
    ...Younger more than older people
    ...Baptists more than Anglicans or Roman Catholics
    ...From England (apart from the South East) more than the
       rest of the UK.

We need to comment on the response of former Baptist church-goers. Baptist church government is probably the most 'democratic' form in existence. A Church Meeting in a Baptist church is the only place of authority where, under the guidance of God's Spirit, final decisions can be taken about that church's life and ministry. Such a meeting provides opportunity for any members to participate fully in discussion and decision-making. This being the case, it seems anomalous that Baptists complain loudest that their views are not taken seriously! I think this reflects their unhappiness when they find themselves in the minority time and again when votes are taken.

However, let us not forget that Baptist Christians have always been Dissenters. They have always had an independent tendency. Maybe we should not be surprised, therefore, if they submit more tamely to authority and question more.

Let us restrict further comment to one point. Scripture teaches the validity and importance of every member of the Body of Christ. Jesus reassured his disciples that they 'are worth more than many sparrows' (Mt 10:31) before he sent them out into ministry. If God cares so much for his children, church leaders need to provide facilities so that all who are a part of the church can feed them their questions and perceptions without fear of rejection or dismissal. Maybe a simple solution is to provide cards and a 'Suggestions box' in the foyer. A sign could explain that the cards were for constructive comments, observations or criticisms about the church and would be given serious consideration by the leaders. Any church which makes it easy for its worshippers to contribute their views is likely to see its membership grow in stature and size as a consequence.

4. 'SHOULD I STOP GOING TO CHURCH IF IT CAUSES TENSION AT HOME?'

This question provokes much heart-searching especially, of course, in homes where one partner is committed to Christ and regular at church and the other is not. It raises important and delicate questions about our priorities in life and causes important issues to be faced. Some 8% of those contacted in our Survey said that domestic conflicts or tensions stopped them attending church; a further 2% responded with a 'maybe' answer.

One minister who assisted with the Survey told of a complicated situation. He said that a couple married, the woman already having a child through a previous relationship. Other children were born, but the woman constantly accused the husband of picking on the child of which he was the adoptive father. The marriage was fraught with tension with the woman as the dominant partner. The family attended church but then the woman bought several dogs and became obsessed with showing them at dog shows which were held on Sundays. She began to miss church, and the husband came for counselling because he could not handle the situation. Friction between him and the oldest child worsened. Eventually the whole family left the church.

This situation shows what can happen when one partner comes to church and the other opts not to join them. It is not unusual for the whole family to be lost to the church in situations like this. Jesus knew only too well that his call to discipleship would provoke splits in families and warned his disciples of this (Mk 13:12). He also made it clear that there would be ultimate rewards for loyalty to him (Mt 19:29), while his Parable of the Great Banquet shows that some will reject him in favour of their marriage partner (Lk 14:20).

This then is a complex subject. It is probably best that we come to no firm conclusions here about what is right in any given situation. Scripture, of course, teaches both the sanctity of marriage and the need for marriage partners to remain faithful disciples of Jesus. Certainly a wife or husband with an unbelieving partner needs to display great sensitivity to their partner's needs and preferences if they are to be used by God to win them for him.

Figure 18 (Chapter 4) told us more about the 13% of those surveyed who left church because of some kind of domestic conflicts or tensions. We know that they are:

- ...Women more than men
- ...Middle-aged more than younger or older
- ...Baptists more than Methodists or Roman Catholics
- ...From South East England more than the rest of England or the rest of the UK.

In exploring reasons for these conclusions, we need to bear in mind that the subject-matter here is different from the previous categories. They focused on problems people had with the church. This however is a home-based problem and does not therefore reflect directly on the church although it does affect church attendance.

It is no surprise that women are much more affected by this problem than men; they account for 58% of the church-goers in

England.[13] In the light of New Testament teaching, Christian women may tend to submit to their unbelieving husbands when they disapprove of their going to church (Eph 5:22). Middle-aged family women, often with children, are maybe most prone to this difficulty. Baptists seem to have a greater than average proportion of problems in this area; this may be because their style of church life can attract family-orientated people.

At this point we have covered the main personal issues raised by the Survey. There are, however, several others that are important although space precludes detailed study.

5. 'SHOULD I STOP GOING TO CHURCH IF I FEEL GUILTY INSIDE?'

Here is a problem we referred to in Chapter 3. Human beings feel more than one kind of guilt. True guilt is what we feel when we stand before God having committed sin. We will consider this more fully in Chapter 8. Feelings of false guilt can consume us when, for instance, others condemn us or point the finger when we have done nothing wrong. People need to understand which kind of guilt they have before making any decision about going to church. Either way, because of God's provision through Christ, they should be able to find release. 1 John 1:9 tells us what to do if we are guilty before God. Romans 8:1 explains that if we are not guilty in God's sight we have no need to feel condemned. In the name of Jesus we can tell Satan to take his lies and leave us. If we still feel guilt we may need counselling help.

6. 'SHOULD I STOP GOING TO CHURCH IF I FEEL UNCOMFORTABLE AND ILL-AT-EASE IN THE BUILDING USED FOR WORSHIP?'

We live in 'space' and are constantly monitoring (often sub-consciously) whether or not we feel comfortable in that space. When we go to church physical space becomes a personal issue. Do I feel comfortable with the way the building is laid out and with this particular seat or pew in relation to others around me?

If the building is stark and aesthetically cold and unwelcoming it can hinder people feeling able to relax there. A relaxed worshipper is much more likely to be a responsive worshipper.

...cold and unwelcoming

We must think carefully and consult professionals when considering the future design and layout of our buildings. This is particularly the case when we consider how to make things easier for those who are disabled. Often we as good as exclude those with poor sight, hearing or mobility from church services quite undeliberately. It happens because we neither understand nor think about disabled people, and fail to make special provision to help them feel fully part of our worship.

7. 'SHOULD I STOP GOING TO CHURCH IF I DON'T FEEL I WANT TO PARTICIPATE PUBLICLY IN THE WORSHIP?'

Some Christians genuinely and sincerely believe that the Christian faith is a totally personal, individual and private matter. They say that it is therefore of no consequence to anyone else what they believe and what their faith means to them. Thus if their church moves towards more relaxed and flowing worship with greater opportunity for worshippers to be actively involved, they feel uncomfortable and threatened. They do not want to participate in this kind of service. If it is all that is available, the protective part of their nature tells them strongly that their only safe course of action is to stop attending.

We probably can help such people best by both the preaching ministry on Sundays and teaching in small groups, although they may not come easily to the latter. It is not just that they need a broader understanding about the biblical perspective on worship as a corporate act. It is also vital that they begin to see the importance of spiritual family life. They are depriving themselves of a whole dimension of Christian experience. Gently and sensitively they need encouragement to open themselves up to others and so begin to experience the joy of two-way Christian fellowship.

8. 'SHOULD I STOP GOING TO CHURCH IF I DON'T FEEL HAPPY TO BE ALONGSIDE THESE OTHER PEOPLE?'

There are probably at least three situations that apply here.

a) A Christian feels that some people also present at worship are not real and authentic. Steve Pogue tells of Mike who says, 'I haven't met very many people who seem to really live the Christian life. My Christian co-workers sure don't act differently to the non-Christians at the office. My wife and I have visited a few churches, and people seem to be there just for show.' [14] This may include the leadership of the church whom he or she may perceive to be hypocritical. 4% of our Survey respondents said that they left church because of the hypocrisy. It does not need to be blatant two-faced behaviour, but merely a sense that these people do not live in the same world and face the same problems as me. Bill Hybels says that when seekers come to church they sense hypocrisy if pastors do not come clean about their problems. After all, seekers know that *everyone* has problems. Every time a pastor admits to problems they breathe a sigh of relief. Here is a member of the human race who is in touch with reality![15] We need more preachers today who are prepared to be open with their congregations.

b) A Christian is unhappy with others in the church due to arguments and disagreements. One minister wrote to say that he had tried to find out why some people stopped attending his church. He asked older members who referred to 'arguments over music, flowers and seating'. Unresolved issues like these, however trivial they appear, provoke many to stay away. They must be opened up even if it is painful for the church for a while. It is likely to be productive long-term.

c) Some Christians know they have a problem—much like Paul in Romans 7:21-24 where he speaks of the war being fought in him between God's law and the law of sin. Not a few Christians experience weakness, for instance, in the sexual area of their life. Others may be aware that they compromise in their witness. The result is a feeling of unworthiness when they come to church. They know the difficulties they have, but presume that they alone in their church are suffering in this way. Their inner torment builds to a pitch where they cannot handle it any more and cease to attend. When Christians learn to be normal, natural, open and honest with each other, those who feel this way will quickly see that *all* believers face pressures. They will then understand that to stop going to church will only make things worse.

9. 'SHOULD I STOP GOING TO CHURCH IF I FEEL I CAN'T HANDLE THE PRESSURE THERE ANY MORE?'

There are some churches which extract every ounce of blood from their willing members. This can easily lead to burn-out, which causes a person to stop attending church because it seems the only way to escape. There are others whose full-time employment puts increasing pressures on them, effectively excluding them from playing any significant part in the life of the church mid-week. If, however, the church refuses to acknowledge and accept this pressure, the people concerned may well feel they have to extricate themselves from the church to remain sane. Church leaders in particular must work hard to keep closely in touch with the pressures of life that affect their congregations. Newspapers, magazines, TV news and documentaries are all vital here. If they take this lightly they will lose people who probably do not want to leave the church at all but find themselves desperate for some time and space.

We move now to consider issues concerning leaders that affect people's attendance at church.

Notes

1 James W Sire, *Discipleship of the Mind* (IVP: Leicester, 1990), p 59-60.

2 Monica Hill, *Rich Christians, Poor Christians* (Marshall Pickering: London, 1989) p 150.

3 Hill, *op cit*, p 150-151.

4 H. Norman Wright, *Overcoming Your Hidden Fears* (Scripture Press: Amersham-on-the-Hill, 1990) p 9.

5 Wright, *op cit*, p 57.

6 John S. Savage, *The Apathetic and Bored Church Member* (L.E.A.D. Consultants: Reynoldsburg, 1976). Also taken from an audio tape, Dropout Track, and used by permission, L.E.A.D. Consultants, Inc. Reynoldsburg, Ohio, USA (1992).

7 From *Church Leaders Handbook* issued at 'Creating a Church for the Unchurched' Conference, Birmingham, UK, 16-18 June 1992, p 10.

8 Michael Green, *Evangelism Through the Local Church* (Hodder & Stoughton: London, 1990) p 289.

9 Ajith Fernando, *Reclaiming Friendship* (IVP: Leicester, 1991) p 15.

10 Alice Fryling, *Disciplemakers' Handbook* (IVP: Leicester, 1989) p 66.

11 Taken from an audio tape, *Dropout Track*, and used by permission, L.E.A.D. Consultants, Inc. Reynoldsburg, Ohio, USA (1992).

[12] Taken from an audio tape, *Dropout Track*, and used by permission, L.E.A.D. Consultants, Inc. Reynoldsburg, Ohio, USA (1992).

[13] Peter Brierley, *'Christian' England* (MARC Europe: London, 1991) p 79.

[14] Steve L. Pogue, *The First Year of Your Christian Life* (Scripture Press: Amersham-on the-Hill, 1990) p 72.

[15] Bill Hybels at the 'Creating a Church for the Unchurched' Conference, Birmingham, UK, 16-18 June 1992.

CHAPTER 6

Problems Over Leadership

L EADERSHIP HAS AN important place in church life as elsewhere in society. Church leaders are entrusted with great spiritual responsibility. As they seek to be faithful to God, and especially when they want to introduce change, it is not surprising if problems surface. Relationships within a church can become stressed, and leaders have a major part to play in trying to resolve tensions that may involve them personally. Sometimes a substantial number of people in a church believe the leaders are themselves the cause of the church's problems. Sometimes this assessment is right. At other times it is the church members who are so out of touch with God's will that they are a real stumbling-block to progress. Before we delve further into this delicate area, we will consider leadership more broadly.

Leadership in the Bible
It was God who first conceived the idea of delegating responsibility for part of his work on earth to imperfect people whom he had created. He insisted, of course, that they had a personal relationship with him, loved and trusted him and were prepared to let him lead them. Once these criteria had been met, he could take and use them. They then shared in partnership with him as he used them to influence the lives of others and accomplish his plans and purposes.

As we read the Old Testament we see God at work in Abram, Joseph, Moses, Joshua, Gideon, David, Solomon and many

135

more. In the New Testament we see him transforming Simon Peter, Stephen, Philip, Saul of Tarsus and Timothy into people he could use. God needed these people because he had elected to work on earth primarily through human beings who were in submission to him. He used them to fulfil his plans despite their vulnerability and temperamental natures.

Leaders of the stature of, say, Moses and the apostle Paul are hard to find today. Nevertheless, God continues to raise up men and women to lead his work. The quality of this leadership is crucial. If churches are to be effective in God's work, then the appointment of the right leaders is vitally important. Peter Wagner says that 'the primary catalytic factor for growth in a local church is the pastor.' [1] Certainly this view coincides with the picture of many leaders in Scripture. Moses for instance, in partnership with Aaron, had a vital role to play in extricating the Israelite people from slavery in Egypt. The project had to be overseen by leaders who were open to God, responsive to him and trusted him implicitly. While the task of leading churches today may be different, God still needs leaders who will serve him and his people faithfully.

Christian leadership today

Are leaders of this calibre at the helm of Christ's church in the world today? The answer seems mixed. David Wilkerson, pastor of Times Square Church, New York, believes that God has shared truth with him concerning the state of Western society and the churches. He told Nicky Cruz, 'Many American shepherds—or, ministers—have become so blind, lazy and sinful that God has had to call upon secular writers and artists to warn this nation it is dying'.[2]

Monica Hill is equally negative but for a different reason. She refers to the many clergy trained in theological colleges by 'academic theologians, who do not regard the Bible as the authentic word of God and who do not have a strong personal experience of faith in God'.[3] She says that this has resulted in a 'sterile intellectualism' that precludes these people from being effective in communicating the Christian faith. This is clearly not the will and plan of God.

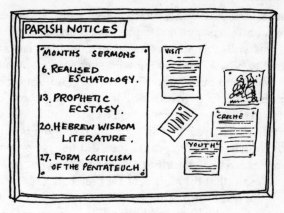

...sterile intellectualism

True Christian leadership is intended to be an agency through which God accomplishes his will on earth. Leaders play a key role in preparing and activating the people of God. Thankfully, contrary to the observations made by David Wilkerson and Monica Hill, there are many leaders who are faithfully serving God, often in demanding situations. Fame is not an accurate indicator of faithfulness in Christian leaders. Some of those whom God knows serve him most loyally and effectively are hardly known beyond their own town or village.

What then are the problems involving Christian leaders that cause people to leave the church? Let us explore some of these factors. The first three are those expressed by former church-goers; the following four are issues that pertain to leaders themselves but spill over and affect their role in the church.

1. BAD RELATIONSHIPS WITH THE LEADER OR LEADERSHIP

The Bible is a book that is very open with its readers. Imperfect relationships are not concealed in obscure corners, but are reported honestly. We are told that Jesus' disciples argued about their status (Mk 9:34) and became angry with James and John (Mk 10:41). We are told of a 'sharp dispute' between Christians in Antioch (Acts 15:2) and a 'sharp disagreement' between Paul and Barnabas (Acts 15:39). Despite these events God, in his mercy, was still able to use these men in his plan as they submitted to him. When dealing with such important issues as the will, plans and purposes of God, maybe it is no surprise that differences develop between individuals—even those deeply dedicated to God.

Our Survey showed that 10% of the respondents said that they left church partially because they did not get on with the leader or leadership. A further 6% gave a 'maybe' answer. A further 2% said that they left because they had a serious problem with the leadership. This sample obviously covers a wide range of leaders, churches and issues. If it is true that the leader has some negative part to play in 18% of the situations where people leave churches, we must take this matter very seriously.

In Figure 19 (Chapter 4) we examined this group of people who left church because of leadership problems. We know they are:

...Women more than men
...Aged 25-54 more than 24 and under or 55 and over
...Anglican and Baptist more than Methodist
...From Wales, Scotland and the Channel Islands more than England

What are the reasons for these findings? The preponderance of men in senior leadership in churches when women form the majority of church-goers probably makes it inevitable that women will feel under-represented and at times misunderstood. It is more likely that a woman will feel intimidated when having to work through a problem or complaint with a male dominated leadership. Older people leave church less over conflicts with the leadership. There are three possible reasons. First, they are not intimidated so easily. Secondly, they refuse to leave church and so change the habits of a lifetime. Thirdly, they think they are a more permanent fixture in the church than the leader who may move on. Methodists may have fewer problems because of their itinerant leadership system which has ministers moving from circuit to circuit more than their counterparts in other denominations.

For what reasons, then, do church members and leaders fall out? Probably anything and everything imaginable! We need to recognize the work of Satan here. If he can destroy respect, trust and love between a church and its leadership he wipes out much of the potential effectiveness of that church's ministry. Unresolved tensions, therefore, must not be allowed to fester. Yet they do. This is partly because we all detest both conflict and the pain associated with it. We often consider it better to let problems lie dormant under the surface than to face them courageously.

Gerald Coates tells of a rumour that spread around a Brethren church he was part of many years ago. One of the elders was supposed to have been seen after church on Sunday morning in a pub having a drink and smoking a cigar—behaviour quite unacceptable in that church. Gerald observes, though, that 'nobody was ever confronted with anything. Things were put under the carpet'.[4] We do this so often. Yet if we pray and let God work, his Holy Spirit gives resources that allow people to come to a common understanding and reconciliation. Most of the 18% of people who left church with unresolved leadership problems could undoubtedly have been helped by God to work these through to a satisfactory conclusion.

Without laying any blame at the door of church leaders, we must recognize a problem that some have. They feel insecure and uneasy with the responsibility entrusted to them. There can be a number of reasons for this:

a) They have not been called by God. I received a perceptive letter from a retired minister. 'Clearly some ministers have never had a call from God and ought never to have been in such a high calling. Though they may be a "very nice man", if they do not possess the spiritual qualities required, then the deep needs of the people cannot be met. He cannot lead farther than he himself has reached'.

b) They find themselves focusing on the obvious spiritual gifts that God has given others in the church and discover strong

feelings of insecurity rising inside. Tom Marshall points out a
common error. A...

> mistake, and the one most often made in the Christian
> church, is to equate leadership with ministry. The leader,
> whether minister, pastor or elder, is therefore expected to
> be the best preacher, the best Bible teacher, the best coun-
> sellor, the best prophet and the best organiser in the
> church. Very often the minister places the same expecta-
> tions on himself, because that is how he has been trained
> to think. Consequently he feels threatened if gifts arise in
> the congregation that appear to threaten his supremacy in
> any area of ministry, particularly the one he favours most.[5]

c) They are aware that some members of their congregation
have high educational qualifications, status in society and
maybe years of experience in secular business. These people,
who may have a forthright manner, leave the minister feeling
intimidated, inexperienced and ill-prepared to cope when confronted.

If leaders feel under threat it affects their performance. When
challenged they become defensive, protective and maybe
unnecessarily intransigent. This harms relationships and causes
frustration and maybe anger in those who want to raise issues
with them. I want to suggest that this problem may be a significant one in British churches. To explain why I believe this I need
to recap on the method I used to obtain data.

In early January 1992 I sent 300 letters to church leaders in
nine denominations or streams throughout Britain. Each was
reminded of the serious losses in church-goers highlighted in
the English Church Census. I explained my project and then
invited them to cooperate by sending me the names of up to five
former attenders who do not go to church any more. I gave two
weeks for the form to be returned in a Freepost envelope. By one
day after the closing date, just seventy-five responses (or a
quarter) had been received. Only twenty-four leaders cooper-
ated by sending names.

Many of the replies were warm and encouraging, but some
ministers said that to send names could be a threat to pastoral

Leaders...become defensive

confidence. It could make it harder for the people involved to return to church in due course. I understood and respected this although it did not help me. Shortly afterwards I was bemoaning this lack of response to a friend who immediately asked, 'Could it be that they feel threatened because things happen in their churches that they don't want made public?'. Undoubtedly both apathy and overwork are some of the reasons why more replies were not forthcoming, but I suspect my friend's comment merits careful reflection.

Whoever is to blame and whatever the nature of the problems between Christians and their leaders, we must take action to stop so many people leaving churches for this reason. My impression is that some people leave church rather than discuss difficulties and problems. They walk away rather than look for solutions and reconciliation, and the church lets them go rather than face difficult issues and criticism. Yet God's help is at our disposal. We need it; so many soiled relationships are a dreadful witness to the world.

2. DISAGREEMENT OVER THE DIRECTION IN WHICH THE CHURCH IS GOING

This is a complicated subject because of the many church traditions that exist. For example, the Roman Catholic understanding of the church is vastly different in many ways from the Baptist understanding on which I was brought up. My only experience of Eastern Christianity is the day I visited the Church of the Nativity in Bethlehem only to discover that the Armenian church was there because it was their Christmas Day. Their style and expression of the Christian Faith seemed a million miles away from all I have known and experienced.

Add to this the way the different segments of the Protestant church in Britain all seem to highlight various aspects of the biblical teaching on the church, and the confusion deepens further. To make it worse, we have to consider whatever childhood experience of the church we may have had (whether good or bad), and the fact that denominational allegiances in Britain today are not what they were. When Christians move home the criteria that guide their choice of a new church are more likely to be the warmth of its welcome and the style of its services rather than the denomination to which it belongs (if any).

All of this greatly increases the likelihood of disagreements over the future direction of any church. A broad mix of people from widely differing backgrounds will include those with substantially different expectations of a church. This concerns leaders because usually they formulate plans that are then presented to the church. If people oppose the plans, therefore, their feelings are largely targetted at the leadership. In our Survey 17% of respondents left church because they did not like the direction in which it was going. A further 10% gave a 'maybe' answer. A later question in the Survey, which we have not discussed yet, suggests that people were saying a number of different things. Of those surveyed 11% said they were not keen to go back to church because 'it's too old-fashioned' while 6%

said 'it's too modern and changed too much'. Frankly, we are facing a major cause of discontent and difficulty here. Over a quarter of those who left churches said that a factor in their decision to leave was the way the church was going.

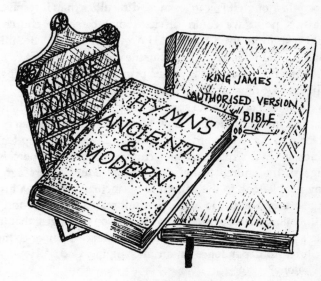

...too old-fashioned

In Figure 20 (Chapter 4) we referred to these people. We know that they are:

...Women more than men
...Aged 25-34 more than 55 and over
...Baptists more than Roman Catholics
...From the rest of England more than South East England and the rest of the UK

What do we learn from this? When the church is not going the way they like, women seem to give up first. Similarly, those in the key 25-34 age-group do the same, both groups possibly concluding that they are powerless to change the church. In this case it seems better to them to leave than be continually frustrated. It is intriguing that Baptists lost proportionally more people through dissatisfaction than the Catholics, although this is not really surprising. Catholics have no say in the direction of their church, but they join knowing this. Again we find ourselves wondering if the Baptist form of church government, democratic though it is, causes more difficulties than it resolves.

At this point we could discuss what direction churches should take to be used by God. However this would be futile because of the wide variety of churches to which we are referring. In the Bible God has given us principles about our corporate life that we must apply to our own churches.

We will not consider the specific direction any church should go in, but instead reflect on how to handle the changes necessary for it to move forward. In *Leadership Explosion* Philip King reminds us that while God and church leaders may perceive change in the church to be vital, not all church-goers agree. 'Many people look to the church as a sanctuary where nothing changes: they want it to act as a windbreak against the forces that threaten to disrupt our lives.' He goes on to suggest that the leader's job is to 'wean people from dependence on an unchanging church to dependence on an unchanging God.' [6] How can this be done?

There is clearly no right or wrong way. The personality of the pivotal leader and the circumstances of the church will tend to influence the decision. Philip King suggests there are various types of leaders who operate differently:

a) The traditional leader who wants to preserve continuity with what has gone before. He will avoid and resist change whenever he can because it will unsettle the church's unity and stability.

b) The charismatic leader who welcomes change and even finds the conflict that accompanies it an enjoyable challenge.

c) The classical leader who plans change in a series of organized steps, even if it takes a long time to complete. Classical leaders are sometimes authoritarian, using their position or status to pre-empt discussion.

d) The human relations leader who will not hesitate to agree with a compromise if it will mean that happy working relationships will continue. This is deemed more important than creating effective policies.

e) The systematic or organic approach can be described as evolution as opposed to revolution. Gradual changes are made continually over an extended period.[7]

What matters most is that a church follows certain principles when its future direction is being considered:

a) that God's will is sought for the church and its future ministry, and that the principles of God's Word form the backbone of decisions taken;

b) that leaders are sensitive to the Christians in the church, especially those who are older and for whom change may be more difficult;

c) that careful thought and prayer is given by the leader not only to *what* changes are proposed but also to the *manner* in which the changes will be presented to the church and implemented;

d) that cooperation is seen as the ideal goal. This is where 'the parties involved work together not just to resolve the conflict but to use it in order to make progress. This is the systematic or organic style which seeks to harness the creative elements in conflict;' [8]

e) that specific facilities are provided by the leadership so that those who are unhappy with proposed or actual changes can discuss their feelings with key leaders as soon as possible.

Satan is undoubtedly keen to capitalize on the conflicts that surface when change is in the offing. Leaders need more sensitivity; members more openness to change. The Holy Spirit needs more cooperation so that he can lead God's people on. Donald Bridge encourages us by telling of a Brethren church which realized it was failing to win people to Christ. The elders proposed changes to Sunday activities that some thought radical. 'There was uproar. Older people were in tears,' he says One elderly man threatened never to come again. Howev elders persevered, a few members left, and within ten y membership was doubled'.[9] Changes can be very pro if painful.

3. DIFFICULTY COPING WITH THE STYLE OF WORSHIP

Since the birth of the church Christians have met together on the first day of the week to worship God. This is utterly appropriate. The Old Testament includes extravagant praise to God, particularly in the Psalms, and Hebrews 13:15 encourages Christians to 'continually offer to God a sacrifice of praise'. When we consider how much he has done to reveal his love to us, it is fitting that Christian people should take time to worship him.

Christian worship in the 1990s, though, is not the predictable thing that it was in, say, the 1950s. In an Anglican church the service probably would have been taken from the 1662 *Book of Common Prayer*. In a Baptist church there would have been a predictable hymn/prayer sandwich. Today the *Alternative Service Book 1980* is the norm in the Church of England. There are some Anglican churches, though, which have almost disposed of liturgy altogether while others have retained Cranmer's Prayer Book.[10]

Within the Methodist, Baptist and other Free churches there are widely differing styles of worship, even within the same denomination. Some worship is much the same as forty years ago. Others have more open, free and flowing worship using largely contemporary music. New churches have emerged since the 1950s. Their worship tends to be charismatic and gives time for open participation under the leading of the Holy Spirit.

This variety is seen by many (including me) as thoroughly refreshing and wholesome, yet the changes to which we have referred have brought pain and trauma to many churches. *In Tune With Heaven*, the Report of the Anglican Archbishops' Commission on Church Music, says 'Many correspondents complain, often with a real sense of hurt, about peremptory change and innovation in parish church music.' [11] I wonder how many of the 27% who were unhappy about the direction in which their church was going were really commenting on the style of the worship. All we know from the Survey is that 2% of respondents added sentiments that said that they left because they could not cope with the current style of worship in their church.

Let us think about two points:

a) Dave Pope reminds us that the English word 'worship' is derived from the Anglo-Saxon 'wercscipe' which means 'to appreciate the worth of'. When we worship God 'we are appreciating His worth in all we do in order to communicate our love for him.' [12] Worship should never be turned into a Christian battleground.

b) Satan is always looking for openings to provoke disagreements and conflicts between Christians. Worship is the central activity in corporate Christianity and Satan targets it. He has plenty of room to work because of the wide range and variety of styles and ingredients in existence. His opportunities to cause disruption become greater when music is a factor. Each of us has differing tastes and preferences in music. At home we can select what we like by tuning in to a particular radio station or playing a favourite record or tape and adjusting the volume. At church, however, we all have to cope with the same selection. *In Tune With Heaven* speaks of 'the unsurpassable power of music to set a mood' [13], but we may simply not appreciate the mood being generated by the music we hear at church. Possibly we find some modern music offensive in church because we do not like its style or the volume at which it is played. Satan clearly makes the most of problems about worship. After all, he is out to provoke conflict in the church.

Another area where Satan scores victories is over traditions. Some worshippers think that past traditions are biblical whereas new forms and styles of worship and music are not. The organ is perceived by some as the *only* instrument to lead hymns. The fact that today's worship bands may be nearer than organs to the biblical picture in Psalm 150 is of little consequence. Some church-goers are offended if a service goes on longer than an hour or if the music is loud.

Where does the Bible teach that this is a right length of time to spend worshipping God or that worship should always be tranquil—or loud? The Bible does not teach that we are to have two or three worship services each Sunday. Paul simply encourages us to 'not give up meeting together' (Heb 10:25). I agree with Donald Bridge who says, 'Christians are human, and human beings find change painful and threatening. The familiar

Come on down, Vic, your time is up

and predictable are much to be preferred: they fix the boundaries and give us a sense of security.' [14] Satan seems to enjoy the disruption he can cause in a church when traditions are under threat.

We will now look at four issues that relate directly to church leaders. None was referred to in the Survey, but my experience suggests these leadership issues affect people leaving churches.

4. REFUSAL TO SHARE AND DELEGATE LEADERSHIP RESPONSIBILITIES

Long ago Moses learned that delegation is God's way for his human leaders to operate (Ex 18:13-26). Yet today some church leaders are uneasy about sharing responsibility with others. Consequently some Christian people in our churches feel the same frustrations as Jethro (Ex 18:14-17).

Many Christian writers advocate the development of true team leadership in churches. One of them, Derek Copley, explains his belief that 'decision-making by consensus' is the right way to involve others in taking real responsibility in God's work. At the college where he is principal he says, 'Each of us (including myself) knows that his views may be thrown out completely'.[15] Nevertheless he feels far more comfortable in this setting than as a boss who directs a group of people who are dependent on him always to take initiatives and find solutions to problems.

Genuinely to involve other people whom God has gifted in shared leadership is taught in the New Testament. Paul in Ephesians 4, for instance, encourages leaders to be what we could call 'benevolent enablers'. In 1 Corinthians 12 he emphasizes the wide-ranging gifts that God has given the Body of Christ to use in ministry. Yet, for a range of different reasons, some churches operate around one key leader. Not only is it unhealthy for that person, it also suggests that in their absence the work cannot go on. John Waterhouse describes the problem from an Australian perspective.

> I recently met with a mature and widely experienced lay Christian. She currently works in a strategic overseas missionary situation. Of her 15 (female) friends, all with years of solid, committed ministry in parachurch work behind them, none now goes to church. This is an astonishing statistic that should pull us up with a shock. Why don't they go? 'Because they got tired of being talked down to as women.' In the institutional church's preoccupation with women's ordination—as complete a red herring as is possible to imagine: the issue is *ordination*, not women's

...some churches operate around one key leader

ordination—we have ignored to our peril the legitimate request of all laypeople, men *and* women, to be treated as partners in, not just objects of, ministry.[16]

Such policies and attitudes are destructive. It is hardly surprising that some Christians get tired of waiting for the impossible to happen.

One further point is worth making. Church leadership in the New Testament was always plural. One advantage of this is that it spares a church from the problems that arise where a sole leader comes under attack personally. Who helps to resolve the problems? Where a team of leaders work together, others are on hand to help bring healing if a church member and one of the team get into difficulties.

5. A BUILD-UP OF WORK-RELATED STRESS

In Chapter 1 we discussed the increase of stress in society. This stress also affects churches and Christian workers, although it is only comparatively recently that the subject has been publicly aired. In 1987 Dr Marjory Foyle's book *Honourably Wounded* gave the Christian community at large the opportunity to understand, maybe for the first time, the extent to which being a missionary serving abroad can be a stressful calling.[17] Two years later Paul Beasley-Murray wrote about the stresses that pastors experience. 'Today, more than at any other time, pastors feel under pressure. Increasingly such terms as "stress", "burnout" and "marital breakdown" are being used in relation to pastoral ministry. Pastors, it would appear, are themselves in need of pastoral care.' [18]

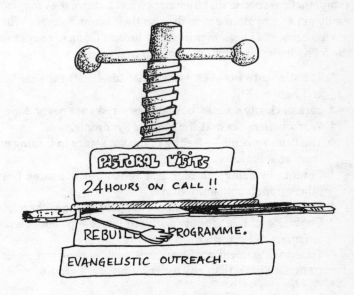

pastors feel under pressure

Dr Roland Croucher, himself a Baptist minister in Australia, founded John Mark Ministries in 1991 following 'eight years almost exclusively speaking to, listening to and counselling pastors, many of whom come to me and say they are thinking of leaving the church.' [19] Dr Croucher says that there are around 10,000 ex-pastors in Australia and estimates that some denominations are losing more church leaders than they are keeping. Back in England a research study by Dr Ben Fletcher among Anglican clergy revealed that 58% of his respondents said, 'There is a lot of pressure but I find I can cope', with 5% saying 'The pressure is so great it is a constant source of stress to me'. One twentieth of the Church of England's 10,000 parish-based clergy means that 500 are in deep trouble.[20] The situation is serious.

Clearly a pastor will not function well if he or she is under relentless, intolerable pressure. Thus a member of the church with a problem may not get the kind of understanding, loving, sympathetic response that they hoped for. Indeed, they may not easily get an appointment to discuss their problem at all. What are the causes of stress in ministers? Roland Croucher says that the following areas keep cropping up in research:

* The disparity between (somewhat idealistic) expectations and hard reality;
* Lack of clearly defined boundaries—tasks are never done;
* Workoholism ('bed-at-the-church' syndrome);
* The Peter Principle—feeling of incompetence in leading an army of volunteers;
* Conflict in being a leader and servant at the same time ('line-support contamination');
* Intangibility—how do I know I am getting somewhere?;
* Confusion of role identity with self image—pastors derive too much self-esteem from what they *do*;
* Time management problems (yet pastors have more 'discretionary time' than any other professional group);
* Too few 'perks';
* Multiplicity of roles;
* Inability to produce 'win-win' conflict resolutions;
* Difficulty in managing interruptions;
* The 'little adult' syndrome (Dittes)—clergy are too serious, they have difficulty being spontaneous;

* Preoccupation with 'playing it safe' to avoid enraging powerful parishioners;
* 'Administration overload'—too much energy expended in areas of low reward;
* Loneliness—the pastor is less likely to have a close friend than any other person in the community.[21]

Steve Chalke, writing about Christian youth leaders (who also suffer high levels of stress) says, 'In this strategic area, where the church needs committed, experienced, consistent and mature leadership, it is often tragic to see the temporary nature of so much that is done...Leaders become wounded, exhausted and burned out.' [22]

The New Testament assures us, though, that the problem is not new. Paul writes, 'We do not want you to be uninformed, brothers, about the hardships we suffered in the province of Asia. We were under great pressure, far beyond our ability to endure, so that we despaired even of life. Indeed, in our hearts we felt the sentence of death. But this happened that we might not rely on ourselves but on God, who raises the dead. He has delivered us from such a deadly peril' (2 Cor 1:8-10). Many leaders need God's help today. Sadly, without it, they may leave the church themselves *and* indirectly contribute to others in their congregations going.

6. A LACK OF PERSONAL SPIRITUAL DISCIPLINE

Anyone called to full-time church-based Christian service is indeed privileged. They do not have to combine a full-time job with making time and energy available to serve the Lord. They can concentrate all their energies on the latter. There is a subtle danger, though. Because leaders have sermons and Bible studies to prepare, and are called on to pray with those in their fellowship, they can easily neglect their own spiritual life. I know—I have done it.

Yet in reality no amount of sermon preparation and prayer ministry can compensate for a deficiency in our own devotional life with the Lord. Christian leaders in active ministry *need* the enriching input of a daily time with him. Without it they impoverish their own lives and run the risk of failing others. It is more than likely that some who leave our churches do so, indirectly, because of ministers' spiritual self-neglect.

I agree with Paul Beasley-Murray when he says that 'the call to pastoral leadership...is in the first place a call to be, rather than a call to do'.[23] The first responsibility is to 'Fix...eyes on Jesus' (Heb 12:2) because it is when walking close to him a Christian becomes most effective in his service. Derek Copley says, 'For those who preach, teach or lead, where hours of preparation are needed, there is a big temptation to use the devotional time as a study period instead.' [24]

Leaders are often tempted to do seemingly more important things than spend time with God. Almost none is ever valid. Leaders who become spiritually dry through lack of regular refreshment in God's presence are a hazard to the church. Their neglect can make it easier for some vulnerable people in their flock to break away.

7. FAILURE OF THE LEADER TO ADOPT A BIBLICAL MODE OF LEADERSHIP

Books on Christian leadership are plentiful. From different perspectives they encourage existing and aspiring leaders to become people God can work through. Some teaching on leadership is relevant to our thinking on why people leave churches. To end this chapter we will focus on two points regularly made by those who write about Christian leadership. It is the absence of these qualities in some leaders that almost certainly encourages some Christians to depart.

a) Vision
Quoting Biblical examples, many Christian writers argue that contemporary church leaders need vision. John Perry encourages us to look at Nehemiah who arrived in Jerusalem when the city walls had been 'razed to the ground'. Its few residents were 'dispirited and listless'. He says that the way Nehemiah 'tackled the colossal task that confronted him is a superb example of visionary leadership'.[25] Peter Brierley takes us back to Abram

who had a vision from God who showed him how big his future family would be.[26]

Peter Wagner talks of the importance of pastors being 'possibility thinkers', which is precisely what provides God with the opportunity to reveal his way forward.[27] Many churches become stagnant because church leaders lack vision. If the leaders have little drive, motivation and enthusiasm for God's work, it is not surprising if the same deficiencies are found in the church. A church with no direction and goals is a church likely to be so dull that even long-standing Christians will find it hard to stay loyal to it.

Dr Kriengsak Chareonwongsak is Founder and Senior Pastor of the Hope of Bangkok Church in Thailand. He believes God has called him to open a church in every one of the nation's 685 districts by 2000 AD.[28] Gradually his vision is becoming reality.

b) Servanthood
The kind of attitude that Christian leaders have towards the people in their churches is very important. It is easy for a trained, experienced and academically qualified ordained minister to feel superior to his flock. Yet Jesus, who had every reason to lord it over his disciples, acted in an utterly radical way when he washed his disciples' feet. He did so, he told them, to teach them a lesson they would never forget. 'Now that I, your Lord and Teacher, have washed your feet, you also should wash one another's feet. I have set you an example that you should do as I have done for you' (Jn 13:14-15).

Philip King suggests how leaders should live. 'The servant leader must be ready to lead by example and not just by exhortation.' Later, he says how important it is not to set unrealistic standards. 'We must remember that even great leaders, such as Moses, David and Simon Peter, experienced major weaknesses and failings...A leader who is ready to admit mistakes and failure may have a much wider ministry than one who always appears highly organized and self-sufficient.' [29]

When church leaders fail to provide the type of spiritual leadership that Christians look for, these leaders, often well-meaning, sincere and dedicated, can indirectly provoke church-goers to leave the church. In today's consumer age, if people do not find what they want, they often look elsewhere. In religious terms this may mean a cult or sect as opposed to another orthodox church. On the other hand they may not look elsewhere and may decide to opt completely out of anything religious. The responsibility on Christian leaders is great.

The prophet Ezekiel had no doubts about this as he castigated the religious leaders of his day. 'You eat the curds, clothe yourselves with the wool and slaughter the choice animals, but you do not take care of the flock.' (Ezek 34:3). In total contrast, Nicky Cruz gives a candid assessment of his friend and colleague, David Wilkerson.

> I thank God for Dave. He is a man unlike any other I have ever known. He knows God intimately. He is a student of the Word, of church history, of the writings of great men of God gone before him. He is a man of prayer—a man who really walks with God. The diversity of the Times Square Church's ministry in New York City is amazing. Holy Spirit discernment is needed to protect the time, emotions and energies of those involved. This comes through intimacy with Christ, having His mind, seeing others through His eyes and sharing His love. This sort of leadership and lifestyle is not learned, it is imparted by association. Only a man who walks with God can reflect His heart. Dave reflects the heart of God—the One Hope for Mankind.[30]

Notes

1   C. Peter Wagner, *Your Church Can Grow* (Regal: Glendale, 1976) p 55.

2   Nicky Cruz, *A Final Warning* (Kingsway: Eastbourne, 1992) p 109.

3   Monica Hill, *Rich Christians, Poor Christians* (Marshall Pickering: London, 1989) p 100-101.

4   Gerald Coates, *An Intelligent Fire* (Kingsway: Eastbourne, 1991) p 53.

5   Tom Marshall, *Understanding Leadership* (Sovereign World: Tonbridge, 1991) p 6-7.

6   Philip King, *Leadership Explosion* (Hodder & Stoughton: London, 1987) p 151.

[7] King, *op cit*, p 148-156.

[8] *ibid* p 157.

[9] Donald Bridge, *How to Spot a Church Split Before it Happens* (MARC: Eastbourne, 1989) p 24-25.

[10] Robert Van De Weyer, *The Country Church* (Darton, Longman & Todd: London, 1991) p 47-50.

[11] *In Tune With Heaven*, The Report of the Archbishops' Commission on Church Music (Hodder & Stoughton: London, 1992) p 79.

[12] Dave Pope, *Giving the Best in Worship* (CWR: Farnham, 1991) p 3.

[13] *In Tune With Heaven*, p 47.

[14] Bridge, *op cit*, p 25.

[15] Derek Copley, *Taking a Lead* (Kingsway: Eastbourne, 1985) p 87-107.

[16] John Waterhouse, 'The Crisis of Evangelicalism, A Movement Gone Sour', *On Being*, Australia, (April 1992): p 4-8.

[17] Marjory F Foyle, *Honourably Wounded* (MARC Europe: London, 1987).

[18] Paul Beasley-Murray, *Pastors Under Pressure* (Kingsway: Eastbourne, 1989) p 11.

[19] Dr Roland C Croucher, 'Loss of Clergy Outruns Gains', *SEE*, Australia, (April 1991): p 3.

[20] Dr Ben Fletcher, *Clergy Under Stress* (Mowbray: London, 1990) p 31.

[21] Dr Roland C Croucher, 'Stress & Burnout in Ministry', *GRID*, Australia, (Summer 1984): p 1.

[22] Steve Chalke, *The Christian Youth Manual* (Kingsway: Eastbourne, 1992) p 78.

[23] Paul Beasley-Murray, *Dynamic Leadership* (Monarch: Tunbridge Wells, 1990) p 198.

[24] Copley, *op cit*, p 34.

[25] John Perry, *Christian Leadership* (Hodder & Stoughton: London, 1983) p 81.

[26] Peter Brierley, *Vision Building* (Hodder & Stoughton: London, 1989) p 81-82.

[27] Wagner, *op cit*, p 57.

[28] Carolyn Boyd, *The Apostle of Hope* (Sovereign World: Tonbridge, 1991) p 66-67.

[29] King, *op cit*, p 130-131.

[30] Cruz, *op cit*, p 186.

CHAPTER 7

Problems of Irrelevance

W E HAVE ALREADY observed that this country is very different now compared with much of the last century when a far higher proportion of the population went to church. During the succeeding years of diminishing attendances, however, there seems little doubt about how the churches have handled the perpetual decline. On the whole they have taken to the security of their shells and shut out a society that was becoming increasingly Godless.

From inside their sanctuaries they have criticized the world out there for becoming increasingly pagan and materialistic. They have concluded that if people wanted to find God they would come to church. After all, the churches are still there in the heart of the community. Their doors are open on Sundays, and if the people are reluctant to come it can mean only one thing. They are happy with their lives as they are and no longer feel a need for God. There is, as Jack Burton puts it, a 'gap' or 'cultural divide' between those with a 'church-going habit' and the rest of society.[1]

However this caricature leaves out something very important. At least since the first evangelistic missions by Billy Graham in London in the mid-1950s there have been some Christians and churches intent on breaking out of their shells. They have recognized the challenge of Jesus' commission to 'Go and make disciples' (Mt 28:19) and have sought to take the Good News about him to the world. Had these believers from so many and varied denominations and streams not caught this vision the Church of

Jesus Christ in Britain today probably would be heading towards extinction. Hundreds of thousands of people have made a personal commitment to Jesus in the past thirty or forty years.

Then what has happened? New converts have been strongly encouraged to go to church. On the Sunday following their conversion, they may go for the first time. Let us imagine what they could find. Possibly a group of sober and intense people engaging in a religious service that feels as if it came out of the dark ages. The hymns were mainly written between 200 and 400 years ago and contain ideas and language that at times are impossible to comprehend. The sermon is not easy to understand and seems to have no bearing on the real world they know and live in with its unemployment, crime, natural disasters and war. The service feels as if it lasts too long, is drab and has little obvious point or purpose. The people who come every week seem content enough with it, but to unchurched people it feels a very strange environment. What is more, they have to admit that coming into a personal relationship with Jesus seemed good; having to get used to going to church is quite something else!

When we stand back and look at the situation, we begin to understand that there is a vast difference between the culture of secular society and that of most churches. Let us recall the responses given in our Survey from those who were churchgoers but who do not go now for varying reasons. Overall, 34% of them said that to differing degrees they found church boring, and the same proportion said that to some extent they found church irrelevant to their everyday life. Some 15% of respondents answered another question by saying that they did not think church is relevant to life today. A quarter said that to some extent they were put off church by the sermons. Between them these figures encompass 55% of those answering the Survey, and therefore represent hundreds of thousands of people who have left our churches over the past decades.

Such sobering statistics tell us that many ordinary British people have had two serious problems with the church: what happens and the way it happens. What happens just does not relate to the rest of their lives, and the way it happens is just plain dull.

COME TO ST. JUDE'S EVANGELISTIC MISSION MEETINGS YOUR QUESTIONS WILL BE ANSWERED

Do you think they will help me deal with my redundancy, Sharon?

Here then is the British church's biggest problem area. Many of those who on average have been to church for thirteen years confirm that it is irrelevant and boring. Of course, these are merely personal views of survey respondents, but the fact remains that many people are leaving due to boredom and what Martin Goldsmith calls 'the dreary cottonwool irrelevance'.[2]

The same is true abroad. Floyd McClung has lived and worked with Youth With A Mission in Amsterdam for many years. His research suggests that while eighty-five to ninety per cent of young people in Holland 'are still interested in God', most 'have turned their backs on formal religion'.[3] These serious findings and two other matters now demand our attention.

1. THE BUILDINGS IN WHICH WE MEET FOR WORSHIP

Recognizing its importance, let us begin with subject-matter not covered by the Survey. Britain is in the grip of commercial forces that are continually attempting to influence ordinary members of the population. A local building society branch, for instance, was remodelled using the latest designs maybe some four years ago. It was attractive and functional. Just recently, however, it was ripped apart and thoroughly redesigned using a different layout and colours. Shopping malls opened a mere decade ago have millions of pounds spent on them to remodel them in ultra-modern styles with glass-sided elevators. It seems that our obsession with newness knows no bounds.

Many people use Saturdays as family days out. Sometimes my wife and I, and our children, visit one of the many sleek shopping centres in our area. We do not in the least dislike the opulence and attractive surroundings; it makes shopping more bearable! The next day we go to church. What kind of building do we enter when we get there? How does the worship centre compare to the shopping centre? Badly is the frank answer in the case of the Church where I serve as pastor. Apart from a scheme partially to improve and modernize the interior of the building in the 1960s it is fundamentally the same as when it was built in 1843. There are bare floorboards under the pews and the whole Centre of which it is part is austere. Yet it is typical of many buildings set aside for worship. For a variety of seemingly respectable reasons, churches have failed to make positive decisions to upgrade them as generations have come and gone. Indeed, some of them date back many centuries, a few to the last millenium and part of their charm is their antiquity.

The impression therefore given to our nation is that Christianity is for and from a bygone age. It does not help at all that the vast majority of our population seems to perceive the *building* to be the church. This is an added complication. Unable to grasp the subtle difference between the building used for services and the people who meet for worship, they just have a vague feeling that this Faith is old, tired and long past its sell-by date. In the circumstances we can hardly blame them.

Our Church's Youth Ministry Worker, Geoff, and his wife, Sam, visited Blists Hill Open Air Museum in Shropshire not long ago. They toured the old stores restored to 1920s style where you can buy goods in pounds, shillings and pence. They appreciated the olde-worlde feel of the exhibits. Then they came to the chapel. They went in and were astounded; it was no different from the inside of churches today! They said that it felt just like a time-warp. Almost certainly the historic nature of most church buildings in Britain does nothing to help the public to think of the Christian Faith as contemporary. Quite the opposite, in fact. Should the minister dare suggest a radical programme of modernization, he or she will often be met with a shrill protest such as Robert Van de Weyer describes in his book, *The Country Church*.[4]

Church planting is firmly on the agenda of many denominations and local churches. This is good for many reasons. One is that new congregations will frequently have to make use of general community facilities. Our own Church's new congregation, planted in September 1991, for instance, meets in a Scout and Guide hall in the heart of the neighbourhood that the 'plant' was set up to reach. It is light and airy, has no fixed seating and is thoroughly versatile. Best of all it does not feel 'religious' and I, at least, find it a delightful environment for worship. The Baptist Church in Conisbrough, South Yorkshire, felt led to plant a church in Mexborough. The Dog Daisy public house was used for worship until a temporary building was delivered to the site on which the new church intends to build a permanent base. Easy solutions to the problems of ageing buildings may be hard to find, but Christians need to be aware of the turn-off factor that these so easily engender in the surrounding community.

2. THE CONTENT AND STYLE OF WORSHIP SERVICES

It can be helpful to view Sunday services as the shop window of the Christian church. While many unchurched people may encounter a Christian at work or on the doorstep, it is only when they venture into a church service that they see Christians together. A welcome exception to this is when a church takes away the walls surrounding its worship and presents something like a March for Jesus event. At such a time the church prays that those who have inaccurate ideas about Christianity will recognize that this faith is more relevant than they had thought.

In Table 21 (Chapter 4) we looked at the 34% of Survey respondents who thought church was irrelevant to some extent. We know that they are:

...Men more than women

   ...Aged 25-34 more than 55 and over

   ...Anglican and Roman Catholic more than from the 'Other' denominations

   ...From England (but not the South East) more than the rest of the UK

Why is this? Men are probably naturally less tolerant of what seems a meaningless church service. Younger people have been brought up in an environment where they think and analyse what is going on around them. If it is incomprehensible or illogical, they will have little time for it. The greater tendency towards liturgical services in the Church of England and Roman Catholic churches makes complaints about irrelevance more likely due to the greater repetition of material week-by-week.

What is it, then, about church services that makes some church-goers see them as irrelevant? I submit three answers.

a) They are fronted by unreal and distant people

Having already raised this matter before we will not pursue it at length here. The problem is that those who lead worship and preach can appear other-worldly. For a start they do not always talk in a normal tone of voice or use ordinary everyday language. They do not come over as having a sense of humour or even seem happy, let alone joyful. Rather they appear as sombre creatures who have the power to make a congregation rise, sit, sing, pray or whatever they suggest. Clerical attire does nothing to make them seem like normal human beings, and any artificiality at the door afterwards just reinforces the view some have that they really are living on a different planet. In short, the image of Christian ministers is not helpful.

b) They seem full of yesterday's religious artefacts.

Some church-goers, ecclesiastical historians and others may feel it is good for the church today to continue using forms of worship, prayers, translations of the Bible and hymns that were first produced two or three hundred years ago. From this Survey it seems fair to say that there are some who do not agree. Coming as they do from ordinary homes and jobs, they find it unnatural to be transported back in time at church. They may find beauty in the style of language in the King James Bible. The traditional hymns and their familiar tunes are almost part of our national heritage. The message that appears to come from those who have left, however, is that a church's determination to parade its history every time it meets is counter-productive. Ordinary people find it reassuring on one hand but aggravating on the other to be confronted with material that is spiritual but antiquated. Like the person at the front, it can feel other-worldly.

Having said this there is, not surprisingly, another side of the coin. In a magazine article, Gordon Miller of World Vision of New Zealand, makes some comments about relevant worship. One of them says:

> Worship is relevant when it manages a happy balance between the old and new. In relevant worship, archaisms may need to be removed from hymns, and modern songs selected with care—anything banal and triumphalistic

should be discarded. Relevant worship neither discards the old nor uncritically accepts the new.[5]

Gordon Miller has a point. Retaining older Christian material in worship is fine if it is still valid. In doing this, though, we should not just be mindful of the group in the church which is very vocal whenever change is threatened. Others need care too. These are the less vocal people who struggle with an old-fashioned format.

c) They don't relate to people's real needs.

Every human being has pain, hurt, anxiety and trauma to cope with at times. None of us is exempt. While undertaking street surveys I met a man in his sixties who served on a battleship during the Second World War. One minute he was taking part in an obligatory service led by the Padre; the next he was summoned to fire fifteen inch shells at the enemy. He told me that he still feels confused at this incompatibility all these years later. When people come to church on Sunday they neither leave their feelings at home nor at the church door. They naturally find feelings surfacing from time to time during the service. Do they expect help with these things when they come to church? Probably not, but almost certainly God has some to give to them. At the very least their Good Shepherd wants to reassure them of his love, acceptance, continual presence and resources. He is keen that they should leave feeling more assured and full of faith than when they came. During the service he desperately wants them to catch sight of his power and authority in a fresh way that will enable them to trust him more. My impression is that those who lead worship seem to overlook the plans God may have. The consequence is that his help and reassurance is frozen right out. People go home as they came.

Yet the outstanding feature of Jesus' ministry was both his desire to minister into people's hurt lives and his capacity to do so. So many physically sick who came into his presence were healed; many demonized people were delivered; many people with inner hurts were restored. Stories abound of those who have been touched by the Lord in worship. Peter Lawrence tells what happened to seventy-seven year-old Daisy at church in Birmingham. Her...

> badly swollen knee...was preventing her from visiting sick relatives and relations. As the Spirit came, Daisy's left leg started swinging backwards and forwards. Team members gathered round to bless what the Father was doing and commanded the knee to be healed in Jesus' name. When the leg stopped moving, all the swelling had gone down and Daisy was able to go visiting again.[6]

Nicky Cruz spoke to someone leaving Times Square Church, New York, where David Wilkerson is pastor. He asked them what the church means to them.

> 'My salvation. Four weeks ago I was in heavy drugs and living in the streets. One of the counsellors brought me in and I was saved. I'm with the Lord now. If it weren't for this church I wouldn't be happy, content, saved. I have a great spiritual feeling right now and I want to devote myself for the rest of my life to our Lord. I couldn't do that in forty-one years of my life. The only thing I was doing was being in the pit of hell with drugs. Times Square Church reached out.' [7]

Yet while some churches particularly gear their ministry to meeting people's needs, many seem not to do so. Their services go on week after week as if no-one present had any problems. Not unnaturally, when church-goers find that nothing in their lives changes *despite* regularly going to church they become despondent. They may hear stories of remarkable miracles preached from the pulpit, but these are never translated into reality in the here and now. It is as if God is now powerless or turns a blind uncaring eye to present-day needs. Worship services that do not link God to people and people to God are the cause of many leaving our churches.

It is more than this, though. Church-goers tend also to take careful note of the extent to which their church has any ministry to prevailing social needs. Maybe they find that prominent local needs are completely ignored and not even prayed about in services. They may also find that the church makes no attempt to minister in any area of local need. It is as if they did not exist. Further, the church *may* virtually ignore world needs and, despite enormous publicity in the media, do nothing positive to help famine, earthquake and war victims. This parochialism and narrow-mindedness is also likely to provoke some who are well aware of these situations to wring their hands in despair.

Baby boomers

Irrelevance also seems the main cause why many people in one particular age-group are being lost to the churches in the United States of America. Rev Arnell Arn, a Director in the American Baptist Churches, has studied the church-going tendencies of the 76 million Americans born between 1946 and 1964, commonly called 'baby boomers'. She reports that a recent survey found only 11% of them say they regularly attend a church or synagogue. Yet, she reports:

> Don't be deceived, baby boomers are a profoundly spiritual generation. Perhaps more than any other group of people, baby boomers are aware that a spiritual world exists. They believe that a person is made up of mental, physical and spiritual. It's been said they are Ghostbusters, Exorcist, Jesus People and New Age Generation. Members of this generation continue to search for a spiritual connection which gives meaning to their daily lives. A recent study...concluded that the single greatest reason for membership decline in most American churches is the failure to reach and retain the baby boom generation. Their lack of interest in most churches has nothing to do with a lack of interest in God. They like the contents of the Gospel. They just don't like the container—the cultural clothing—they find it wrapped in. New wine needs new wineskins.[8]

Maybe, though, her most perceptive comment comes later. 'Many aging churches and denominations are trapped behind a cultural and religious "stained-glass barrier", unable or unwilling to break out.' On this side of the Atlantic too, churches seem 'trapped' and are unable to stop their congregations diminishing because people find church irrelevant. This is a complicated problem to deal with, partly because of differing factions in some churches. There are people, especially those contemplating leaving, who hope and pray for greater relevance in church services. There are others who are content for things to stay just as they are. Indeed, they positively oppose change.

Handling change

Things become complex when we see that it could be a mercy if a group left the church because they are frustrated. Their departure would stave off conflict that may have erupted if these people had stayed and demanded change. What then is the best course of action in such circumstances where maybe young and old fundamentally disagree? Again, a definite answer is hard to give. Honesty, openness and straight-talking in love that allows the problem to be aired and hopefully resolved with God's help is hard to beat. In practice some kind of compromise may be necessary to keep the church together.

George Carey tells how he had to settle for this when he was Vicar of St Nicholas's, Durham, and the Church Council turned down a recommendation to undertake a major building modernization project. 'I shared the feeling of bitter disappointment. And yet now that the moment of truth had arrived it all seemed so obvious. The Council had made the correct decision because the church was not ready.' [9]

A seeker-led church

Outside Chicago is a church that seems to have overcome the problem of irrelevance. Located in Barrington is Willow Creek Community Church, now North America's fastest-growing Protestant church. In 1975 a small group of young Christian leaders sensed God was guiding them to reach people in their community for Christ. In a community survey they discovered the many reasons why people did not go to church. High on the list were irrelevance and boredom. In response, they believed God was leading them to establish a church that put the needs of people seeking Christ first. Therefore the weekend services were organized and planned with this as a priority.

> The services are designed for people who are in the process of making a decision for Christ or evaluating Christianity, and for those who have recently committed their lives to Him. The weekend services are intended to supplement the evangelistic efforts made by members of the body as they build relationships with unchurched Harrys and Marys. These services communicate the message of Jesus Christ to those unfamiliar with it. To accomplish this the message needs to be presented in such a way that unchurched individuals understand and relate to what is being said, and wish to learn more.[10]

It works because 15,000 people now attend the four weekend Seeker Services and almost 6,000 go to the two New Community mid-week services for Christians.

Having been to the Willow Creek Conference in England in 1992 I firmly believe that this Church has much to teach us. It is a church that seriously attempts to meet people's real needs. With vision from God and a minimum of adaptation for the British situation, this model could be the instrument that God will use to help show this generation that he is thoroughly relevant to people today. It is encouraging to know that some British churches for the unchurched are now being planted.[11]

3. THE BOREDOM FACTOR

So many people in our Survey said that church is boring that I have to believe it! To be honest, I have been bored so often myself that I know they are right. How is it that Christianity can be made so dull and uninspiring?

In Table 22 (Chapter 4) we discovered more about the 23% of Survey respondents who left church at least partly because they found it boring. There was a further 11% who gave a 'maybe' answer. We know that they are:

"TODAYS SUBJECT IS JOY"

…Male more than female

…34 and under more than 35 and over

…Anglicans and Roman Catholics more than Methodists and those in 'Other' denominations

…From the rest of England more than South East England and the rest of the UK

Why is this? Maybe, on the whole, men are less tolerant and will leave church more quickly if they detect a lack of imagination or incompetence. The same is probably true of younger people as opposed to older people. After all, they have grown up in a society where professionalism and creativity are expected. They had to be imaginative at school and probably have had the freedom to flip TV channels at home whenever a programme seemed boring. In church, however, no such facility exists. Therefore the only choice to be made is whether or not to come again. Martin Goldsmith observes, 'Boredom is the one thing young people today will not tolerate'[12] Denominationally, maybe the Anglican and Roman Catholic churches' greater reliance on liturgy in worship seems more boring.

Reasons for dullness at church

Let us contemplate possible reasons why church services can be so dull and tedious. We will consider four.

a) There is a lack of awareness by those leading worship. It is quite possible for those leading a service to become so preoccupied with what they are doing at the front that they become oblivious to the people for whose benefit they are doing it! Their practical involvement means they are not bored. Their introspection is such that they presume it is fine for everyone else too. People can be very insensitive.

b) There is a lack of spiritual vitality by those leading worship. We know how essential it is for any Christian to be closely in tune with God before he can use them effectively. Therefore it is obvious that anyone daring to lead worship when out of relationship with him will have nothing to give and no spiritual life to share. While they may attempt to introduce some of their human personality into what they do it will be in vain for worshippers who have come expecting to meet God. It will seem hollow and empty.

c) There is a lack of spiritual readiness on the part of the congregation. It is not always the fault of the worship leader if a service fails to ignite. Many is the time when I felt really motivated and prepared for worship, only to find the congregation stodgy and unresponsive. In such circumstances most people find it a dry experience. Consequently some may decide not to return next Sunday and Satan will be on his way to scoring more victories.

d) There is a lack of creative imagination in the planning. The God whom we come to meet in worship is the God of creation. It is this God who designed our planet and decided on the different species of flowers, grasses, insects and animals. This same God can come to worship leaders during their preparation and give them thought patterns to follow that will lead to much more creative worship. There is hardly any limit to the variety that can be included in a service of worship. Why have one person read the Scriptures when, using *The Dramatised Bible*, two, three or four people can share a passage? Why not say a hymn or worship song sometimes instead of singing it? Why not include a personal testimony from a member of the congregation? Current testimonies are evidence that God is at work in lives today. People find other people's stories fascinating.

In his book *The Irrelevant Church* Robin Gamble raises the subject of our services. He says that it is possible 'to cut out the huge slices of dullness that haunt much of our worship, and to inject new life.' [13] It is vital that this happens. Two ministers explain why. From Lancashire one says, 'There is so much else to do, like watching TV, videos and the like.' From New Zealand another says, 'Frankly, I don't think I would keep attending half the churches I get glimpses of! Life elsewhere is simply so much more interesting.'

We need to understand how much more interesting church could become, although Satan will do his best to keep Christian churches producing boring services. No-one ever complained that Jesus was dull. On the contrary, the life that flowed from him was instrumental in changing multitudes of people's lives. Jesus' call to his church today is simply to follow his example.

Maybe the first thing to do is to create a team that plans special worship services if not those for every Sunday. Steve Gaukroger, basing his experience on the church of which he is Senior Pastor in Stopsley, Luton, advocates the creation of a special team to plan, what he calls, 'user-friendly' services. Others may call the same thing, 'seeker services'. He says the team needs six giftings: the Minister (someone with spiritual authority), a person who is creative (to handle visual and dramatic material), a technician, a musician, an evangelist and an administrator.[14] The team meets maybe a month before an event to plan and organize it. The various members then oversee responsibility for the material in their own area. Stopley's experience is that it works well and enables them to present well coordinated material.

4. THE TEACHING AND PREACHING MINISTRY

Some comments made by former church-goers in our Survey about irrelevance and boredom undoubtedly include their feelings about sermons. They were asked separately, however, for their response about sermons. 15% of them said they were put off by them, and a further 10% gave a 'maybe' answer.

In Table 23 (Chapter 4) we learned about these people and know that they are:

> ...Aged 34 and under more than 35 and over
> ...Anglicans and Baptists more than Roman Catholics and those in the 'Other' denominations
> ...From the rest of England more than South East England and the rest of the UK

The only new point to make here is how inevitable it is that younger people who have been brought up in a very visual age find it hard to cope with sermons. Spoken presentations that they have experienced during school and higher education have probably been largely accompanied by visuals. A straight monologue, therefore, is hard for them to cope with.

While considering preaching we need to turn our attention not only to the style of presentation, but to the content. We have already established that the average time our Survey respondents went to church was thirteen years. In that time what did they learn about the Christian Faith? Being inquisitive, I produced a supplementary questionnaire about Christian doctrine and practice. I sent it to a small random number (15) of those who had already submitted a main Survey form. While inconclusive because of the small number researched, the results, nevertheless, are interesting, not least because the average length of time these people went to church before leaving was fifteen years.

These are some examples:

* 12 believed God exists and always has.
* 5 believed God is a Trinity (Father, Son, Holy Spirit).
* 7 believed God is wholly loving.
* 7 believed God is wholly just.
* 8 believed God possesses all power.
* 5 believed God has plans to save his fallen world.

* 9 believed Jesus was God's Son who came to earth.
* 7 believed Jesus was born to a mother who was a virgin.
* 6 believed Jesus came to earth on a major rescue mission.

* 3 believed that when Jesus was on earth he was wholly God and wholly man.
* 10 believed that Jesus rose from the dead.

* 4 believed that Satan does not exist and never has.
* 4 believed Satan is the father of lies and deceit.
* 5 believed Satan is committed to destroying people.
* 2 believed Satan is behind the occult, cults and New Age Movement.
* 1 believed Satan is in charge of numerous demons and evil spirits.

* 6 believed God wants to use every Christian to reach others because he wants everyone to be a Christian.
* 8 believed the Bible is a special book in that its writers were inspired to write by God's Holy Spirit.
* 5 didn't see anything wrong with reading their horoscope.
* 1 had been taught to tithe (give a tenth of their income) to God.
* 4 said that their last church had a structure for pastoral caring that meant they always knew who to turn to if they needed some kind of help or support.
* 7 said that they had been taught about the spiritual gifts that God gives to his church (as described in 1 Corinthians 12).

If these responses are typical of those who are still with us as well as those who have left, the churches are failing badly. Many of these figures reveal ignorance, inconsistency and confusion with the teaching of the Bible. People are not being taught the basic doctrinal truths of the Christian Faith. We are not providing what people need in order to grow and develop spiritually. In short, it is no wonder that people leave our churches; the miracle is that they stay as long as they do!

How can people who do not understand the basic tenets of the Faith make any sense of, say, a small section of the Bible they hear read or preached on in church? Christianity is an intellectually credible and logical Faith—once certain key blocks of basic truth are understood. Those surveyed, however, reveal appalling omissions in their understanding. Now for my most serious comment of all; probably it is not their fault. In the same way that a baby needs to be breast-fed and spoon-fed until it can grasp a spoon for itself, so those who do not yet have this capacity spiritually need help. Yet this kind of nurture seems woefully thin on the ground.

God's word through Hosea is wholly appropriate here. 'My people are destroyed from lack of knowledge' (Hos 4:6). God's heart must be heavy because people are rejecting his church and the Christian Faith when, in reality, they are ignorant of what they are rejecting. They have never understood. We can expect little else when, for instance, a respected churchman is featured in a national newspaper as saying, 'I'd like to drop Christmas for fifty years. It's the hardest thing to preach on because I think some of it is legend'.[15] The lack of solid Biblical teaching and preaching in some churches is having disastrous effects.

What then should be taught in our churches? Let us list some absolute essentials:

* The Person and character of God the Father.
* The Person, life and work of Jesus Christ.
* The Person and work of the Holy Spirit.
* The current spiritual condition of mankind.
* Man's need for salvation and redemption through Christ.
* How to receive God's grace.
* The transformation that takes place in a person who begins to trust Jesus Christ personally.
* How to grow as a Christian.
* The reason for the existence of the Church.
* Who Satan and his compatriots are and what is their goal.
* The need for Christians to obey the Great Commission.
* The point and purpose of Christian worship.
* The ways in which God meets people's needs today.
* The holy lifestyle God calls Christians to live.
* How to lead other people to Jesus Christ.
* The eternal security Christians have through faith in Jesus Christ.

Only a balanced diet of spiritual truth based on the Bible, clearly presented, will adequately feed hungry people. So many of those who left church must have been aching inside for some nourishment—and it never came. How Satan must rub his hands with glee that the church does so much of his nasty, evil, destructive work for him! No wonder numbers in the cults and New Age movement are growing. Their teaching may be obscure and illogical—but at least it is presented with conviction and passion. To disillusioned Christians it must seem like a breath of fresh air!

5. RELATING TO OUR YOUTH CULTURE

It is always a struggle to keep up with the latest aspirations and fads that occupy our young people. A survey among 15-24 year olds suggests that they tend to go out with friends, watch TV and spend the largest proportion of their money on going to the pub, buying clothes and eating out. They also spend a fair amount on records, tapes and cigarettes. Many 16-24 year olds

...pub...clothes...eating out...records

are sexually active having had at least one partner in the past year. Half those surveyed claimed to be faithful to one partner; 11% said they had two or more partners. Some 60% of both sexes believed alcohol is a dangerous drug, yet on average this age-group spends £14 a week on alcohol although 88% said they would never drink and drive. One fifth of the men liked to feel drunk by the end of an evening's drinking.[16]

If these young people are typical of those in our nation, to what extent are the churches either keeping them or reaching them? The English Church Census shows that between 1979 and 1989 the churches had 194,500 fewer children, partly because of the low birth rate in the early 1980s. There was a 'massive drop-out among older teens', however, with 155,000 fewer 15-19 year olds in church in 1989 compared to a decade before. '20% of the church-going loss in the 1980s was among those in their twenties, and thus 87% of the total drop in church attendance in these ten years is accounted for by all those under 30.' [17] The churches do not seem to understand young people or be concerned about them and the pressures they face. This appears to be the way young people themselves perceive the situation.

Steve Chalke explains the situation more fully. A survey in 1984 showed that half the sixteen to twenty year olds...

> wanted to hear about personal relationships, sex, marriage, homosexuality, racism, law and order, the third world, work, the environment, unemployment and pop music. Just under half wanted to talk about the occult, cults, prayer, the Bible, television and politics. These findings indicate just how big the gap is within the churches between what many young people want to explore and what the adults are prepared to talk through with them. So the little contact that most teenagers have with Christianity and the church convinces them that it is muddled and has nothing real to say to today's world. It seems to exist within a vacuum, with a lot more to say about our heritage and tradition than the difficult business of twentieth-century life.[18]

Clearly our churches have to invest more time and attention

in relating to our youth. For the sake of God's church in future generations we must act now to stem the flow of young people leaving it. It will be neither easy nor cheap. An encouraging development in some churches has been the emergence of specialist full-time youth leaders. In some situations churches may find that joint initiatives with their local or county council may allow public funds to be made available to them from the Youth Service budget. This is partly how my own church is able to employ an extra full-time staff member in youth ministry.

Other churches may need to invest resources in sending gifted youth leaders to some of the varied training courses now available. For some it will be to gain experience; others will be glad of refresher courses to keep them in touch with changes and developments. It is crucial that those called and gifted by God to relate to today's young people are equipped and encouraged in this sphere of ministry.

To conclude we reflect on a statistic from our Survey that may have been missed earlier. Quite spontaneously, 3% of the former church-goers surveyed said that they had been made to go when younger and it put them off for good. I wonder if this proportion applies to the 1000 people leaving English churches each week, many of them younger people. If it does, this resentment may be felt by thirty people a week or over 1500 people a year who leave. What to do about it is not easy to see. Naturally, Christian parents want to encourage their children and teenagers to go to church with them, yet it seems that for some it becomes counter-productive.

There is really only one course of action the British churches can take to overcome all the problems featured in this chapter. Take a leaf out of Jesus' book; relate to ordinary people at *their* level. We will continue discussing how this can be done in the last two chapters.

Notes

[1] Jack Burton, *The Gap* (SPCK: London, 1991) p 26.

[2] Martin Goldsmith, *What in the World is God Doing?* (MARC: Eastbourne, 1991) p 94.

3 Floyd McClung, chapter: The Streets of Amsterdam, *No Stranger in the City* (IVP: Leicester, 1989) p 59.

4 Robert Van de Weyer, *The Country Church* (Darton, Longman & Todd: London, 1991) p 110.

5 Gordon Miller, 'Dear Tim...About Making Church Relevant', *Christian Leadership Letter*, World Vision of New Zealand, Issue 116 (May/June 1991): p 2-3.

6 Peter H Lawrence, *Doing What Comes Supernaturally* (Kingsway: Eastbourne, 1992) p 197-198.

7 Nicky Cruz, *A Final Warning* (Kingsway: Eastbourne, 1992) p 182.

8 Rev. Arnell P.C. Arn, 'Baby Boomers...Can we Reach Them?', *The Good News Link*, Vol. 15, No. 2 (Summer 1991): Board of National Ministries, American Baptist Churches U.S.A., Valley Forge, PA.

9 George Carey, *The Church in the Market Place* (Kingsway: Eastbourne, 1989) p 59.

10 From *Church Leaders Handbook* issued at 'Creating a Church for the Unchurched' Conference, Birmingham, UK, 16-18 June 1992, p 8-9.

11 Martin Robinson, *A World Apart* (Monarch: Tunbridge Wells, 1992) p 157-216.

12 Goldsmith, *op cit*, p 95.

13 Robin Gamble, *The Irrelevant Church* (Monarch: Tunbridge Wells, 1991) p 166-167.

14 Steve Gaukroger, speaking at Baptist Union 'Roots' Conference, Gravesend, 12 November 1992.

15 Ysenda Maxtone Graham, 'In the Beginning was the Word', *The Sunday Telegraph*, 15 December 1991, p iv-v.

16 Statistics from 'Young Britain: A survey of youth culture in transition', Euromonitor & Carrick James Market Research. Reported in *LandMARC*, MARC Europe, London (New Year 1991), p 5.

17 Peter Brierley, *'Christian' England* (MARC Europe: London, 1991) p 82-83.

18 Steve Chalke, *The Christian Youth Manual* (Kingsway: Eastbourne, 1992) p 97.

CHAPTER 8

Problems of Not Finding God

WHEN I WAS IN CHELMSFORD gathering data for my Survey I met a man in his forties. 'I used to go to a church school when I was a kid,' he said. 'The reason I don't go to church is because God don't stick his head out of the clouds and say "I am here".' His response is common in people who have had some kind of Christian or church input in their past but who seem to have what I have to call an unrealistic expectation of God.

The Survey figures show something of the extent of this problem. Some 7% of respondents said that they did not go to church any longer partly because they felt that God had let them down in some way. A further 6% gave a 'maybe' answer to this question which means that 13% of former church-goers have questions and problems about who God is and what he is like.

In Figure 24 (Chapter 4) we learned more about these people and know that they are:

   ...Female more than male
   ...Aged 35-54 more than 34 and under
   ...Methodists (predominantly) and Baptists more than Roman Catholics and those in the 'Other' denominations
   ...From England (excluding the South East) more than Scotland, Wales and the Channel Islands

Why is this? The fact that no-one can prove that God has let them down means that their views can only be subjective.

Women are said to be more intuitive and maybe more likely to sense what they would call betrayal or failure by God than men. Possibly the simple fact that 35-54s have lived longer and have experienced more of life is why they feel more let down. Yet this would not be so had their faith also grown over the years. The number of former Methodists who feel God has let them down is unexpectedly high. It forces us to ask whether the teaching these people received helped them sufficiently to understand God as the Bible portrays him.

The question that must occupy us now is whether it is really possible for God to let people down. Does God fail people? Can God fail people—or is it that our human expectations of him are faulty? To find out we have only the Bible to guide us. Some Psalms speak about the presence of God. Psalm 46 begins by describing God as 'our refuge and strength' (v1) and later expresses the words of the Lord himself, 'Be still, and know that I am God' (v10). The writer of Psalm 118 experienced God's help during difficult times. 'In my anguish I cried to the Lord, and he answered by setting me free. The Lord is with me; I will not be afraid...The Lord is with me; he is my helper' (v5-7).

Psalm 121 was sung by pilgrims as they approached Jerusalem to worship. The second verse refers to the 'help' that 'comes from the Lord', and the remainder of the Psalm expands on the practical ways that God helps his people. 'He who watches over you will not slumber...the Lord is your shade at your right hand...the Lord will keep you from all harm...the Lord will watch over your coming and going both now and for evermore.' These human writers knew the loyal, purposeful and thoroughly practical support of God in their lives.

Jesus spoke of the relationship God will have with those people who come to him through his Son. He saw it as a mutual bonding. 'Remain in me, and I will remain in you' (Jn 15:4). He also instructed the disciples about the ministry of the Holy Spirit. 'You know him, for he lives with you and will be in you', he said (Jn 14:17). Later, the writer to the Hebrews reminds his readers of God's long-standing promise, 'Never will I leave you; never will I forsake you' (Heb 13:5). God promises to be with and to support his people in Christianity. So why do some people become disillusioned and leave churches believing God has deserted them?

There are two points to make. The first is that God's promises are always to *his* people. By this we do not mean those who vaguely believe he exists and who choose to call themselves Christians. Instead, we are talking about those who have come into a covenant relationship with him. The Old Testament reveals the covenants God made with his chosen nation Israel (notably at Sinai) that bonded them together in partnership. Both God and the Israelites made promises of loyalty to each other that they were then obliged to keep. The New Testament focuses on the New Covenant made as Christ died on the cross. It is a covenant of pure grace dependent wholly on God pouring out his love and forgiveness to those who deserve only judgement. It is those people who receive this forgiveness to whom God promises his presence and constant support.

The second factor to consider is the conditional clauses in some of God's promises. God promises Joshua his presence in the words, 'the Lord your God will be with you wherever you go' (Josh 1:9), but they are preceded by strict instructions. 'Be careful to obey all the law my servant Moses gave you; do not turn from it to the right or to the left...Do not let this Book of the Law depart from your mouth; meditate on it day and night, so that you may be careful to do everything written in it' (Josh 1:7-8). God clearly ties together obedience to his will with the promise of his presence. Indeed, only a few chapters later in Joshua we see how serious God is about this. He showed Joshua how the city of Jericho could be overcome, which it was (Josh 6). Yet when Joshua sent up troops to conquer Ai they were routed and chased away (Josh 7:4-5). It was not long before Joshua learned from God that Israel's disobedience was to blame (Josh 7:11-12). When that was resolved, the Israelites followed God's blueprint and were successful in taking Ai.

Another promise of God that is tied in with precise instructions is found in Jesus' last words to his disciples. He promises to be with his followers when he says, 'Surely I am with you always, to the very end of the age' (Matt 28:20). Yet these words follow his mandate to 'Go and make disciples...baptizing them...and teaching them'. It is when disciples of Christ obey his instructions that this promise of his presence comes into operation.

So Scripture teaches us that God does not fail those with whom he has a relationship if they are seeking to be obedient and submissive to him. Hosea 5:6 shows how out of touch with reality some people can be. This prophet ministered at a time when God's people were very rebellious and pagan. He says that 'when they go with their flocks and herds to seek the Lord, they will not find him; he has withdrawn himself from them'. The next verse tells why: 'They are unfaithful to the Lord'.

While God is forever loving, merciful and gracious, he neither can nor will force people into obedience. When they live in rebellion and disobedience they cannot count on him as they could before. There is, however, always a way back. Hosea revealed that God would judge his people—but then wait for them to be repentant. 'I will go back to my place until they admit their guilt. And they will seek my face; in their misery they will earnestly seek me' says God (Hos 5:15).

How then do we interpret the answers to the Survey question about God letting people down? Here are some possibilities.

a) It is probable that some who feel God has let them down did not have a true covenant relationship with him through Christ in the first place. Despite their sincerity, their 'faith' was little more than wishful thinking and hoping for the best.

b) Possibly others have had a relationship with God but have also rebelled. While unrepentant, they have expected God to act with and for them as if they were following Christ as dedicated disciples. In these circumstances they are as deluded as the people in Hosea's day.

c) It is likely that there are others for whom neither of the above comments is appropriate. God's silence and lack of clear-cut help at a difficult time was an absolute mystery to them. They found themselves as baffled as Job when a string of disasters struck his life (Job 1:13-21).

In one sense it is quite understandable for people to turn against God when he seems absent and uncaring at a time when they feel they need him most. Let us explore this matter further, and try to understand why people do this.

1. THE WAY GOD WORKS

We must never forget that Christianity is a faith. By definition a faith cannot be intellectually proven. Those who follow it accept and believe the tenets of that faith although they cannot necessarily prove them completely in words. The Bible contains teaching about the person and nature of God the Father, the Son and the Holy Spirit. It reveals truth about man's plight. It reveals how the Father's love provoked him to send his Son, Jesus Christ, to redeem sinful man. It tells how God can totally change a person's life from the inside out. He gives purpose for living and eternal security too. As Jesus told Nicodemus, 'You must be born again' (Jn 3:7). When a person is 'born again' he or she receives God's gift of salvation. The definition of a true Christian is one who responds by faith and receives God's love in this way.

Some new believers seem to think something magical happens when they are born again, something that will utterly change their lives. In one sense this is wholly true. God has forgiven them and changed their nature. 'You have been set free from sin and have become slaves to righteousness' (Rom 6:18). If however the new convert to Christianity imagines that this means that problems in life are now a thing of the past they are badly mistaken. God has never made such a promise to anyone. In 2 Corinthians 11:23-28 Paul relates the harsh treatment that he received since becoming a follower of Jesus. In the following chapter he tells of a persistent problem he had to cope with daily, almost certainly some kind of physical difficulty (2 Cor 12:7-8). God declined to remove it, preferring to force Paul to trust and depend on him more. 'My grace is sufficient for you, for my power is made perfect in weakness', God told Paul.

The first paragraph of Hebrews 12 is about God's discipline. 'The Lord disciplines those he loves, and he punishes everyone he accepts as a son. Endure hardship as discipline; God is treating you as sons' (Heb 12:6-7). At times God wants to test and stretch the faith of his children to make it develop and grow. He wants 'to purify for himself a people that are his very own' (Tit 2:14). Therefore Christians should expect some times in their lives to be harder than usual. When they come, pressures increase and God may seem distant. This is not a sign of his anger or absence, but an indication of his love. He is using the flames of the furnace to refine and purify us. In our desperation as we cling to him tenuously by a single thread of faith we will discover him in a new and fresh way. Through this hard and maybe painful process our faith and trust in God as Father will grow immeasurably.

When we understand the way God works, we see that he wants to use these experiences to draw us closer to himself, not have us go further from him.

2. THE DEPRIVATION OF FULL BIBLICAL TEACHING

Another reason why people blame God is because of the paucity of instruction they have received. They have never been helped to understand the nature and character of God and the way he works. This deficiency starts from the beginning of their Christian life.

Inadequate presentations of the Gospel

For many years I have had a high regard for the Evangelism Explosion Gospel presentation. I did not find it easy to memorize when I first went to a training course, and I have struggled to keep it fresh in my mind ever since. Its strength lies in three things. First is the fact that it is used in a training context so that one trained person teaches two others how to share the Gospel on the job. Secondly is the fact that the EE training encourages recipients to ask questions and not be rushed into making a response. Thirdly, and maybe most importantly, is the breadth of material covered. Unchurched people are not just told who Jesus is, what he has done and what he can do for them, but also what the 'implications' will be. Here it is made clear what the long-term effects will be if they commit themselves to Christ.

John MacArthur spent some years studying how Jesus dealt with enquirers. He says:

> The message being proclaimed today is not the gospel according to Jesus. The gospel in vogue today holds forth a false hope to sinners. It promises them they can have eternal life yet continue to live in rebellion against God. Indeed, it *encourages* people to claim Jesus as Saviour yet defer until later the commitment to obey Him as Lord...The good news of Christ has given way to the bad news of an insidious easy-believism that makes no moral demands on the lives of sinners. It is not the same message Jesus proclaimed.[1]

This type of inadequate evangelism is unhelpful to the lives of the individuals concerned and also to the life of the church they attend. The people themselves have a faith that is brittle, fragile and shallow. For them God's grace was cheap. Andrew Brandon says that for these people to become Christians 'is no more costly than filling in a form with the appropriate responses, or receiving a gift from a cereal packet'.[2] He goes on to see evangelism of this kind as a subtle trick of Satan to confuse and demoralize the church. 'To compromise the integrity of the gospel in an attempt to attract converts can be the devil's work', he says.[3] It is. It leaves the new convert with a faith that has such a small root that he or she cannot easily grow. It also brings discouragement into the church when it sees new believers falling away when pressures come. Presentations of the Gospel need to be more complete. This will enable those who respond to Christ to enter a relationship with him which can grow and become increasingly enriching.

Inadequate nurture
In the last chapter we gave some thought to the diet of spiritual teaching Christians need if they are to be properly fed and grow. Never is this more important than when they are new to the faith. In the same way that a new-born baby needs special food regularly to remain healthy and grow, so new believers need special help too. If deprived of this they will be weak and

vulnerable. One pastor told me about a man whom he believes was incompletely converted. 'Despite much time on my part trying to help him grow, he did not seem to have the ability to stick at his faith', he said. 'Very much a case of the seed in shallow soil.' In my own pastoral experience, I have found three important areas in which new Christians often receive very little teaching. Others have written about the same areas.

a) The greatness and majesty of God. David Needham says, 'There are times when Paul had to put down his pen'.[4] He goes on to explain that there are times in his writings when Paul seems overcome with the wonder of who God is and what he is like. Needham argues that this happens when Paul writes to the Christians in Rome. He has taught about the plans and purposes of God and finds himself caught up in praise and wonder. Consequently it is as if he just blurts out:

> Oh, the depth of the riches of the wisdom and knowledge of God! How unsearchable his judgments, and his paths beyond tracing out!...For from him and through him and to him are all things. To him be the glory for ever! Amen (Rom 11:33-36).

Much time needs to be invested in helping new Christians recognize the wonder of God. The more we find ourselves astounded at his greatness, power, authority and grace the more we are likely to respond to him in humble obedience and submission.

b) The miracle of God's grace. One of the hundreds of ministers to whom I wrote said, 'The only "hunch" I have as to why people stop attending is that they don't fully understand what God has done for them.' I agree with him, as I do with Terry Virgo who tackles the same subject from a different perspective when he argues that 'Nothing has hindered the growth of the kingdom more than the ugly face of legalism'.[5] Many Christians today find themselves bound by continuing sin in their lives and become disillusioned because they let God down. Yet despite all their good intentions they find themselves unable to change. Romans 5-7 contain complex truth, so the teaching is not passed on to new converts. Yet Paul knew that an explanation of what happens when a person is converted to Christ is essential. They need to understand what God does in a person's life when they make a commitment to him. They need to grasp the fundamental change of nature that takes place within them. Paul explains it clearly. He says, 'By dying to what once bound us, we have been released from the law so that we serve in the new way of the Spirit, and not in the old way of the written code' (Rom 7:6).

Many Christians today do not know the new freedom and liberation available in Christ because these are aspects of the Christian life they have never been taught. Here again we see a tactic of Satan. As Terry Virgo says, it is a very effective strategy. 'The devil realizes that undermining the very character of the gospel is far more effective than opposing it blatantly because he then reduces it to the level of an irrelevant religion.'[6] Some Christians experience inner and personal frustration because they seem to keep failing. If it seems that there is no obvious help or support from God they become prime candidates for abandoning both church-going and the Christian faith. In such circumstances the lack of vital teaching is a major factor.

c) The justice of God. As an experienced Christian leader, Selwyn Hughes knows how self-centred some Christians can be. In his *Every Day with Jesus* Bible reading notes, he helps his readers understand why God acts in the ways and at the times he does. We bring prayers that, if answered, would benefit us far more than God. We tend to be concerned about our own welfare far more than other people's. We are not really concerned about God's glory. Selwyn Hughes works this problem through.

> If He (God) lets something happen to us today that we think He should not have let happen, then we will find it very difficult to have confidence in Him should we have the same requirement tomorrow. Often in these situations we end up developing a deep rage or disappointment with God, which, in the interests of the Christian faith, we learn to suppress. This is largely because we do not understand God's "bottom line". So what is the "bottom line" in God? I suggest it is His *justice*. By this I mean the truth that whatever God does, He does because it is right. Not that it

is right because God does it, but that God does it because it is right. There is a world of difference between those two things.... Unless we are gripped by the belief that God acts justly in everything—*everything*—then we will not have the sure-footedness we need to negotiate the rocky slopes that are up ahead.[7]

Christians need to be properly nurtured so that the seed of the Gospel grows and becomes fully mature within them. They will then 'no longer be infants, tossed back and forth by the waves, and blown here and there by every wind of teaching' (Eph 4:14). When difficulties come they will have both the faith and the understanding of the way God works so that they keep trusting him instead of abandoning both him and his church.

3. THE PROBLEMS OF A CRISIS OF FAITH

We have almost described this already. It is where Christians find themselves thrown into confusion because of traumatic and demanding events taking place in their lives. The worst thing, perhaps, is not the events themselves but their inability to discover God's presence and support at this difficult time.

Maybe one of the greatest areas of neglect by Christian leaders is their failure to warn believers that at some time in life crises of faith are inevitable. As Gavin Reid observes, 'The parable of the soil should lead us to expect this.'[8] In one of his lectures Dr John Savage teaches that there are certain times of life when natural crises occur:

Early twenties

Mid-life

Retirement[9]

At each of these mileposts we find ourselves moving into another phase of life. Naturally, we need time to work through the effects this has on us. If a number of problems arise in our life at the same time it can precipitate a crisis. We feel like a ship which is out of control being tossed around mercilessly in a storm.

During times of strain we can easily make premature decisions. A minister colleague once invited me to go sailing on the Solent with him and one of his Deacons. Chris told me how wonderful sailing is and in a hesitant kind of way I looked forward to our afternoon out. The journey from the English mainland to the Isle of Wight was fine, but on the way back Chris wanted me to experience *real* sailing. He insisted on going as fast as we could with the yacht balanced at some strange angle, almost (it seemed to me) on its side. I had grave reservations about the wisdom of this and felt no easier when we had to tack backwards and forwards to get back to Lymington, with the Sealink ferry constantly bearing down on us. I decided very quickly never to go sailing again. I never have!

At times when everything seems in a state of flux in our lives we look for *anything* to hang on to. It is when under this kind of pressure that some people decide to abandon Christianity. When God does not seem to come running to their aid they feel he has deserted them. This decision may be as premature as mine never to go sailing again. I have no doubt that experienced sailors would tell me that had I gritted my teeth and gone through the experience a few more times I would have grown to love this sport. Deep down I concede they may be right! We can make the same point about Christianity. When the ground seems to fall away under my feet, is it a good time to make ultimate decisions about God? Is it the best time to decide to cope on my own? Or would I do better to conclude that although I cannot sense he is there I will hang on to him tightly by faith and just see what happens? Crises of faith are critical times. They can make or break our faith.

Let us look at John 6 in this context. After Jesus spelled out what following him would mean, some concluded, 'This is a hard teaching' (v60). Jesus explained that he knew that some who were apparently his disciples did not really believe in him at all (v64). Then he made the point that only those 'enabled' by his Father can come to him. After this it says, 'From this time many of his disciples turned back and no longer followed him' (v66). It may be provocative to say that Jesus encourages crises of faith to sort out the sheep from the goats. Perhaps we can conclude that while he is not keen to lose followers, he is committed to seeing a high quality of discipleship among those who continue with him.

Sammy Tippit tells how he and his wife were called by the Lord to work in a ghetto area of Chicago where they ministered to drug addicts, runaways and street gangs. They prayed for 'a mighty spiritual awakening' and worked hard among the people to give God the opportunity to move. They not only saw people coming to Christ; they also felt opposition from nightclub owners. One night after a man knelt in the street and gave his life to Christ there was a violent reaction and Sammy and his colleague found themselves in jail. They sat in their cell, he says, 'in utter disbelief'. It could have been for them a time of disillusionment. On the contrary they decided to worship, and before being let out of jail on bail had the privilege of leading another man to Christ. As a direct consequence of their arrest, Sammy says that through the media as well as personal contacts they had the opportunity to witness to hundreds of thousands of people.[10]

Of course not all crises turn out to have such positive consequences as this, but the principle stands firm. Crises of faith either make or break us.

4. THE PROBLEM OF GUILT-FEELINGS

Sometimes people leave churches because they feel guilty. This may be a guilt complex or an awareness of an indiscretion, misdemeanour, neglect or omission in their lives. They sense they are bound by sin and guilt, and a way out seems hard to find. In these circumstances some feel that the easiest course of action is to bury what they feel and give up their faith and their church. They plan to carry on living life with neither.

This is not necessary. Like physical pain, feelings of guilt are actually there to help us. They alert us to problems that we might otherwise overlook. A general guilt complex can prompt us to think through even big theological issues like the doctrines of original sin and total depravity. John Gunstone helps by defining this both negatively and positively. It has never been, he says, 'a doctrine declaring humanity to be as bad as it can be.

What it does maintain is that there is an element of fallenness in all that human beings think, speak and do, and that therefore they are incapable of perfection in their own strength.'[11] A guilt complex can therefore help us to see our need of Christ although it also can make us claim that sin is not our fault.

Specific sins are frequently drawn to the attention of those intent on walking God's way. Both through our consciences and the ministry of the Holy Spirit, God tells us how and when we stepped beyond the boundaries that he set around us. However if we choose to ignore what we hear we put ourselves in a state of rebellion before him. Our relationship will naturally grow cold and our faith will come to mean less and less to us. It is not unusual in these circumstances for God to allow crises in our lives to try to draw our attention to our clear need of him. At times like this the prophet's words apply:

> Seek the Lord while he may be found; call on him while he is near. Let the wicked forsake his way and the evil man his thoughts. Let him turn to the Lord, and he will have mercy on him, and to our God, for he will freely pardon (Is 55:6-7).

Whenever God's people are in danger of blaming God because they feel he has let them down and they themselves feel guilty, there is always a way out. John Gunstone points us to the healing of the paralysed man, let down in front of Jesus. Maybe, he says, the man was initially startled or disappointed to hear Jesus refer to his forgiveness. After all, it was physical healing that he was looking for. Eventually, however, Jesus told him to get up, take his mat and go home. As he obeyed Jesus' words the gift of healing was his. John Gunstone then says this. 'The miracle demonstrated powerfully that Jesus Christ had come as the bringer of God's forgiveness to men and women. Sin need no longer paralyse God's people. His mercy was available for all.'[12] Through Christ's death sin and guilt can be dealt with. There is now no reason why they should cause people to blame God for inaction or lack of care. Yet, sadly, God is still blamed, and at this point only two courses of action may remain open to us. We can pray that God will be able to penetrate people's lives, and we can continue to love and support them—even if they find it difficult to respond.

5. THE TRICKS OF THE ENEMY

So far we have commented on ways in which Satan appears to be at work encouraging Christians away from allegiance to God and his church. That is the subject of our next chapter, but there is another way in which he works. Satan is delighted if believers are not grounded firmly in their faith and have not understood some of the truths about God that we listed earlier. It means that he can attempt to dislodge even the minimal security they have.

Also, if Christians have not been taught about Satan and his devious ways, he can have a field day by taking full advantage of their ignorance. They will be unaware that he and his colleagues are planting seed-thoughts intended only to provoke confusion and disbelief. They will believe that they are asking normal, natural and intelligent questions—even if they do tend to undermine their own belief in God.

In 2 Corinthians 11 Paul has to deal with problems in the church in Corinth caused by people he sees as false apostles. He tells the believers that he is 'afraid that just as Eve was deceived by the serpent's cunning, your minds may somehow be led astray from your sincere and pure devotion to Christ' (v3). Later, having discussed the problem more fully with them, Paul refers to those whom he believes are leading the church astray. They are, he says, 'false apostles, deceitful workmen, masquerading as apostles of Christ. And no wonder, for Satan himself masquerades as an angel of light. It is not surprising, then, if his servants masquerade as servants of righteousness' (v13-15).

Paul's warning applies whether the deceivers are human or spiritual beings. Satan is determined to cause confusion and disillusionment among Christ's followers wherever and whenever he can. If he can find a way into a Christian's life when they are vulnerable he will do so. If through some devious means he can undermine their trust and belief in God he stands to gain a convert. His 'convert' may simply leave the church and become uninterested in spiritual things; that is enough. If however the disillusioned Christian can be enticed into a cult or even the occult so much the better. When we understand the dangers we see how important it is that Christians are taught the truth of the Bible. At times when they could find themselves questioning God's love and care for them, they will be more alert if Satan attempts to deceive them.

A broader view

In the past four chapters we have considered areas of Christian and church life where people have problems that may provoke them to leave their church. What we have not yet done is look at the other side of the coin. While some people are leaving churches, many tens of thousands of others continue to attend regularly. For the sake of both completeness and comparison, I undertook a further small-scale survey of current church-goers.

Initially I asked for co-operation from twenty-six ministers and leaders. Eight agreed to help. They circulated a questionnaire to some people in their churches. Most churches used the envelopes I supplied so that members' responses would not be seen by their own church leaders. This kept their replies confidential. I received ninety-one replies from six denominations.

These people display a high level of Christian commitment.

23% attend church once a Sunday.
77% attend more than once.
67% were christened.
86% went to Sunday School.
77% have been baptized by immersion.
81% consider themselves a born-again Christian.
62% have been in leadership.
95% see themselves as an active, committed Christian.

The questionnaire asked the respondents what they do on Sundays apart from going to church. They could tick as many activities as was appropriate. Their replies are noticeably different from those of former church-goers in Figure 8 (Chapter 2).

Table 7: How respondents use Sundays

87% spend time with family and/or friends
63% relax at home
35% go on relaxing trips out
5% work in paid employment
4% go shopping
4% go to DIY stores
1% go to car boot sales

These people were also asked why they go to church. They could tick as many reasons as were appropriate.

Table 8: Reasons why respondents attend church

99% said they go to worship God
90% said they go to receive biblical teaching
87% said they go to hear God speak to them
66% said they go to meet friends
60% said they go to receive a spiritual boost
30% said they go to display loyalty to the church
12% said they go because they have always been
None said they go because they are coerced

This is a very positive response from people who largely seem determined to take God seriously in their lives. They appear to understand the purpose of Sunday worship services and, on the surface at least, go for thoroughly biblical reasons. These same people were also asked how they feel about their church. Again, they had the freedom to select as many answers as were appropriate.

Table 9: How respondents felt about their church

76% felt their church is where God wants them to be
73% were happy and content in their church
27% felt thoroughly fulfilled in their church
10% were neither happy nor unhappy in their church
4% were dissatisfied in their church
1% were discontent and unhappy in their church
1% were considering leaving their church

It is encouraging to see just under three-quarters of the respondents saying how happy and content they are at church. Maybe it is even better news that 76% see the guidance of God as a major factor here. They believe that their current church is where God has called them to worship and serve him. This conviction is enormously valuable because it means that they see themselves as answerable to him as far as their church-going is concerned. With this attitude, they will not stop going to church or change churches at the slightest provocation. Having responded positively so far, we must not ignore the group that is at risk. The bottom four lines of Table 7 reveal that 16% of those surveyed (none ticked more than one box) have feelings about their church that could lead to movement away from it. We cannot foresee, of course, what will happen from this point on, but they probably will take one of four courses of action.

a) They will remain in their church but continue to have feelings about it that are not very positive.

b) They will drift away from it and begin to explore other local churches to find one they identify with more.

c) They will stop attending their church regularly and before long become yet another former church-goer.

d) Something will happen that changes their situation radically and leads to them becoming happy, content and fulfilled in their church.

What can we learn from this third survey? Most people take their faith reasonably seriously and are at least fairly content with their church. There are others, however, who are vulnerable. They are possibly apathetic about church or unhappy and discontented. This group is at risk. They may not just leave their current church, but may stop attending any church. This in turn means that their whole spiritual life and experience is at stake. A lot hangs on the decisions they will make. These decisions, in turn, will be greatly affected by any action (or lack of it) taken by their church to help and encourage them. If, for instance, their church took time to hear and understand what they feel unhappy and dissatisfied about and responded in an appropriate way, their feelings could change quickly.

This scenario alerts us to the spiritual battle that is going on for those who are not securely rooted in their church. In a change of direction we now look at some biblical and theological issues that will help us move towards some positive suggestions.

Notes

[1] John MacArthur, Jr., *You Call Me Lord?* (Marshall Pickering: London, 1988) p 15-16.

[2] Andrew Brandon, *Enjoying God* (Kingsway: Eastbourne, 1991) p 209.

[3] Brandon, *op cit*, p 210.

[4] David C Needham, *Close to His Majesty* (Frameworks: Leicester, 1987) p 9.

[5] Terry Virgo, *Restoration in the Church* (Kingsway: Eastbourne, 1985) p 9.

[6] Virgo, *op cit*, p 38-39.

[7] Selwyn Hughes, *Every Day with Jesus*, January-February 1992 (CWR: Farnham, 1992), Friday 24 January.

[8] Gavin Reid, *Good News to Share* (Falcon: Eastbourne, 1979) p 121.

[9] Taken from an audio tape *Why Active Members Stay Active* and used by permission, L.E.A.D. Consultants, Inc. Reynoldsburg, Ohio, USA (1992).

[10] Sammy Tippit, *Worthy of Worship* (Scripture Press: Amersham-on-the-Hill: 1990) p 85-87.

[11] John Gunstone, *Free in Christ* (Darton, Longman and Todd: London, 1989) p 8.

[12] Gunstone, *op cit*, p 18.

SECTION 3

Responding To The Truth

CHAPTER 9

Looking Under The Surface

T O BEGIN THIS FINAL Section we will look at declining
church attendances from a different perspective. I have
already made some observations about the part Satan
plays when people leave churches, but we will now explore this
more deeply.

We begin with Job 1. In v1-5 we are introduced to the key
human characters in the story, but in v6-12 are transported to the
heavenly realm. Here we find God and Satan discussing Job's
life on earth. Very soon Satan is revealed as the orchestrator of
the serious difficulties that afflict Job and his family (v13-19).

Is there a parallel with the situation we are discussing? Is it
possible that Satan is in some way contributing to the decline in
attendance in British churches at this time? To answer this we
will explore Satan's key stratagems, but first need to ensure that
we are fully aware of the sovereignty and authority of God.

The person of God and his plans

The Bible begins by revealing an eternal God who determines to
undertake a mammoth and magnificent work of creation. The
pinnacle of his created works is man whom he made in his
image. God's deep desire was that man, who has been made
with freewill and a genuine freedom of choice, should volun-
tarily elect to submit to him, worship and serve him. God is
shown as loving, just and holy, and when man rebelled and
sinned, God had no choice but to adjust the relationship
between himself and man. The result of sin was that fellowship

was now no longer possible, and God had to impose a separation between them. His heart was sad, however, and he formulated a plan that would allow man to be salvaged and reinstated.

He chose the Israelite people to be his human instruments to bring this to the rest of the world, but their failure to live his way brought continual dismay. Eventually God sent his only Son, part of the eternal Godhead, to the world. His blameless life and sacrificial death allowed repentant human beings to experience God's true forgiveness and new life in Christ from that time on. Through him there is genuine hope for all men to discover the purpose of their birth and to find fulfilment in their lives. The message of the Bible is that God loves and cares about lost people and made even the ultimate sacrifice of his Son to bring them back to himself.

The person of Satan and his plans

There is however another character trying to squeeze into the spotlight much of the time. The origins of Satan are not revealed clearly in the Bible, but it is likely that he is a former senior angel who rebelled against the sovereignty of God. He first surfaces in Genesis 3 when he enticed Adam and Eve to reject God's authority over them. As Scripture unravels he is shown to be the originator of all sin, evil and rebellion and is the epitome of filth and depravity. He is the archenemy of God who is intent on causing disruption and havoc that will stop God's plans and purposes from reaching fruition. Any pain, hurt or destruction caused by his actions is of no consequence to this evil spiritual being without a heart.

In *The Screwtape Letters* C.S.Lewis gives his understanding of Satan's prime intention. 'Do remember', Screwtape tells Wormwood, 'the only thing that matters is the extent to which you separate the man from the Enemy' (the 'Enemy' here being God).[1] Peter Horrobin also perceives Satan as serious in his intentions.

> Satan is a filthy fighter, he is no respecter of persons and he hates God so much that he will stop at nothing to destroy those whom God has created...Satan has never forgotten the defeat of Calvary and is working to the limits of his

capacity to keep people away from finding out the truth, that in the name of Jesus people can be set free.[2]

Satan, however, does not work alone. There is no way that he could because, unlike God, he is not omnipresent. Therefore he needs a willing army to serve him and carry out his perverted desires. He finds his troops in what Paul describes as the 'rulers...authorities...powers of this dark world and...spiritual forces of evil in the heavenly realms' (Eph 6:12). This list includes evil spirits that Jesus and early church leaders encountered who had people in their grip. Yet through the power and authority of Jesus, those in bondage were freed. Jesus' disciples learned this for themselves when their Master sent them out (Lk 9:1,10; 10:1,17). Both C.S. Lewis in *The Screwtape Letters* and Frank Peretti in *This Present Darkness* and *Piercing the Darkness* have written Christian fiction that gives their understanding of the subtle and devious work of demons in influencing human beings and situations on earth. While both writers clearly go beyond the revelation of Scripture, they help Christians to understand the sheer intensity of hatred and hostility that Satan and his forces have towards God and people who belong to him.

When Jesus met satanic forces during his ministry he faced them without hesitation. He was confronted by Satan in the wilderness (Lk 4:1-13) and later, the same chapter tells us, met a demon-possessed man in the synagogue at Capernaum (4:31-37), and many other demonized people (4:41). In these and other situations Jesus demonstrated his greater authority and power. In the synagogue at Nazareth he used Isaiah's prophecy to show what he understood to be the purpose of his earthly ministry. He told his audience that, among other things, he had come 'to proclaim freedom for the prisoners' (Lk 4:18). The way he brought liberation to so many is a clear demonstration that God has far greater authority than Satan. Although Satan continues to interfere with and disrupt God's will, he has insufficient resources to withstand the power of God's Word when directed to a given situation. When Jesus had been crucified, it was God's supreme power that routed Satan's perceived victory. Jesus rose victorious from the dead and is now triumphant over death for all time. No wonder Paul quotes Isaiah's words, 'Death has been swallowed up in victory' (1 Cor 15:54).

Paul's letters include several passages on this subject. Clinton E. Arnold traces this very comprehensively in his recent book.[3] Paul's best-known teaching is in Ephesians 6:10-20 where he begins by highlighting the extent of the opposition. He then teaches about the protection and weaponry available to believers to counteract the attacks they will endure. He has no doubts at all that with God's power all Christians can live victoriously even when the enemy directs many hostile missiles towards them.

The nature of the spiritual battle is varied. Paul speaks of being subjected to a continuing attack in 2 Corinthians 12:7-10. His 'thorn in my flesh, a messenger of Satan, to torment me' is never defined although commentators tend to believe he had some type of permanent physical disability. When he writes to the Corinthians, Galatians and Colossians he warns them about erroneous teaching being promulgated in their churches that can lead them away from the Truth (eg 2 Cor 11:13-15). Satan works in a variety of ways although they all have the same goal: to stop God accomplishing what he desires to do in the lives of people who need him.

Satan's main tactic

When Satan's activity is analysed, there is one technique he uses time and again—and to great effect. This is deception, something other writers call Satan's 'primary tactic',[4] his 'diabolical method',[5] and his 'stock in trade'.[6] Nigel Wright refers to Satan's power as 'inherently deceptive',[7] while in Revelation 12:9 Satan is called the one who 'leads the whole world astray'. Jesus says about him, 'he was a murderer from the beginning, not holding to the truth, for there is no truth in him. When he lies, he speaks his native language, for he is a liar and the father of lies' (Jn 8:44). The Bible teaches that Satan is a perpetual liar who is committed to deception as a strategic device for undoing the work of God.

Having said this we must not be tempted to exaggerate. Although Satan is dedicated to deceit we should not give him credit for every known deception chronicled by the human race since the world began. Man was made with free will and has to accept responsibility for his actions and decisions. Even when converted to Christ he has remnants of this sinful nature left within him. These engage in battle with the new nature that Christ plants inside us. This is why Paul admits with great honesty, 'What I want to do I do not do, but what I hate I do' (Rom 7:15).

Clinton Arnold refers us to Ephesians 2:1-3 where we see Paul's balanced view of the nature of the evil influences that affect man:

1. The World: 'the ways of this world'
2. The Devil: 'the ruler of the kingdom of the air' 'the spirit who is now at work in those who are disobedient'
3. The Flesh: 'the cravings of our sinful nature...its desires and thoughts'.[8]

Having made this separation, however, we have to consider both Jesus' description of Satan as the 'father of lies' (Jn 8:44) and Peter's observation that he 'prowls around like a roaring lion looking for someone to devour' (1 Pet 5:8). Timothy Warner suggests that 'if he finds a person, especially a Christian, having a struggle with the flesh, he would be a fool not to jump in and try to take advantage of the situation'. Therefore, in practice, it is more likely to be 'Satan and the flesh, rather than one or the other' that are responsible when sin is committed.[9]

Deception in Scripture

Earlier I said that deception is Satan's main tactic for influencing people against God and his will. Let us see how this is taught in the Bible. It starts after the Lord created a perfect world in which he invested vast resources. Then he made man, the pinnacle of his creation, and gave him free will. This meant that man could operate independently of his creator if he chose. God knew this but was prepared to take the risks involved. C.S. Lewis, in devil Screwtape's words, says 'the Enemy takes this risk because he has a curious fantasy of making all these disgusting little human vermin into what he calls his "free" lovers and servants'.[10]

Before long Satan, suitably camouflaged, entered God's ideal creation with one simple intention: to capture the allegiance of those who until now had been happily under God's authority. Genesis 3:1 reports Satan's apparently innocent question to Eve, 'Did God really say, "You must not eat from any tree in the garden?"' to which Eve responded by repeating the instructions God had given Adam and herself. At this point Eve had no intention of rebelling against God; the thought had probably not even occurred to her. In v4, however, we find Satan planting doubts in her mind by the simple act of questioning the authenticity and validity of God's word. Here he began cleverly to undermine God's truth and authority.

His trump card was his daring suggestion that what God had spoken to her and Adam was not wholly true and that God cannot be trusted totally. This unsettled Eve, particularly as Satan's indirect message to her was that he can be trusted fully. It was at this point that she looked more closely at the fruit on the forbidden tree. She found that it 'was good for food and pleasing to the eye' (3:6)—which was enough to convince her of her next move. Among Satan's devious expressions was his (true) statement that if she took that fruit she would 'be like God, knowing good and evil'.

In her naivety she was tricked into believing that this was desirable, not realizing that this kind of 'being like God' was totally against God's will for her and Adam. Eve was thrown into confusion by Satan's subtle and devious use of words. Once she and Adam became disobedient, however, mankind was saddled with a sinful nature that would be an inherent part of every new-born human being from that day on.

There are many other instances in Scripture of Satan's attempts to trick and deceive. Matthew 4:1-11 tells of Jesus' forty days in the wilderness after his baptism. Here he encountered Satan who had a well-prepared plot to disarm him and render him wholly unsuitable to redeem the world. Satan knew why Jesus had come to earth; he knew that the whole spiritual future of the human race hung in the balance. He was aware that God's final plan to rescue lost men could be ruined if only he could entice Jesus to compromise in some way. He had history on his side. The last time a sinless human (Eve) was given one of his presentations, she succumbed. Satan believed it was just possible that Jesus would do the same.

Satan's first stratagem was to make Jesus question whether or not he really was God's Son (4:3), a very similar ploy to the question that began to undermine Eve's trust in God's integrity. When Jesus rejected this, Satan suggested that Jesus jump off the temple. He attempted to get Jesus to put on a dramatic display— which it would have been when angels caught him before he reached the ground (Mt 4:6). The attraction was instant popularity and success, with droves of people following him. Jesus knew, however, that the kind of obedient discipleship he came to introduce included self-denial and the isolation of a painful cross. To get immediate adulation was not his Father's way and Jesus rejected Satan's second attempt to deceive him too.

Satan's final thrust had an unusual start (4:8-9). In describing the kingdoms of the world Satan said that they were his. That was true to the extent that he hijacked them when Eve succumbed to his earlier deceit. What he offered Jesus was precisely the world that he knew Jesus had come to reclaim. Jesus knew that he would do this through the torment of the cross, but Satan offered him a short-cut. He could be spared the intense physical and spiritual pain if he just bowed and worshipped Satan now. That was all it would take, and at a stroke he would achieve his life's goal. Again Jesus saw that the easy path was not at all compatible with his Father's perfect plan. He also recognized that if he worshipped Satan, he would acknowledge Satan as greater than God. This would make Jesus a follower of Satan and the world would then become Satan's in a fuller sense. He rejected the proposal and Satan withdrew knowing he had failed.

He did not leave it very long before he tried again. Simon Peter had just recognized Jesus as 'the Christ, the Son of the living God' (Mt 16:16). Jesus acknowledged that Peter could only have said this because God had revealed this truth to him (16:17). What better opportunity for Satan to rush in and use this same mouthpiece to try to knock Jesus from his intended course? Soon afterwards Jesus explained to his disciples that before long, and in accordance with his Father's plan for his life, he would suffer and die. At this Peter reacted emotionally and impulsively, 'This shall never happen to you!' (16:22). Without a moment's pause Jesus recognized this for what it was—another attempt by Satan to deceive him and divert him from his Father's will. Immediately he rejected Peter's words (16:23).

Satan failed to stop Jesus accomplishing God's plan for his life. While Jesus' death at first looked remarkably like a victory for evil, his resurrection was a defiant witness to Satan that the power and might of God was beyond comparison. Yet Satan was still there, and when the church had been founded and local Christian communities were springing up around the Mediterranean, he began to cause disruption in a new way. Some churches were infiltrated by false teaching. Paul wrote to the church in Corinth to say that 'just as Eve was deceived by the serpent's cunning, your minds may somehow be led astray from your sincere and pure devotion to Christ. For if someone comes to you and preaches a Jesus other than the Jesus we preached...you put up with it easily enough' (2 Cor 11:3-4). Later he calls these people, 'false apostles, deceitful workmen, masquerading as apostles of Christ. And no wonder, for Satan himself masquerades as an angel of light' (11:13-14).

In Galatia also Paul found false teaching. Here some declared that to be a true Christian you had also to be a Jew and follow the regulations that Moses introduced. Paul saw this as an attack on the Gospel (1:6-9) and regarded any move in that direction as a return to slavery (Gal 4:9). The Christians at Colossae also were subjected to erroneous teaching that threatened to stop them trusting fully in Christ for salvation. Paul's advice to them was simple. 'See to it that no-one takes you captive through hollow and deceptive philosophy, which depends on human tradition and the basic principles of this world rather than on Christ' (Col 2:8).

This kind of deceit by Satan was all too common and Paul could see it as a stratagem to undermine God's work in various churches. When he wrote to Timothy, he highlighted the problem. 'The Spirit clearly says that in later times some will abandon the faith and follow deceiving spirits and things taught by demons' (1 Tim 4:1). Yet Satan's work to thwart God's will on earth was not confined to deceiving those who have become followers of Christ. Paul says, 'the god of this age has blinded the minds of unbelievers, so that they cannot see the light of the gospel of the glory of Christ' (2 Cor 4:4). As Clinton E Arnold says:

> The church's mission is to bring sight to the blind. The gospel must be proclaimed in the power of the Spirit because the church faces an enemy of supernatural proportions, who commands a host of angelic powers seeking to prevent the spread of the kingdom of Christ.[11]

These are not the only ways in which Paul saw Satan active while he engaged in ministry for the Lord. We have already seen that Paul called his thorn in the flesh a 'messenger of Satan' (2 Cor 12:7). He told the Thessalonian Christians that 'Satan stopped us' when he tried to visit them (1 Thess 2:18). Paul's message about Satan in his letters is the same. Satan is intent on hampering God's will being done in and through those who trust in Christ. His main tactic is deception and it seems to be an effective stratagem. Be careful, Satan will trick Christians if he can just as he deceived Eve. He has no new stratagem but perpetually uses the old one that has served him well in the past. Through Christ, however, you can live in victory over him.

Christian writers tell how they were deceived. Johannes Facius, co-ordinator of Intercessors International, came to believe he had committed the unforgivable sin.[12] In the testimony, *A Brilliant Deception*, Chris Kline tells how, at last she came to see that 'The Voice' which spoke frequently to her and guided her was not in fact God as she had earlier concluded.

> "God didn't do this", I said. "He wouldn't have come and turned me into a chronic alcoholic, and then left. Satan did this to me, didn't he?" Her friend agreed. "Yes Chris, it was Satan... You've been deceived." The word 'deceived' had an ugly, hollow ring. It was an awful revelation, yet its truth was overpowering. I felt tricked and horribly used. All these years I'd been thinking I was being used by God

> when in fact I'd been a fool, manipulated by the devil. And
> what a brilliant job he'd done.[13]

Recognizing that Satan continues to use this same stratagem
today, we must face up to what we are dealing with here. Maybe
the decline in church attendance in this country is not purely a
sociological and ecclesiastical phenomenon. Perhaps the reasons
people gave for leaving their church are not the whole story and
Satan is being deceitful to deplete the strength and resilience of
Christ's church. Clinton Arnold comes to similar conclusions in
his chapter on Spiritual Warfare. Having introduced Ephesians
6:12 as one of 'the most misunderstood, misconstrued and practically neglected texts of the Scripture', he suggests some Christians suffer from 'double-mindedness'.

> When dealing with a personal problem such as illness or
> depression, medical and psychological services are the
> only considered alternatives. Little thought is given to the
> spiritual side. Even in Christian ministry the spiritual
> dimension is often ignored. Ineffective evangelism, for
> example, is often attributed to a lack of training or persua-
> sive skill rather than powerful demonic hindrance.[14]

I see Satan hard at work today as the deceiver. He is deceiving the world at large through materialistic philosophies and
New Age teachings, but has also infiltrated the Christian
church. I am certain that some of the decline in church attendance is due to the success of his tactics. These need uncovering
without delay. There is no way we can take Peter's advice in
1 Peter 5:9 to 'resist' the devil unless we first grasp what he is
doing.

We need to look again at some areas of life both inside and
outside the church in order to discern where Satan is active. We
will do this under three headings.

1. Areas where we detect no direct activity by Satan

Earlier as we looked for reasons for a decline in church attendance we covered different areas of human life: unemployment,
redundancies, the presence of ethnic groups in our communities

and the growing level of stress in many of our lives. We touched on the increasing number of single-parent families, the level of prosperity that some children enjoy and the many changes in education. Technological advances have been significant and leisure patterns have changed. In these areas of life Satan is not clearly apparent. These are human issues and human problems. Not every situation is ideal, but none is fundamentally sinful to the core and in direct conflict with God's principles.

2. Areas where Satan and humans together take responsibility

In *The Screwtape Letters*, senior devil Screwtape encourages his junior partner, Wormwood, to influence the man with whom he is working. 'Remember you are there to fuddle him…make his mind flit to and fro…keep him in that state of mind as long as you can'.[15] This correlates perfectly with Paul's perception that Satan and his compatriots are always looking for vulnerable people to influence. They search for cracks in the armour of those who belong to Christ. All the time Satan is looking for situations to exploit so that he can make some gains.

Paul comments on our sinful nature in Romans 7. He tells us that human beings, even when committed to Christ, have a continuing capacity to sin. Often all Satan has to do is to trigger a person's thinking processes in a certain way and before he knows it they have strayed from God's will. At times like this he can sit back and watch as often well-meaning people help him accomplish his goals. People, then, are often very vulnerable and Satan capitalizes on this whenever he can.

The growing levels of crime come in this category as do the practices of cohabiting and divorce. The increasing amount of debt, the abuse of alcohol and the liberal way Sunday is spent are issues where Satan works to destroy and undermine people's lives and society at large. Man's destruction of his planet through contamination of the atmosphere probably suits Satan's plans quite well. He also triggers many of the problems within the Christian church and then waits for people to develop them into battle areas. Conflicts over worship, the problems of nominality, burn-out in spiritual leaders, bad media publicity, sour relationships and people feeling they do not belong in a fellowship are all instances where Satan can make substantial gains. In these circumstances no-one can identify him categorically as the chief trouble-maker. Yet when we find conflict, pain, apathy or embarrassment in a church, it can often be traced to Satan. At such times his actual role was maybe no more than lighting the touchpaper and then quickly getting out of sight. As Donald Bridge concludes, 'He is after success, not recognition'.[16]

3. Areas where Satan seems to have a fairly free rein

In some areas of life Satan scores major victories. Through stark lies and blatant untruth he encourages what will destroy, erode and undermine God's work on earth. Alcohol and substance abuse, crime, violence, homosexuality, the profusion of abortions, child abuse and pornography all fit in here. Some situations (abuses and crime especially) fit into the previous section too; it depends on the specific circumstances. People's obsession with newness and prosperity, together with the growth of the cults and the emergence of New Age teaching are included in this category too. Other examples are to be found in the churches. The hypocrisy and introspection, people's loss of faith and inner confusion plus the wastage, broken vows and pain are all evidences of Satan's activity.

Let us take the contents of this last paragraph and look in more detail at the ways Satan can be at work in the church. We will attempt to uncover where Satan is peddling his lies and deceit to keep people from the truth of God. Once exposed and detected, we can reject them with the help of the Holy Spirit and begin again to walk in God's way.

The deceit of Christians and churches
There are many ways in which Satan seeks to score successes by deceiving believers and churches. These are so-called 'truths' he likes Christians to believe.

* You can call yourself a Christian but ignore any teaching in the Bible you do not like or agree with.
* Belief in God is all that matters. It is not important whether you go to church and become an active and integral member or not.
* The Bible is not really the inspired and inerrant word of God. It is just another religious book with some useful teaching in places.
* The Devil does not really exist; he is no more than a figment of the imagination of ancient writers who knew no better than to invent an evil power. Demons and evil spirits do not therefore exist either—and never have.
* There is therefore no long-standing war between God and the Devil or good and evil.
* Jesus Christ is not the only way to God. Other religions teach equally credible alternatives.
* The occult, spiritism, New Age teaching and the cults are fascinating alternative philosophies to Christianity and are harmless to explore.
* Other things in life like family, career and the accumulation of financial and material security are just as important as God.
* Christianity is essentially private and personal. Others must not intrude and interfere in 'what I believe'.
* To become a Christian and go to church once a Sunday is enough. None of us must go over the top and let our faith dominate our lives.
* It is not realistic to expect people to have loving, trusting relationships, even within a church. It is therefore foolish even to strive for them.
* Bad and unhappy relationships in a church are best ignored.
* Leaders in every church are just ordinary vulnerable people like anyone else. Therefore I will not allow myself to be influenced too greatly by any of them.
* It is not harmful for Christians to read their horoscopes, do the pools and buy raffle and lottery tickets.
* You need only give anything in the offering if you like the church and agree with everything it does.

* It is not important whether Christians have any non-Christian friends or not.

So many of these thoughts seem commonplace within churches today and are held with great conviction. Yet each one is a distortion of the truth contained in the Bible and is flawed. Satan is having a field day by confusing God's people.

The deceit of church leaders
By virtue of their office and consequent ability to influence and guide, church leaders are especially targeted by Satan. Numerous lies and part-truths seem to be believed by some of those who lead churches today. Here are some:

* People who are spiritually lost and outside the churches are not a major source of concern when great needs exist within the church community.
* As leader, I am the most, or one of the most, important people in the church.
* It does not matter if there are some doctrinal or practical issues in the Bible that I never preach and teach about.
* It is controversial to preach about the Holy Spirit, the Devil, evil spirits and spiritual warfare, so I won't.
* Money is short in this church, therefore we will keep on appealing, emotionally if necessary, until the income increases.
* It is very time-consuming to keep preparing for sermons. Having been a preacher for a long time, I will now rely on my years of experience to get me through as I stand in the pulpit.
* The lack of good quality relationships in my church is not a major concern or anything to worry about.
* The only people who come to my church are those who have been coming for years. Therefore it does not matter whether services relate to non-Christian people—as long as we keep 'the faithful' happy.
* My major responsibility is to undertake all that is expected of me in the church even if I don't take much time to develop my personal relationship with God.

Leaders can be deceived by Satan just like anybody else. Maybe their calling, training and experience should give them a greater resistance to his cunning plots designed to trick and deceive them. In practice, however, many of them appear to be equally vulnerable. This of course leads to distortions and lies being spread throughout the churches as they exercise their influential leadership roles. Satan must be very satisfied that his plots are proving effective.

Thwarting Satan

In summary, the Enemy is out to inflict as much harm and damage as he can on God's work in the world. The more he can hamper the growth and development of Christians and churches the more content he is. He does not use new and original ploys to hold back God's work, but often relies on his well-established tactic of introducing deceit, half-truths and total untruth into people's minds. He is angry that his successful campaign to eradicate Jesus from this world was transformed into a mighty victory for God when Jesus rose from the dead. He knows now that he has lost the war, but is taking any and every opportunity to win individual battles meanwhile. Therefore to whatever extent the world, Christians and churches allow themselves to be infiltrated with his lies, he will take advantage.

Certainly he must view each church-goer who 'independently decides' not to go any more as a victory and triumph. It is by reducing the numbers one by one that he will make a major impact. While it is a gentle and often overlooked trend, his stratagem will not be noticed and his eroding work will not be exposed. Johannes Facius reminds us to '...get used to the idea of having the Enemy hanging around in everything we do and everywhere we go'.[17]

In the light of what we have seen thus far, we are right to wonder whether tens or even hundreds of thousands of Christians, church-goers and Christian leaders are being deluded and deceived in different ways. Is this then at least partly why we are seeing such erosion in the church? If so, we must not agree with this conclusion and then push it aside. In Amos 6:1-7 God condemns his people for their complacency, casual lifestyle and for putting off taking vital action to obey him. His final word to them is very serious. 'Therefore you will be among the first to go into exile; your feasting and lounging will end' (v7).

Scripture makes it clear that God wants to help his people out of dilemmas caused by their straying from his will. Paul tells Timothy that 'those who oppose him he must gently instruct, in the hope that God will grant them repentance leading them to a knowledge of the truth' (2 Tim 2:25). Through confession and genuine repentance all who fall into Satan's devious traps can be forgiven and restored.

The really important lesson to learn here is that it is not necessary for Christians to succumb frequently to Satan's lies and deceit. Christians are no longer 'slaves to sin' (Rom 6:6), we are 'alive to God in Christ Jesus' and need to live this way (Rom 6:11). When Jesus rose from the dead he was triumphant over Satan and shares this with his followers (1 Cor 15:57). Jesus intends them to live in victory too. This cannot and will not happen if human resources like intellect and determination are our main strengths. Satan will fool us time and again. It is when we take and use the spiritual armour described in Ephesians 6 that we effectively thwart Satan. In that situation it will be God's resources, not ours, that are our strength.

God's call to us today as we continue to lose church-goers is to understand the practical problems that exist in our churches. Even if we tackle every difficulty that has surfaced in the areas covered by Chapters 5-8, we will make only limited headway unless we counteract all of Satan's activity in God's strength. We need God to teach us how to pray in the Spirit, engage in spiritual warfare and how to win a succession of victories over Satan as we seek to emulate Jesus.

Notes

[1] C.S. Lewis, *The Screwtape Letters* (Collins: London, 1942) p 64.

[2] Peter Horrobin, *Healing Through Deliverance* (Sovereign World: Tonbridge, 1991) p 60.

[3] Clinton E Arnold, *Powers of Darkness* (IVP: Leicester, 1992) p 87-166.

[4] Timothy M Warner, *Wrestling with Dark Angels*, ed. C. Peter Wagner & F. Douglas Pennoyer (Monarch: Tunbridge Wells, 1990) p 113.

5 Arnold, *op cit*, p 129.

6 Horrobin, *op cit*, p 59.

7 Nigel Wright, *The Fair Face of Evil* (Marshall Pickering: London, 1989) p 26.

8 Arnold, *op cit*, p 124.

9 Warner, *op cit*, p 116.

10 Lewis, *op cit*, p 17.

11 Arnold, *op cit*, p 135.

12 Johannes Facius, *God Can Do It—Without Me* (Sovereign World: Tonbridge, 1990) p 41.

13 Chris Kline, *A Brilliant Deception* (Kingsway: Eastbourne, 1990) p 123.

14 Arnold, *op cit*, p 148.

15 Lewis, *op cit*, p 14, 16, 19.

16 Donald Bridge, *How to Spot a Church Split Before it Happens* (MARC: Eastbourne, 1989) p 178.

17 Facius, *op cit*, p 93.

CHAPTER 10

Looking Again At Jesus

I T WOULD BE NO SURPRISE IF, because of what we have considered up to now, we felt depressed and disillusioned with the state of the churches in the UK. What we have seen is neither attractive nor effective. Certainly many problems exist within our churches. Not everything, of course, is bad, but it seems a million miles away from the biblical description of Jesus' church. This may not necessarily be a disaster. After all, new motor cars today are so utterly different from the earliest models in the National Motor Museum that you could be forgiven for not recognizing them as having the same function. The problem with the church, however, seems to be two-fold:

a) What we see today seems on the whole to be inferior in many ways to, say, the first Christian church in Jerusalem. The most positive features of that church seem fairly scarce today.

b) To some extent the effectiveness of a church can and must be measured in terms of its ability to relate to and reach ordinary people surrounding it. We have already noted the extent to which former church-goers perceive the church to be irrelevant and boring.

We find ourselves coming to a sad conclusion that many British churches appear to be successful at obscuring God. I find this painful because I have been linked with a church since I was a tiny baby. Yet it does seem that much of what we call 'church' hides the way to God. Sometimes church-people themselves are the hindrance; at other times it is the structures, organizations and traditions. In Mark 10:14 Jesus became indignant with his disciples because they stopped people bringing children to him. It seems that the contemporary church has disobeyed Jesus' instruction that his disciples should let people come to him.

The teaching and practice of Jesus and of the early Christian churches show us the principles on which Christian ministry should be based. This is God's will and purpose for his church on earth. We cannot recreate a first-century church in the late twentieth century, and it would not work anyway, as Michael Harper has argued in his book, *Let My People Grow*.[1] As we study these principles we see how some churches have gone astray, and how to correct the problems caused. Let us explore different facets of the ministries of Jesus and the Early Church in order to understand what God's will and purpose is for his church on earth.

1. JESUS CAME TO COMBAT THE EFFECTS OF THE FALL

After Adam and Eve succumbed to Satan's deception three things followed:

a) All humans are born with a sinful nature. It is impossible for any human being to live on earth without sinning.

b) All humans are vulnerable to the deceit and lies of Satan. Furthermore, Satan is aware that some humans are vulnerable enough for him to send evil spirits to infiltrate them and take up residence in them.

c) Humans are subject to disease and decay in their bodies.

However, immediately after Jesus returned from the wilderness and his personal victory with Satan, he demonstrated that he had the authority and power to reverse these three effects of the Fall in men's lives.

a) He offered forgiveness to the man let down in front of him on a stretcher which in turn made possible his physical healing (Mk 2:5).

b) He drove out an evil spirit that possessed a man he met in the synagogue in Capernaum (Mk 1:26).

c) He brought healing to people whose lives were restricted by illness (Mk 1:31-34).

In the Gospels we observe Jesus exercising a pioneering ministry characterized by power, love and authority. He sought continually to reverse the effects of the Fall in the lives of people he met. The reason the crowds pursued him was that he offered them precisely what they needed and wanted.

The public today does not perceive that British churches have anything relevant to offer. If long-established church-goers are ceasing to attend because they find it irrelevant and boring, others who have never been will get that message clearly too. British people today may think Jesus and the church irrelevant, although when he was on earth the people who met and saw him had a quite different opinion. He met people's needs.

The New Testament tells us that during the first decades of Jesus' church, his disciples continued his work in a similar way to his three years of public ministry. Luke's account of the advance of Christ's work shows that sins were forgiven (Acts 2:38-41), evil spirits cast out (Acts 16: 16-18) and people received physical healing in Jesus' name (Acts 3:7). Between then and now, however, something has happened that has brought enormous changes to the style of ministry initiated by Jesus.

Some churches, usually those that call themselves 'evangelical', take opportunities to preach the Good News that Jesus came to save lost people. Some people in our communities therefore have the opportunity to hear or read the news that Jesus can and does forgive. Mercifully, because of answered prayer and the quiet but penetrating ministry of the Holy Spirit, some respond and find new life in Christ.

Not all of those that preach the Gospel also take seriously the bondage some people are in because Satan holds them captive in one way or another. There is a danger, of course, that we can start imagining Satan's grip everywhere. This is why we need the gift of discernment. The other hazard is that we can believe that any possession of evil spirits as recorded in the New Testament was a phenomenon that is unknown today. That is another lie Satan likes us to believe. Because so many do believe this or are scared to explore in this area, comparatively few people seem to be released from spiritual bondages. I recall vividly the scene at The Brighton Centre during the *The Battle Belongs to the Lord* Conference in June 1991. Sitting in a balcony where I could see and hear across the auditorium I was amazed at how many of the people present, most of whom I assumed to be committed Christians, needed deliverance ministry.

Healing ministry is more common in the life of churches today. It is not unusual for churches of many denominations and theological backgrounds to provide opportunity for personal prayer ministry for healing. While we may pray for physical healing, God's response may be broader than we expect. I have prayed for people for physical healing whom God has touched, but maybe with a renewed sense of his peace or with a fresh insight into an emotional problem from their past. Tom Walker tells of a man who was terminally ill and who had never made a commitment to Christ. He was only conscious for short periods of time, but after prayer by a local church, the church leaders always found him awake when they visited. They were able to talk with him about Jesus, and he became a Christian before he died.[2]

We must return to the priorities of Jesus if God is to use the British churches to win new converts and to stem the flow of those leaving. The effect of the Fall in people's lives is serious. Every living human is functioning in a sub-standard way compared to our Maker's plans. Jesus came to give a new start to those who trust him. The church must focus on people's needs—as Jesus did, allowing the Holy Spirit to flow through them.

Ralph Neighbour, writing about reaching the people of Auckland, New Zealand, under the heading, 'The Institutional Church is in Trouble' says:

> The churches of Auckland have talked to themselves for too long. At present, few in the unchurched community are listening to what they practise or preach. In discussing the matter with an interviewer on 1ZB Radio, I was pointedly told that the church had lost touch with society. The night-time call-in host indicated that when he was a boy, the Anglican pastor would come to the house for a cup of tea, even though his parents were not active church members. He indicated that in those days his family even knew a few of the leaders in the church hierarchy. However, he

had nothing but contempt for the church of today, and said he had no interest in it or what it did. The only thing which has impressed him were the 'charismatic churches' who seemed to still care about people. He suggested that the church leaders return to the policies of 'their founder' (Jesus) and instead of asking people to 'come', they should 'go' among those who live in the city.[3]

2. JESUS DEVELOPED A CARING COMMUNITY OF LOVE AND TRUST

Mark's Gospel records that when Jesus appointed the twelve apostles he 'called to him those he wanted...that they might be with him' (Mk 3:13-14). He was clearly keen to surround himself with men who identified with his mission. He also wanted them to value and appreciate the very best relationships with him and each other. Not all went perfectly to plan during his ministry. Sometimes they argued (Mk 10:41), but there were times when Jesus really needed them. In Gethsemane his distress and trauma was so deep that he specifically asked Peter, James and John to stay close to him as he prayed. Jesus' teaching and example had an effect on the disciples. Once the Holy Spirit had fallen on them and the church had been born, Luke records that 'all the believers were together and had everything in common. Selling their possessions and goods, they gave to anyone as he had need' (Acts 2:44-45). The caring community of love and trust that Jesus desired now existed.

Love
Our earlier look at the Survey results paints a different picture, however. Some churches do not emulate that Christian community in Jerusalem where people felt they belonged and were cared for. We need to acknowledge the shift that has taken place. Selfless love seems scarce in God's church. We may talk about it, but in practice it is all too rare. Why is this, especially when Jesus instructed his followers to share this kind of love (Jn 15:12)?

Clifford Hill tells how God spoke to him in a dramatic way while he was in Switzerland. A child slipped on a narrow mountain path and began to slide down towards a precipice. Straight-away a man started to run down the steep slope and ignoring all danger to himself caught up with the little girl and managed to stop her just ten feet from the edge. He was her father. Through witnessing this, Clifford tells how God spoke so clearly to him. He reminded him that if a human father's love can be so strong as to respond like that, how much stronger is God's for his children? 'Tell my people I love them' was the message Clifford Hill was given by God that day.[4] As he has shared it with many people, God has used it to make many more of his children aware of the depths of his love. It has had a radical and dramatic effect on them. When more of us get this message, there will be more of God's love shared in his church.

The First Priority

When he was with his disciples Jesus took care to show them that the kind of community he was building had his Heavenly Father at its centre. Mark shows us that Jesus took time alone to enjoy prayer fellowship with his Father (Mk 1:35). The Fourth Gospel reveals most about the intimacy of the Father and Son. Jesus declared in John 5:17-23 and 8:28-29 that he and his Father worked together. Later he said that he and his Father 'are one' (Jn 10:30) and that 'the Father is in me, and I in the Father' (Jn 10:38). The climax of this teaching comes in John 14 where Jesus tells his disciples that they can experience the same close rela-tionship with God. Each one must make an appropriate response before they can experience the relationship. 'If anyone loves me, he will obey my teaching. My Father will love him, and we will come to him and make our home with him' (Jn 14:23). As disciples of Jesus allow this relationship with God to develop, so their relationships with each other will be enhanced because they have their priorities right.

Disordered priorities

Many problems in today's church are caused by disordered priorities. It seems that many Christians do not make the deep-ening of their intimate relationship with God their prime goal.

Other things have taken over. For some, simply going to church on a Sunday is the be-all and end-all of their Christian faith.

> It is well to remember that neither St Paul nor any of the apostles ever 'went to church'. They never saw and probably never imagined a building built and set apart exclusively for Christian worship.[5]

Other Christians feel that seeing long-standing traditions of the church perpetuated should be their priority. Michael Harper lists styles of worship, festivals and head covering as examples of issues where traditions can easily dominate over the teaching of Scripture.[6] In an open letter to his former church, David Coffey says, 'As you will know, I honour traditions which serve to help the people of God to worship. But when worship becomes a habit and worshippers become dull-eyed with meaningless rituals then it is time for a hard question: Do we allow our beliefs to shape our services?'[7] When a deepening relationship with God is our priority it will help keep the focus of our lives fixed on him *together*. In this way our caring community of love and trust will grow.

When Jesus detected problems among his twelve disciples he took positive action. Instead of putting his head in the sand, he worked to resolve the problems. When the disciples argued over which of them was the greatest, he used a child to teach them a lesson (Lk 9:46-48). When ten of them were angry because of James and John's request to Jesus, he 'called them together' and taught them (Mk 10:35-45). Jesus believed that the quality of relationships mattered. Raymond Bakke tells how he regularly visited eighty-three churches in Chicago when he moved there as a pastor so that he could attempt to establish good relationships with ministerial colleagues.[8] Juan Carlos Ortiz describes a similar situation.[9]

Michael Harper quotes Cardinal Mercier of Belgium, whom he calls 'one of the great ecumenical pioneers'. 'In order to be united with one another we must love one another; in order to love one another we must know one another; in order to know one another we must come out and meet one another'.[10] Tom Walker recounts the impact of a youth weekend many years ago

Perpetuating long-standing traditions

with the young people from St Mark's Church, Gillingham. There was, he says, 'a tremendous spirit of love that was evident in the way a group of mostly quite young people behaved towards each other. Usually on self-help weekends there are groans when the list of washers-up is given out. But here there were willing helpers and constant mutual care'.[11] He then goes on to describe the enriching worship he experienced with this group. When we get and keep our relationship with God right, our sharing becomes a delight and encouragement.

3. JESUS BELIEVED IN DISCIPLESHIP TRAINING

When we listed the reasons Jesus chose his twelve disciples I omitted one—deliberately. Mark says he appointed them 'that he might send them out to preach and to have authority to drive out demons' (Mk 3:14-15). From the very beginning Jesus knew that he had a limited amount of time in which to train, equip and prepare them for ministry. They were a mixed selection of Jewish men; they were raw recruits in need of specialized training. His method of teaching them was simple. He did not send them away to a theological college, but invited them to follow him. This meant that as he engaged in ministry they were there too. They heard him preach to the crowds, saw him heal the sick and cast out demons. They witnessed his encounters with Jewish religious leaders. They had special times with him privately, when he taught them the principles of life in the Kingdom of God. He answered their many questions.

In due course a significant day came. Luke tells us that Jesus called the Twelve together and prepared to send them out on his behalf and in his name. They had to do three things (Lk 9:1-2):

a) Preach the kingdom of God

b) Heal the sick

c) Use the power and authority he gave them to drive out all demons.

Once he had given them other instructions he sent them off, and when they returned he listened as 'they reported...what they had done' (Lk 9:10). They must have absorbed so much through this kind of training. Nine of the Twelve learned from a negative experience when Jesus and Peter, James and John were away up a mountain. They found themselves powerless when confronted with a boy with an evil spirit that controlled him (Mk 9:18). When Jesus had released the boy, the disciples asked him why they had not been able to do this. Jesus' reply taught them the vital importance of prayer in the life of a disciple (Mk 9:29).

We must question to what extent Christians today are nurtured. Disciples of Jesus in any era need help in many ways. They need teaching so that they develop a living faith in God. When people are as confused as the former church-goers whose beliefs we saw in Chapter 7, it is no wonder that they abandon Christianity. If faith does not make sense it is useless. This is why Jesus told his disciples in the Great Commission to teach new converts (Mt 28:20). It is also why teaching has been a priority of the Christian church since the very start (Acts 2:42). Jesus devoted about three years not only to public ministry but also to training his disciples for their work when he would no longer be with them.

If Christian churches are to be strong and effective, the disciplined teaching and training of believers must become a priority again. A ten-minute sermon once a week is inadequate. Even a twenty-minute expository sermon straight from the Bible is likely to leave Christians under-nourished. If we reflect on our eating habits we see that we maybe eat three meals each day with the occasional snack in-between. This is what provides us with the energy to live active lives. If we severely reduce our food intake our capacity to function is severely restricted. Most Christians would have enhanced ministries if their level of spiritual intake increased.

We are referring here to consistent personal study and meditation on God's Word together with opportunities to hear God's Word preached with clarity and passion. We also need the stimulation of corporate Bible study with others who want to grow and mature in their faith. We need, with others, the courage to dig into rich chapters of Christian teaching, like Romans 5-8, to understand the wonderful liberation from condemnation there is in Christ. It often helps if we can discuss our understanding of a passage in a group until we grasp God's truth and the way it can affect our lives in practice.[12] Jesus intended that Christian discipleship training should be practical. He told his disciples to teach 'them to *obey* everything I have commanded you' (Mt 28:20) (my italics).

When our churches see purposeful, relevant teaching as a priority, with trained leaders sharing the fruits of their own training and experience, a thrilling revolution will take place. Body ministry of the kind that Jesus and later the Apostle Paul were clearly longing to see develop will become commonplace again. God never intended most of the ministry of the church to be undertaken by a few. Emil Brunner summarizes how he perceives the New Testament church functioned.

> Co-operative action in fellowship might be regarded as its decisive feature. It is especially emphasized that *all* were active in it. What we have already discovered concerning the intrinsic structure of the community—namely that it knows no distinction between the active and the passive, between those who administer and those who are recipients—this is evinced anew in the character of divine worship. Each made his contribution and for this very reason no one was allowed to monopolize the hearing of the assembly. Thus everyone could have his turn (1 Corinthians 14:31). This cult, therefore, knows nothing of the distinction between priests and laymen; its members are aware that they form a priesthood (1 Peter 2:9) and this holy priesthood is built up of each and all (1 Peter 2:5).[13]

A church can function like this only when it has provided discipleship training that allows the growth and development of those in the fellowship. While Christians remain 'infants, tossed back and forth by the waves, and blown here and there by every wind of teaching' (Eph 4:14), a church cannot easily be strong and effective for God. Jesus knew that it was imperative for the future of his work on earth that he should invest time and effort in training his disciples. This principle still stands firm today.

4. JESUS SET THE EXAMPLE FOR CHRISTIAN LEADERSHIP

Across the many Christian denominations and churches today we see a wide range of leadership styles and models. In practice they vary considerably, even within any single denomination. Of course, there will always be differences in the way leaders function because of their varying personalities, gifts and the particular work for which they are responsible. However, in Jesus' own leadership and teaching we see certain principles that are relevant to every Christian leader's ministry.

Jesus had the right when he walked on earth as a man to lord it over everyone. He was, after all, 'in very nature God', but that same passage goes on to remind us that he 'did not consider equality with God something to be grasped, but made himself nothing, taking the very nature of a servant, being made in human likeness' (Phil 2:6-7). Jesus set a memorable example in humble leadership when he washed the feet of his disciples, normally a task that only a lowly servant would undertake.

Christian leadership is definitely no place for those seeking status and recognition. Michael Harper points out that there are several words in the New Testament that can be translated 'servant', of which two, *diakonos*, meaning 'service', and *doulos*, meaning 'slave', are the most important. He sees them as distinct from each other.

> 'The word *diakonos* is a functional word, meaning a person who renders acts of service to other people, particularly waiting at table. When Jesus said, 'I am among you as one who serves' (Lk 22:27), he is using this word. But the word *doulos* is a 'relationship' word. It means literally a 'slave', one who is owned by another person, with no rights or independent status whatsoever. Thus Paul could speak of himself and Timothy as the slaves of Christ' (Phil 1:1).[14]

It was on New Street Station in Birmingham that David Coffey found God speaking to him about his life as a leader. He ~ad been trained to be a professional and competent minister, ~ there, he says, 'I saw that God enjoyed seeing spiritual ~.'[15] It warms the heart of God when his people, including those in leadership, recognize that they have nothing of any consequence to offer him. It does a church good to see that its trained leaders recognize their emptiness before God and their need of him in a new way. David Coffey goes on to quote five mistaken beliefs that cripple the ministry of church leaders:

1. 'I must be constantly available to meet all the demands my people make upon me.'
2. 'I must be capable of meeting any need they bring to me.'
3. 'I must tower as a paragon of virtue.'
4. 'I must have no spiritual needs of my own as chinks in my emotional armour.'
5. 'I must never let on that I have any material needs.'[16]

One of the most encouraging aspects of the *Creating a Church for the Unchurched* Conference in Birmingham in June 1992 was the unassuming Christ-like and open ministry of Bill Hybels from Willow Creek Community Church. In one sense his genuine humility said more about that Church than all the words spoken and written about it. His transparent honesty as the pivotal leader of North America's fastest-growing Protestant church was utterly refreshing—and challenging. It helped me to see one of the reasons why God is able to use that Church's ministry in such a powerful way. Christian leaders seem so often to be locked into a professional model of leadership that provides a sense of security. The example of Jesus asks for a thorough re-think of this. It is our poverty and vulnerability that make us usable—not influence, status and prestige. Then God can work in a new way. Tom Walker tells of the way he had to learn this at St John's, Harborne, as the church began to hold a weekly meeting called 'Open to God'.

> Our determination was to be in the presence of the risen, living Lord, and to wait on him until we knew for sure that we had dealings with him. For this to happen, the clergy felt that they were not to dominate with prepared texts and expositions, but were to be as open to God's leading by his Spirit as any other members of the group. We sat in the circle with other members of the body of Christ, and had

no clerical authority over others. This did not mean that we did not recognize our call to a teaching ministry...It was just that on this occasion we had to learn to listen to what God was saying to us through his word, rather than fill the time with our own platitudinous pronouncements.[17]

We notice from Tom Walker's account that he was the senior spiritual leader of St John's, and leader of the clergy team. More than twenty years ago he had learned the lesson of shared leadership that others still need to learn today. In this area we cannot take our example directly from Jesus. He had a unique solo ministry, but obviously he taught and encouraged team ministry. Luke 10:1 tells how he appointed 'seventy-two others and sent them two by two ahead of him'. David Watson perceived many Anglican churches as having a cork in place, that restricts the whole life of the church from developing. It is called 'the vicar'.

Nothing can go in or out except through him. No meetings can take place unless he is the leader or chairman. No decisions can be made without his counsel and approval. I know of some parishes where the laity cannot meet even for Bible study or prayer unless the vicar is present.[18]

We have already seen that the ministry of the church must involve the whole Body of Christ, but we must go further. Michael Harper quotes two other writers as he summarizes the main features of the Apostolic church as revealed in the New Testament. Both observe that it was mandatory for the local church to function under a plurality of elders.[19] There is clear wisdom in this. It ensures that only a limited degree of responsibility or influence is entrusted to any one individual. It also means that where the shared leadership is working closely together, divisions and quarrels of the kind that Paul alluded to in 1 Corinthians 1 are less likely. There is the added bonus that where a team member is taken ill or led away to other work by the Lord, there is less disruption to God's continuing work in the church. When today's churches understand the principles of

IDEAS
MODERN MUSIC
NEW SERVICES
YOUNG PEOPLES VIEWS
P.C.C. WANTS

leadership that Jesus introduced *and apply them*, some of our contemporary problems will begin to be solved.

5. JESUS KNEW PRECISELY THE MISSION WORK HE HAD COME TO DO

The Bible tells us clearly that Jesus came to earth on a rescue mission. 'The Son of Man did not come to be served, but to serve, and to give his life as a ransom for many' (Mk 10:45). Besides his teaching about the lost sheep, lost coin and lost son, he devoted time to finding and talking with Zacchaeus, a wayward tax collector. When Zacchaeus responded to Jesus' ministry and repented of his past, Jesus declared that 'the Son of Man came to seek and to save what was lost' (Lk 19:10).

Such was the force of this message in Jesus' life and teaching that once he had ascended and the Holy Spirit had fallen on his disciples, they automatically continued this work of mission. Their goal was to save lost people and bring them into God's Kingdom. Peter had no time to prepare his open-air address on the Day of Pentecost. He could only depend on his training by Jesus and the inspiration of the Spirit. He proclaimed the Truth about Jesus and told them about God's forgiveness. Peter and his colleagues saw 3000 people respond in repentance and faith that day.

The response in Jerusalem at Pentecost was significant in another respect too. Many of those who formed the crowd that heard Peter preach were visitors to Jerusalem from all around the eastern Mediterranean. Some of those who believed soon returned to their homes elsewhere as Christians. The rest of the Acts of the Apostles describes the way in which the Good News of Jesus spread throughout an ever-widening geographical area. Evangelizing and church planting in new territories became commonplace, and God saw to it that pioneer missionaries were raised up within the Christian churches so that this vital work was continued. In the Apostolic church we see a great deal of vision, drive and momentum. God used this to work through his people so that the Good News of Jesus was taken to many who were lost.

Churches in the UK now seem very different. The vast majority of churches seem so locked into a maintenance or survival mentality that they have comparatively little, if any, vision or motivation for reaching the lost. If lost people decide to come to church, that is fine. Yet the instruction of Jesus to 'go and make disciples' (Mt 28:19) is conveniently overlooked. In contrast to Jesus' determination to reach lost people, today's church seems utterly complacent about people's ignorance of the Good News of forgiveness and salvation through faith in Christ. The missionary vision of Jesus and the Apostolic church is then, at best, patchy. Paul's words to Timothy about God's deep desire are ignored. 'God...wants all men to be saved and to come to a knowledge of the truth' (1 Tim 2:3-4).

Maybe Hosea's prophecy gives us the deepest insight into the heart of God. The prophet tells the Jews how God sees their lives. They are wilfully sinful, disobedient and rebellious. What is more, they are utterly unrepentant. Therefore God will have no alternative but to judge and punish them. In Hosea 11, however, we see the other side of the coin. The God who is holy, righteous and just is also filled with love and compassion for his children. He reminds them of the way he brought them up and nurtured them (v1,3,4), and then recalls their obstinate desire to go their own way. In the light of this, God concludes, he will have to 'put an end to their plans' (v6) by allowing the punishment to come. Then God reflects again and his deeply passionate love for his obstructive and disobedient children comes out.

> How can I give you up, Ephraim?
> How can I hand you over, Israel?
> How can I treat you like Admah?
> How can I make you like Zeboiim?
> My heart is changed within me;
> all my compassion is aroused.
> I will not carry out my fierce anger,
>   nor will I turn and devastate Ephraim.
> For I am God, and not man—
>   the Holy One among you.
> I will not come in wrath. (Hos 11:8-9)

When God sent his Son, Jesus, into our rebellious world he made an incredible investment for the future. His love for sinful human beings is deeper than any earthly language can describe. The great Almighty Eternal God desired personal relationships and friendship with ordinary people born on planet Earth. Through the death, resurrection and ascension of Jesus, together with the sending of the Holy Spirit, relationships of this kind can now exist. God is looking forward to Heaven itself being populated by former residents of Earth who have become his children through faith in Christ. He is, however, dependent on those who have a relationship with him now to spread the news. He promises the resources of his Spirit so that they do not have to undertake this vast task alone. Such is his commitment to this strategy of winning the world to himself that he has made no other plans to reach mankind. The priority of mission in the Christian church is not optional. It is God's calling to us.

As less than 10% of the population of England attends church, one tenth of people have to reach the other nine-tenths. This is an enormous task and will not be easy. It is so daunting that unless all of the 10% have a strong sense of calling and a vision of what God can do through them, they are unlikely to make much progress at all. The problem today seems to be that this calling and vision are missing in our churches. Consequently many churches are inactive in reaching out with the Good News of Jesus. The result is that millions are being deprived of the most vital information about themselves and God that they could ever hear.

Jesus was dedicated to this vital ministry of touching more and more lost people's lives with his love. Today our churches need a fresh awakening to the depth of love that God has for these hopeless people. He wants to share fellowship with them. He wants to relieve them of so much of their pain and distress. He wants to enrich their lives and give them fresh hope. He needs the willing, active and obedient cooperation of Christians so that he can reach them. He could—if the churches of our land understood their mission as Jesus knew his.

Barriers
The introduction to the book about the ministry of churches in Auckland, New Zealand, says:

> Every city has a 'logo'—something which symbolises the religious lifestyle of its citizens. There are three elements in the Auckland Logo, depicted in the cover picture: A church building, a wall and a hurting life beyond it. The photograph seeks to reflect a disturbing situation. Central in the photo is a wall. It symbolises the enormous barrier which exists between the many church buildings and the activity which takes place in them, and the sea of totally

unchurched all around them who live untouched, unreached by it all. The lass in the picture who faces the wall in despair adds the important dimension of human suffering which is taking place outside the church buildings. Without exception, those who seek to exist apart from Christ live with colossal inner turmoil. They are not related in any significant way to the God who loves them, who wishes to have a personal relationship with them. Sadly, they do not equate the church buildings and the meetings in them as being strongly related to their needs, their problems. With each week of interviews among the unchurched, it became obvious to the researchers that the unchurched in Auckland have cynically rejected the institutional churches of their city. As later pages will explain, the unchurched and churched segments of Auckland's society might as well live on separate islands. Neither group communicates sincere interest in the other one, and both seem to be convinced those on the opposite island have no intention of trying to make contact. This 'logo' needs to be challenged by a new one! The new logo would picture a wrecking crew tearing down walls, with people with bandages and ointment binding up the wounds of broken people. Let us pray for the hour when the people of God in the city of Auckland will aggressively undertake this task, and become preoccupied with caring for the unreached![20]

Comments made by respondents in our Survey in the UK include, 'the Christian religion has little to do with what Jesus said' and 'Jesus presented a simple uncomplicated faith'. We need the wrecking crew in this country too so that walls are torn down. The Baptist Union of Great Britain has launched a programme called 'Roots' to help its churches to communicate the love of Jesus far more effectively than before.

We often think people have rejected Jesus, when in fact they have simply been put off by the church! We have a duty to confront people with the cost of Christianity by a clear explanation of the demands of discipleship, but God

help us if we erect other 'cultural' barriers which keep
them apart from His love![21]

This is God's calling to us.

Notes

[1] Michael Harper, *Let My People Grow* (Hodder & Stoughton: London, 1988)
p 194.

[2] Tom Walker, *Renew us by Your Spirit* (Hodder & Stoughton: London, 1982)
p 96-97.

[3] Dr Ralph W. Neighbour, Jr., "An Urban Strategy for Auckland", *Auckland...Resistant and Neglected* (Touch International Ministries: Auckland)
p 404.

[4] Clifford Hill, *Tell My People I Love Them* (Fount: London, 1983) p 9-13.

[5] Mark Gibbs & T.R. Morton, *God's Frozen People* (Fontana: London, 1964)
p 27.

[6] Michael Harper, *That We May Be One* (Hodder & Stoughton: London,
1983) p 84-91.

[7] David Coffey, *Build That Bridge* (Kingsway: Eastbourne, 1986) p 86.

[8] Raymond Bakke, *The Urban Christian* (MARC Europe: London, 1987) p 114.

[9] Juan Carlos Ortiz, *Call to Discipleship* (Logos International: Plainfold,
1975) p 127-130.

[10] Harper, *Let My People Grow*, p 170.

[11] Walker, *op cit*, p 33.

[12] Some helpful material on this subject is to be found in Chapter 4 of Terry
Virgo, *Restoration in the Church* (Kingsway: Eastbourne, 1985) p 38-47.

[13] Emil Brunner, *The Misunderstanding of the Church* (Lutterworth: London,
1952) p 61.

[14] Harper, *Let My People Grow*, p 86.

[15] Coffey, *op cit*, p 39.

[16] Louis McBurney, *Every Pastor Needs a Pastor* (Word Inc.: Irving, 1980)

[17] Walker, *op cit*, p 91-92.

[18] David Watson, *I Believe in the Church* (Hodder & Stoughton: London,
1978) p 246.

[19] Harper, *Let My People Grow*, p 195.

[20] The Introduction to *Auckland...Resistant & Neglected*, An Urban Strategy Study of New Zealand's Largest City (Touch International Ministries: Auckland).

[21] From *Roots*, A Different Way of Doing Church (Baptist Union of Great Britain: Didcot, 1992) p 3.

CHAPTER 11

Searching For Lost Sheep

I N COMMON WITH OTHER Old Testament prophets, Jeremiah heard God speaking to him about the dreadful state of the relationship between him and his chosen Jewish people. In Jeremiah 3:6-10, for instance, we find an account of the unfaithfulness of God's people. God is distressed and disturbed that his people have gone so far from his purposes for them. He has a plan for their future and is not content to leave them in their sinfulness and rebellion. Instead, he offers them another chance.

> "Return, faithless Israel," declares the Lord,
> "I will frown on you no longer,
> for I am merciful," declares the Lord,
> "I will not be angry for ever.
> Only acknowledge your guilt—
> you have rebelled against the Lord your God,
> you have scattered your favours to foreign gods
> under every spreading tree,
> and have not obeyed me," declares the Lord.
> (Jer 3:12-13)

The rest of the chapter is a passionate call by God encouraging the people of Judah to respond to him. God wants his people back. He cannot and will not force them into a relationship with himself, but he sends his spokesman to ensure that they hear his message clearly.

In one sense, Jesus came to earth for the same reason. As he sent out his disciples he told them to go 'to the lost sheep of Israel' (Mt 10:6). After his ministry to Zacchaeus, a 'son of Abraham', he said that 'the Son of Man came to seek and to save what was lost' (Lk 19:9-10). Jesus told the stories of the lost sheep, coin and son to the Pharisees and the teachers of the law so that they understood that God wants lost people to be found (Lk 15:1-32). God is not content for lost people to stay lost. This is why he expends so much time, energy and so many initiatives in helping them hear the good news that can change their lives. Jesus speaks to seven Asian churches in Revelation 2 and 3. He makes it clear that, as his people repent and turn back to him, major changes are possible (Rev 2:16; 3:19-20).

It is probable that most people reading this book are active Christians in a local church. Let us remember that the people who provided the data for our Survey are *not*. They have gone now. That is the only criterion we looked for when inviting potential participants to complete a questionnaire. These people, now outside our churches, have helped us see things from a different perspective. Because of them we have looked at areas of weakness, error and decay that we may not have seen before. We are indebted to them, even if we did not always like what they showed us, but we must not leave them where they are. *They* took the initiative to leave *us*, but, because the Bible tells us to seek the lost, *we* now have an obligation to go looking for them.

Let us go back to Jesus' parable of the Lost Sheep. The shepherd discovered that while ninety-nine sheep were present and safe, one was missing. He felt a duty and desire to search for it. That one sheep mattered; it was worth spending time and energy to find it and bring it back safely. In the days of the Old Covenant God sent prophet after prophet so that his faithless people could hear what was on his heart and mind. God did not desert his people when they deserted him; he was always active, trying to win back their love and obedience.

The New Testament teaches what God wants the Christian church to be and do. As we survey the church in history as well as at the end of the twentieth century, we see that it has so often failed God. Yet despite its failings and unfaithfulness, God has never withdrawn his Holy Spirit or given up on his church. On the contrary, with infinite patience and love he seeks to minister whenever and wherever his people are open to him. Even if progress is slow or at times non-existent, God persists with Christians and churches.

Most Christians know what God has called them to do, in theory even if they do not do it. They should go and share the Gospel so that people can respond and become disciples of Christ (Mt 28:19-20). After this these young Christians should be baptized and continue to receive teaching of the same kind that Jesus gave to his followers. Then they should go—but to whom? Obviously to people who are not disciples already. This large body of people can be divided into various categories. There are those who have never heard of Jesus, and those who have heard a little but have a complete misunderstanding about him. There are those who follow alternative faiths, and others who belong to cults that appear Christian but on closer examination are found to proclaim a message of salvation by works. There are also those who used to be identified with the Christian church but no longer are. Some were once keen followers of Jesus but have given up as others did during Jesus' ministry (Jn 6:66). Others were steady church attenders, but only had a limited amount of real faith in God. Because people in both these latter categories are now not practising disciples of Jesus, they are within the group which needs to be reached by the church. They are lost and need to be found again.

We can easily produce credible-sounding arguments when suggestions like this are made. We convince ourselves that former church-goers are more resistant than those who have never attended regularly. This may be correct. If they came away hurt or disillusioned they may be 'once bitten, twice shy'. They may not wish to recall the pain they felt as they went away from church the last time. We need to remember what God's desire is for these people.

If their situation is similar to that of the lost sheep in the Parable, God's deep yearning is that they reconsider their relationship with him and his church. Yes, in the short-term this may induce pain, but it will be worthwhile if ultimately another sheep is returned to the fold. My belief is that there is a mammoth harvest waiting in the United Kingdom. There are hundreds of thousands, if not a million or more, people who in the past have been committed to Christ, the church or both. Now they have a relationship with neither.

God wants them back, and he wants to use Christians, active within his church, to reach out to them in love. God wants to stem the flow of people from the churches *and* win back many of those who were once with us but have now gone. How can this be done? Christians and churches of all denominations and streams need to do five things...

1. IDENTIFY THOSE WHO HAVE LEFT CHURCHES AND BEGIN TO PRAY

The shepherd in Jesus' parable only knew he had lost a sheep by going through the laborious process of counting his flock. In the same way, we must accept that those who God uses to reach people who have fallen away from the churches will have to work hard, and with dedication. Initially we have to find out the people in our locality who used to go to church. We are looking for those who were involved in our own church and those from others, often in different parts of the country. We can then do two things.

First, we need to check church records, directories and membership lists to create a list of people who used to come to our church. Because some relationships stay alive when people stop attending church, we can discuss this informally and discreetly with people still in the church. We want to discover as much useful information as possible. We need to know how many former church-goers still live nearby and, if possible, whether they now attend any other church. We are not intending to steal sheep now in other folds.

Secondly, we can undertake independent research to find people who live in our locality and who once used to attend a church somewhere. We can do this by three methods at least:

a) Asking our current congregation about those who used to attend a church but no longer do so.

b) Creating an appropriate questionnaire that we encourage volunteers to take door-to-door in our area . . .

c) . . . or into the main local shopping area, stopping people in the street at random.

Once we have a list of people who once were church-goers we can begin to pray. Many or few can be involved, but we pray for these people by name and ask God to work in their lives. Even if all we know is their name and address at this stage we can still pray. God knows their circumstances and we can ask him to soften them and use other Christians in different ways to prepare them for our contact later. What we need is faith that God will work. He, alone, can delve deeply into people's lives by His Spirit.

Loren Cunningham, founder of Youth With A Mission, tells a remarkable story of how God responds to simple faith and belief. He arrived in Nigeria to minister with $45 in his pocket and knew he would need it later when he moved on to Khartoum, Sudan. In the meantime he was to preach in a number of remote villages and was being taken around in a truck by his host. One day a tyre burst and the only money they had between them was Loren's $45 which he had reserved for Khartoum. He sensed, however, that God was leading him to make it available, so he did and was left with just $3 in his pocket. He knew the time to leave was drawing closer and was aware that he had inadequate funds to survive once he arrived in Sudan. Out of the blue on his last day a letter arrived from friends in Los Angeles who had never given him money before. Inside was $150.[1] God honours simple trust. We need this kind of faith when we pray for those who do not go to church any more.

What should we ask him to do? It obviously helps if we can pray imaginatively and creatively because we understand something about those who used to come regularly to church. At this point some of the data we have already examined can be helpful. Figure 8 in Chapter 2 told us how former church-goers spend Sundays. . .

70% stay at home relaxing and doing jobs around the house and garden

66% spend time with family and/or friends

41% go on relaxing trips out

16% work in paid employment... and so on

With this information we can visualize the Sunday lifestyles of many people on our prayer list and begin to ask God that they will become hungry for something spiritual in their lives once again. We can ask him to make them increasingly flexible in their Sunday activities so that they will have time to fit church in again at some point in the future.

There is some vital information that we need here from the Survey that I have not yet given. The final Survey question was, 'How do you feel now about attending church?' The replies are fascinating.

Table 10: Participants' feelings about attending Church now

Response	% of total surveys
I sometimes wish I could go back	32
I'd like to try again, but life is too busy	21
I'm glad I don't go; I've no desire to return	20
I do not think it's relevant to life today	15
It's too dull and boring for my liking	11
I suspect it's too old-fashioned	11
I'd like to try again, but work is in the way	8
I suspect it's too modern and changed too much	6
I'd like to try again, but my family wouldn't approve	3

These replies are significant because only 20% of former church-goers interviewed said that they have no desire at all to return to church. Some, and often with good reason, said that they have reservations. The largest response in this section, however, is from those who wish at times that they could return. Across the nation this represents very many people.

The English Church Census tells us that between 1975 and 1989 the number of adults who stopped going to church totalled just over 386,000.[2] Let us surmise that 32% of these people would say if asked, 'I sometimes wish I could go back to church'. This would mean that there are 123,520 adults in England alone who might respond favourably if approached sensitively by a Christian. We must not take this lightly, especially as Table 8 shows that the number who may react this way is *more* than the 32%. Admittedly, some have different pressures on them, but they are not ruling out a return to church. If some of these people thought about the gap left in their lives when they abandoned church (and probably God), eventually they might readjust their lives to make God and his people a priority again.

This point is important. Our research shows that to identify people and to start praying for them is a responsible thing for Christians and churches to do. When we start this process we are in tune with the heart of God.

2. TAKE A CAREFUL AND DETAILED LOOK AT OURSELVES, OUR CHURCH MEMBERS AND LEADERS

We saw earlier that people who have been going to church for years do not stop without a good reason. Something is behind their action. Sometimes it is a matter directly to do with the church; at other times it is hardly related to the church at all. There is something we need to recognize here. If a person is still aware of pain caused before or during their departure from church, it will be virtually impossible to win them back unless and until that pain is dealt with.

There are several ways in which they may have absorbed this pain and hurt. One is that there was something in the church that caused them grave offence. It may have been that they responded badly to the direction in which the church was going or felt that people at church were insensitive and uncaring. If either is true, we can be sure that at some stage they will ask direct questions about that part of church life. After all, as they understand it, this is what caused their pain before. They do not want to be hurt again. No-one can blame them for that.

As we can see by now, it will not be easy to win back former church-goers. We must try to see things from their perspective. They simply will not come back to what they have rejected once before, especially if they experienced pain there in the past. Before we can expect any change in behaviour by them, *we* must be prepared to go the extra mile to prepare the way. I found the following analogy both illuminating and helpful.

'In the mid 1980s a national cinema chain decided to try to encourage people back to public theatres and away from their TVs and video recorders.

"Come and see your favourite films on a large screen with a Nicam digital mega-warp stereo system! It's far better than being huddled round that little box in the corner of the living room, being disturbed when the phone rings. Come back to the cinema for a great night out".

Once this style of advertising had been agreed on, it dawned on someone that people might turn up at the cinema, see frayed carpet, be greeted by the rude, gum chewing usherette, perch on the broken seats while sitting cross-legged to avoid visiting the foul smelling dirty lavatories! Things must change. Uniforms were introduced, staff re-trained, buildings and furnishings upgraded. The advertising worked, people enjoyed their night out and cinema attendances in the UK continue to increase!'[3]

Most of our churches are in desperate need of the same kind of treatment. We must look at our church as the average outsider would. Much useful material exists and we need courage to use whichever diagnostic tool looks best for our own local church. We need to pray, and open ourselves to the research to hear what God is saying to us through it. We need to face the fact that we may uncover things that will not be easy to accept. We may have slipped unwittingly into traditions and practices that hinder God working. It is possible that we will find areas of church life where the Devil has led us astray by deceiving us.

As we invest time, prayer and effort in exploring our church's life in depth, so we will begin to see why people have left in the past. It will dawn on us that some attitudes, together with aspects of church life, will need to change. We may wonder how we have been so blind. We may marvel that we ourselves have stayed at church when some things were so off-balance. A regular diagnostic exercise of this kind is very important for a church. In other areas of life we take it for granted. Cars and buildings are given diagnostic examinations periodically so that problems are discovered before they become serious. When we consider the eternal consequences of the work in which the church is involved, we cannot afford to be complacent or sloppy.

3. BE PREPARED TO MAKE CHANGES TO OURSELVES, TO CHURCH LIFE AND STRUCTURES

When Paul writes to the Christians in Corinth he explains how imperative it is for him to preach the Good News of Jesus. He will, he says, 'put up with anything rather than hinder the gospel of Christ' (1 Cor 9:12). 'I am compelled to preach. Woe to me if I do not preach the gospel', he says later (1 Cor 9:16). His burden is for the lost who do not have a relationship with God through Christ. He continues by explaining how far he is willing to be flexible in his approach in order to see people won into God's kingdom. The principle by which he operates is fixed, 'I make myself a slave to everyone, to win as many as possible' (1 Cor 9:19). On this basis he became 'like a Jew, to win the Jews', 'like one under the law...so as to win those under the law' and 'weak, to win the weak' (1 Cor 9:20-22). Paul was never prepared to change his message because the Gospel is fixed, but he adapted his approach and method of communication to suit the culture and background of his hearers. 'I have become all things to all men so that by all possible means I might save some', he said (1 Cor 9:22). Paul has much to teach today's church.

Let us look at some areas where, if we initiated change, it would make it far easier for those who have left us to return. Something else is worth noting too. While a new flexibility will undoubtedly upset some who have no desire for change in their church, others who are vulnerable and prime candidates to drop-out may be held. Prevention is better than cure.

Two-way participation

Bishop Gavin Reid helps us understand a fundamental need that all Christians have.

> Every Christian has two needs that church membership should meet. He or she needs support and he or she needs

to be able to contribute. We have our weak areas and crises where we need help, and we have our gifts which need to be exercised. A well-pastored church will help its members at both levels. They will be helped to grow in grace, finding strength in their weaknesses. And they will be enabled to minister to others through the use of their God-given abilities. Failure at either point can give rise to the dissatisfaction that leads to dropping-out.[4]

The larger a church is, the harder it is for this policy to be applied. God can see the potential in each member of a church, and he wants them all to be genuinely and deeply fulfilled.

Church centre buildings

One area where the Devil has scored many successes with Christians is over their attitude to material church buildings. None of the churches mentioned in the New Testament had a suite of buildings reserved for worship and Christian activities. There were undoubtedly advantages and disadvantages to this. Buildings help Christians to have an identifiable presence in the local community and allow a church great freedom to organize its life as suits itself. The associated financial burden can be enormous, however, and can drain resources that could otherwise be used in local and world mission. Some writers see other problems. David Watson observes that church buildings 'can often be no more than monuments of religion. They can often fail to speak of the reality of the living God.'[5] Howard Snyder goes further. He includes these points as he gives a critique of present-day church buildings.

First, church buildings are a *witness to our immobility*...Christians are to be a mobile people...The gospel says, 'Go,' but our church buildings say, 'Stay'. The gospel says, 'Seek the lost,' but our churches say, 'Let the lost seek the church'.

Second, church buildings are a *witness to our inflexibility*...The Sunday morning service allows the direct participation of only a few—dictated by the sanctuary layout...Communication will be one-way—dictated by architecture and the PA system...

Thirdly, church buildings are a *witness to our lack of fellowship*. Church buildings may be worshipful places, but usually they are not friendly places. They are uncomfortable and impersonal. Church buildings are not made for fellowship.[6]

The cinema chain knew that its buildings and furnishings would have to be upgraded before customers got the message that things were different now. Work of this kind is extraordinarily expensive and Christians will have to evaluate what their priorities are with the limited funds available. There are no easy answers, but we can only agree with David Watson when he observes that, 'a dirty and unkempt church building is no witness to our majestic creator God. A cold and dingy church is no witness to an outsider.'[7]

If church buildings are not to be a major deterrent in winning new people for Christ and encouraging former church-goers back, we may have no choice but to invest money in upgrading the facilities they offer. This may seem a daunting prospect initially, but God is on our side. Colin Charlton tells how his Anglican parish church in Essex produced a scheme to add a much-needed church hall that they called 'Project Nehemiah'. They were inspired by a huge building project undertaken by a church in Sheffield and believed God was calling them to pray and give. They started to pray and then held a Day of Giving and Thanksgiving. He records,

> On the morning after the day, having asked for £30,000, we had been given or promised exactly £30,000. For our small church this represents a certain sacrifice in giving. It also ably demonstrates the power of positive prayer.[8]

Attitudes and biases
Christians can be narrow, critical and condemnatory and these attitudes have played a major part in others leaving churches. Part of the problem seems to be that some Christians have developed strong but unbiblical views on a wide range of

Church-related issues. This guarantees problems over worship services and church policy time and again.

God's call to his people is that they should love him, live holy lives and be open to however he chooses to lead them. Terry Virgo tells of a 'flourishing church in Kent' that 'recently hired a local wine bar and invited contacts to a meal (yes, with wine!) where the gospel was clearly shared'.[9] The people who came, he reports, were those who were befriended at the local golf club that the leader and others from the church had joined. The thought of evangelism being undertaken in a wine bar is enough to make some Christians explode!

Yet when we closely examine Jesus' own ministry we find that he went into some risky situations that provoked criticism from the religious leaders of his day. After Matthew's response to follow Jesus, he invited his friends, 'tax collectors and "sinners"' (Mt 9:10), to share a meal with Jesus and himself. Jesus was obviously delighted to be there in order to reach lost people who might otherwise have been neglected.

God's call to us today is to be as bold as Jesus. It is not easy, though, for those who have been Christians in a static church to accept or agree to changes that will turn upside down much that has become to them almost a part of the Christian faith itself. Like Paul, however, we have to be able to distinguish between the unchanging Truth of God which is not negotiable, and peripheral issues that are. If we fail in this our numbers will continue to decline. Admittedly, if we dare to make courageous changes so that we relate more to ordinary people today, it may provoke some to leave. In the short-term our numbers may decline further although we pray this will not happen, but our eyes must be on the longer-term future. Like the cinemas we must be prepared to adapt, even if those who strangely like the hard pews and unsavoury toilets object.

4. BE PREPARED TO PLANT NEW CHURCHES AND CONGREGATIONS

There is something refreshing about new things. The new-born baby has such a soft skin and angelic appearance. A new car has unblemished paintwork and, inside, a rich aroma of the materials used to make it. Sandy-coloured labrador puppies have won the heart of the nation and have made a certain brand of toilet tissue a best seller. At the opposite end of the spectrum things are very different. Our skin becomes wrinkled and baggy as we get older, elderly cars become rusty and tatty, and old dogs get arthritis and cannot run. Looking at churches, we can almost imagine that they have a sell-by date after which they become entrenched in stagnant traditions. This is not how it should be.

This is one of the best arguments for churches to adopt an active policy of church or congregation planting. There are others too. There are some geographical areas that do not have easy access to a Christ-centred church. There are people-groups that existing churches seem unable to touch. My own church agreed in 1991 to plant a congregation on an estate with some 2,800 homes and without a church of any kind as the Anglican parish church is located some distance away. Because the satellite congregation meets in a youth hall, the feel is different to the more 'religious' setting of our town-centre building. The worship often feels more fresh, vibrant and spontaneous. The congregation has no fixed traditions, and while its ultimate leadership comes from the mother church, it is flexible and able to adapt more speedily than a long-established church.

Although he is not directly advocating church planting, Michael Green has some helpful observations to make about the early church which, he says...

...made evangelism its first priority

...had a deep compassion for people without Christ

...was very flexible in the ways it preached the good news

...was very sensitive to the leading of the Holy Spirit

...was not unduly minister-conscious

...expected every member to be a witness to Christ.

In the early church, he continues...

...buildings were unimportant

...evangelism was the spontaneous, natural chattering of good news

...the policy was to go out to where people were, and make disciples of them

...the gospel was frequently argued about in the philosophical schools, discussed in the streets, talked over in the laundry

...whole communities seem to have come over to the faith together

...the maximum impact was made by the changed lives and better quality of community among Christians.[10]

These ideals are worth striving for, and are often easier to implement in a new plant than a long-established church.

Multi-congregations

Peter Wagner highlights the 'multi-congregational model' in his book, *Your Church can Grow*. He refers to Temple Baptist Church in Los Angeles which has 'three separate and semi-autonomous congregations: Spanish, Korean and Anglo.'[11] While the senior minister has oversight of the whole church, he serves as pastor only of the Anglo congregation. 'The Spanish and Korean congregations each has its own pastor and lay leadership and congregational life-style.' Once a quarter they share in a special 'Sounds of Heaven' celebration.

I am writing this having recently launched a different worship service in the church where I am pastor. It seeks to cater for those who prefer a more-traditional style of Baptist worship. Like so many other churches which have sought gradually to up-date the style of worship and particularly the music, we have found a reaction from some who prefer worship to be fairly sedate and predictable with more gentle and mellow music. I do not see this as a reflection of anyone's spirituality, but rather an expression of personal preferences.

Two of our church members are missionaries to the many Asians in our community. Another of my prayers and goals is to see a Punjabi-speaking congregation established as part of our church's ministry. Maybe in due course we will discover other groups of people for whom we could provide a specialist ministry and so win them to Christ. This is surely no different to the BBC's policy over its radio broadcasting. The Corporation provides five national radio services for different sectors of the community together with other regional and local services. We listen to whichever of them we find most personally appealing and satisfying.

This raises, of course, the question of Christian unity. Can a church be truly one if it is made up of many different composite parts that have little to do with one another? Let us consult the apostle Paul. When he likens the church to a body in 1 Corinthians 12 he differentiates between the various parts of the body. They are all separate entities that function to a large extent independently of each other, and yet cannot function at all unless they are part of the whole body. On this basis it seems reasonable for any church to have numerous strands of ministry functioning concurrently under one coordinated leadership which binds the whole together and monitors the progress of the complete church.

Seeker-led churches

While evangelism was the priority of the early church, it is probably fair to say that few churches today exist primarily for those who are not yet disciples of Christ. Like it or not (and I do not), most churches exist supposedly to cater for the needs of those who attend. This is one of the Devil's major victories over the church of Jesus Christ in the world. It has made us self-centred and selfish. It means that we have an uphill struggle to encourage Christians to engage in active outreach and mission work. In Chapter 7 we referred to Willow Creek Community Church, Barrington, Chicago, which is so refreshingly different. From its inception it has been a church utterly committed to putting first the needs of those seeking a faith in Christ.

Before Willow Creek Church was launched, many of those involved had shared in the Son City Spectacular, a youth ministry based in South Park Church, Park Ridge, Illinois. Associate Pastor of Willow Creek, Don Cousins, says that what they did 'was totally radical, even sacrilegious to a lot of people'.[12] They did more than just break traditions; they created a whole new approach about how church could be done. Bill Hybels, the leader of Willow Creek, had difficult decisions to make before they launched the church.

He had no money, no members, no structure, no facility,

no precedent, no influence, no way to support himself and his wife, no seminary degree, no elders and not even a hint of logic. What he had was this: the unmistakable and unrelenting leading of the Holy Spirit. 'I decided to do this by myself if I had to,' Hybels says. 'I felt like I didn't really have a choice.'[13]

We have already seen how God has greatly used this different approach. In seventeen years this church has grown to the largest in the United States of America. It has succeeded because Bill Hybels and his colleagues founded the church on Biblical principles. Reaching lost people is their priority and God has blessed them.

With Christian churches being shunned by so many people in the United Kingdom today, there is plenty of room for alternative styles of church to emerge and blossom. There are several possible ways forward. A mature church can begin to hold seeker events which are user-friendly in that they cater especially for people who are not currently practising Christians. An alternative is for a church to catch the vision for a seeker-led congregation and rather than disrupt its existing ministry, release some members and plant a different style of congregation nearby. Trevor Waldock, formerly a staff member of Above Bar Church in Southampton, has recently launched 'Just Looking' in that city.[14] Since attending the Willow Creek Conference in Birmingham in 1992 I have made this a personal goal for our Church in Gravesend in the not too-distant future.

Today God is looking for those who, like Joshua, are prepared to take new ground. To these he promises that as they are 'strong and courageous' and obey his word, so he will be with them wherever they go (Josh 1:7-9). Having read over 500 Survey forms from former church-goers, and knowing that only 20% of them say that they have absolutely no desire to return, I believe that many could be drawn back to something quite different. The changes would not be in the teaching about our unchanging God, of course, but in the way we 'do church.' As we said earlier, 'we often think people have rejected Jesus, when in fact they have simply been put off by the church!'[15]

Church planting is a vital part of letting God's people grow...We shall be accused of triumphalism and empire-building. But let us not allow the strident sounds of our critics to ring in our ears, but the call of the One who is both the Sower and the Lord of the harvest, and who wants us to respond to his command to plant where there is no seed and gather in where there are no harvesters.[16]

5. BEGIN MAKING CONTACT BY USING TRAINED VISITORS

When we have spent time to pray specifically for people, and have tried under the guidance of the Holy Spirit to make our church different from the one that people left, the time will come when we begin to contact former church-goers. This may not be a ministry for the faint-hearted! It will take careful preparation and specific training to cope with the pressures of this specialist work.[17] We must not expect a casual, friendly social visit to be enough. Pain, hurt and disappointment may have to surface before problems and issues that prompted people to stop attending church can be resolved. We will need to show genuine love and understanding to former church-goers, perhaps over an extended time. Visitors will need patience, sensitivity, skill and spiritual openness if their ministry is to be productive. Strong faith and trust in God's ability to work through them will be essential. These people will need to be risk-takers for him and they will require the prayer support of the rest of the church membership.

David Coffey tells of an American pastor in Chicago in 1943 who invited an unknown twenty-five year old evangelist to take his weekly radio programme. Later the same evangelist was invited to speak at the opening rally of a season of twenty-one nights of evangelistic meetings in a 3,000 seat auditorium in the city. 2,800 people came and when the invitation was given forty-two people were counselled. The evangelist was Billy Graham.[18]

It was only when a Christian took a spiritually calculated risk that this now deeply-respected Christian leader had an opportunity to be used by God. Maybe it will only be when churches take risks and are prepared to invest time and training in this kind of visitation ministry that we will see any significant return of former church-goers to Sunday worship. Of course, we really want far more than this. Our deep desire is that their commitment to Christ will start to grow, either again or maybe for the first time. We have been called to make 'disciples', not church-attenders (Mt 28:19).

We must not confine ourselves to ministering in this way just to former members. Dr Roland Croucher of John Mark Ministries says that some Australian denominations are losing more clergy than they keep. One of his publicity leaflets explains.

> For most ex-pastors the emotional and spiritual strain associated with their transition out of parish ministry is considerable. One writes: 'My denomination and colleagues treat me as if I were a leper...' Another: 'The only contact from the Superintendent of my denomination when I left the pastorate was a terse request for the keys to the manse!'[19]

It will be more difficult for church visitors to go to former clergy living in their area. They will encounter people who have probably been deeply hurt. The visitors may feel intimidated. Yet the picture of the shepherd relentlessly searching the countryside for the lost sheep still applies. These men and women may appear to have fallen a long way, but they still matter deeply to God. They are in need of much love and understanding. Erwin Luther refers to a dilemma he faced. He tells of a friend of his who 'had to resign as pastor because of an adulterous relationship. Within two days after the affair was discovered, he left the area with his wife and family. Now my problem is how to reach out and restore him back to the fellowship of the saints.'[20]

God will undoubtedly equip, use and bless those who catch a vision for reaching former church-goers with his love. He will be glad to make their sensitive ministry effective because he is so keen for lost sheep to come back to the fold.

CONCLUSION

To end, a story about what happened at Ellel Grange during the lunch hour on 13 March 1992.

> The wind was howling, the rain lashing down, and the last thing I wanted to do was take the dog for a walk! As I struggled down the lane, my eyes focused on a tiny bedraggled lamb, hardly able to stand on its legs and unable to move. There were no other sheep around and it was against a tree totally alone, sopping wet and freezing cold. Immediately my heart went out to this vulnerable, weak little lamb. I ran back to the house, grabbed a towel, left the dog and raced back to the spot where the lamb was. My heart so much wanted to rescue the little lamb that I did not stop to think of my best coat, trousers and shoes. I climbed over the fence and into the mud. The lamb took one step towards me with what seemed its last strength. I knew it was dying as I scooped it into my arms, wrapping the towel around it. Back over the fence the lamb was taken to the Christian farmer whose land adjoins ours. I knew that there it would be looked after. Once the lamb was in safety, I then looked and saw my muddy clothes. The Lord spoke directly into my heart, 'Don't you see that this is what I have called you to do. I have called you to rescue my lambs, those who have been abandoned, without shelter or food, and who are bleeding and dying with no-one to help. Many have been neglected. I have called you to bring my lambs to safety, to bring healing to them and to bring them to those shepherds who will care and tend for my flock. It will not be easy and you may get muddy and hurt but the joy I will give will be everlasting'.[21]

With so many former church-goers throughout our nation, God is calling us to reach them again for him. As we reconsider the priority that this ministry should have for us in the future, we must not forget the exhilaration of the shepherd in Jesus' story. 'Rejoice with me; I have found my lost sheep', he cries to his friends and neighbours (Lk 15:6). There will be deep joy both in Heaven and on earth as former church-goers come back to church and God again. Let's go for it!

Notes

[1] Loren Cunningham, *Daring to Live on the Edge* (Sovereign World International: Tonbridge, 1992), p 11-13.

[2] Peter Brierley, *'Christian' England* (MARC Europe: London, 1991), p 30.

[3] From *Roots*, A Different Way of Doing Church (Baptist Union of Great Britain: Didcot, 1992) p 2.

[4] Gavin Reid, *Good News to Share* (Falcon Books: Eastbourne, 1979) p 121.

[5] David Watson, *I Believe in the Church* (Hodder & Stoughton: London, 1978) p 117.

[6] Howard Snyder, *New Wineskins* (Marshall, Morgan & Scott: London, 1975) p 61-65.

[7] Watson, *op cit*, p 120.

[8] Chapter by Colin Charlton in: Donald English (editor), *Ten Praying Churches* (MARC: Eastbourne, 1989), p 23-37.

[9] Terry Virgo, *Restoration in the Church* (Kingsway: Eastbourne, 1985) p 103.

[10] Michael Green, *Evangelism through the Local Church* (Hodder & Stoughton: London, 1990) p 400-401.

[11] C Peter Wagner, *Your Church Can Grow* (Regal Books: Glendale, 1976) p 122.

[12] From *Church Leaders Handbook* issued at "Creating a Church for the Unchurched" Conference, Birmingham, UK, 16-18 June 1992, p 31.

[13] *Church Leaders Handbook* as above, p 37.

[14] Documented in: Martin Robinson, *A World Apart* (Monarch: Tunbridge Wells, 1992), p 157-169.

[15] From *Roots* leaflet as above, p 3.

[16] Michael Harper, *Let My People Grow* (Hodder & Stoughton: London, 1988) p 129.

[17] Probably the most comprehensive training in the world in this area of ministry is that provided by L.E.A.D. Consultants Inc., P.O. Box 664, Reynoldsburg, Ohio 43068, USA.

[18] David Coffey, *Build That Bridge* (Kingsway: Eastbourne, 1986), p 145-146.

[19] John Mark Ministries is based at 7 Bangor Court, Heathmont, Victoria, Australia 3135

20 Erwin W Luther, *When A Good Man Falls* (Scripture Press: Amersham-on-the-Hill, 1988) p 150.

21 Anonymous article, "Feed My Sheep", *Ellel Ministries News Letter*, May 1992: p 1.

APPENDIX A

Areas of the UK from which survey data has come:

	No. of surveys		% of whole
A South East England			
East Sussex	23		
Essex	33		
Kent	83		
London	40		
Surrey	38		
West Sussex	8	Total = 225	44%
B The Rest of England			
Avon	21		
Berkshire	6		
Cheshire	1		
Cumbria	6		
Derbyshire	1		
Devon	3		
Gloucestershire	12		
Greater Manchester	3		
Hampshire	26		
Isle of Wight	57		
Lancashire	8		
Leicestershire	3		
Merseyside	8		
North Humberside	6		

Northumberland	1		
Nottinghamshire	2		
Oxfordshire	1		
South Yorkshire	3		
Suffolk	18		
Tyne and Wear	4		
West Yorkshire	3		
West Midlands	6		
Wiltshire	7	Total = 206	41%

C The Rest of the United Kingdom

Clwyd	3		
Dyfed	24		
Jersey	5		
Lothian	22		
South Glamorgan	7		
West Glamorgan	1		
Unknown	16	Total = 78	15%
		Grand Total = 509	100%

APPENDIX B

Locations Where Street Surveying Has Taken Place

Surveys have been procured at random in the following:

Alfreton, Derbys
Ashford, Kent
Bexleyheath
Birmingham
Brading, IoW
Bristol
Bromley
Canterbury
Chatham
Cheltenham
Colchester
Crawley
Dartford
Derby
East Cowes, IoW
Edinburgh
Eltham
Farnham
Folkestone
Gillingham, Kent
Gloucester

Ipswich
Llanelli
Locks Heath, Hants
London
Lowestoft
Maidstone
Matlock
Newport, IoW
Portsmouth
Rainham, Kent
Ryde, IoW
Seaford
Sidcup
Swalecliffe, Kent
Swanley
Tilbury
Tonbridge
Tunbridge Wells
Weston-Super-Mare
Wootton Bridge, IoW

APPENDIX C

Final Survey Results

Participants: Sex—Male		50%
Female		50%
Age—Under 25		19%
25-34		21%
35-54		37%
55 & over		23%

1. **What do you do on Sundays?**
   a) i) Go shopping — 12%
      ii) Go to DIY stores — 14%
   b) Relaxing trips out — 41%
   c) Stay at home relaxing and doing jobs around the house and garden — 70%
   d) Go to church — 10%
   e) Spend time with family and/or friends — 66%
   f) Go to car boot sales/markets — 14%
   g) Work (paid employment) — 16%

2. **Have you ever been to...**
   a) Sunday School or equivalent? — 73%
   b) Church? — 100%
   Which denomination?
      Church of England — 45%
      Baptist — 15%
      Methodist — 10%
      Roman Catholic — 10%
      Others — 20%

3. If you used to go to church on Sunday and don't any longer, is it because...

		Yes	Maybe
a)	People didn't seem to care about you as a person?	9%	8%
b)	You didn't get on with the leader or leadership?	10%	6%
c)	Of domestic conflicts or tensions because you attended church?	8%	2%
d)	You felt God let you down in some way?	7%	6%
e)	You found it boring?	23%	11%
f)	You didn't like the direction the church was going?	17%	10%
g)	You felt you didn't belong?	20%	9%
h)	You found it irrelevant to your everyday life?	24%	10%
i)	You were put off by the sermons?	15%	10%
j)	Sickness or old age?	3%	1%
k)	Your questions and/or observations weren't taken seriously?	7%	6%

4. If you used to go, how committed and active were you?

a)	Attended once a Sunday	54%
b)	Attended more than once a Sunday	31%
c)	Attended monthly	5%
d)	Attended occasionally	9%
e)	Attended only at Easter and/or Christmas	3%
f)	Attended only for christenings, weddings, funerals	11%

5. Were you ever...

a)	Christened?	83%
b)	Confirmed?	41%
c)	In leadership in the church?	8%
d)	Baptized in water as a believer?	17%
e)	A born-again Christian?	16%
f)	An active, committed member?	29%

6. How do you feel now about attending church?

a) I'm glad I don't go; I've no desire to return   20%

b) I sometimes wish I could go back   32%

c) I'd like to try again, but life is too busy   21%

d) I'd like to try again, but work is in the way   8%

e) I'd like to try again, but my family wouldn't approve   3%

f) It's too dull and boring for my liking   11%

g) I suspect it's too modern and changed too much   6%

h) I suspect it's too old-fashioned   11%

i) I do not think it's relevant to life today   15%

APPENDIX D

Complete Tables of Data

**FIGURE 10: Comparison of responses between
males and females**

Category	Male	Female
Total people surveyed %	50	50
PART A: Expressed commitment %		
Of those who...		
...Went to Sunday School	47	53
...Went to church once a Sunday	52	48
...Went to church more than once a Sunday	54	46
...Were christened, baptized or dedicated as an infant	46	54
...Were confirmed	53	47
...Were in leadership within the church	54	46
...Were baptized by immersion in water	44	56
...Considered themselves a born-again Christian	41	59
...Considered themselves an active committed member of their local church	43	57
Average of above	48	52

PART B: Reasons for leaving church %
Of those who left church because of...

a) Personal issues...

...With some feeling that people didn't seem to care about them as a person	42	58
...Because of some kind of domestic tensions	33	67
...Because they felt they didn't belong to some extent	41	59
...Because they had some awareness that their questions and observations weren't taken seriously	44	56

b) Leadership issues

...Because they didn't get on with the leadership in some way	44	56
...Because to some extent they didn't like the direction it was going	45	55

c) Relevance issues

...Because they found it boring to some extent	54	46
...Because to some extent they found it irrelevant to their everyday life	60	40
...Because they were put off by the sermons to some extent	50	50

d) God issues

...Because they felt in some way that God had let them down	44	56

Total (= 100%)	509 respondents

. . . .

FIGURE 11: Comparison of responses between age groups

Category	-25	25-34	35-54	55+
Total people surveyed %	19	21	37	23
PART A: Expressed commitment % Of those who.....				
...Went to Sunday School	19	19	37	25
...Went to Church once a Sunday	22	20	37	21
...Went to church more than once Sunday	12	17	40	31
...Were christened, baptized or dedicated as an infant	17	20	39	24
...Were confirmed	13	19	47	21
...Were in leadership within the church	10	23	44	23
...Were baptized by immersion in water as a believer	13	22	44	21
...Considered themselves a born-again Christian	17	27	42	14
...Considered themselves an active committed member of their local church	14	22	39	25
Average of above	15	21	41	23
PART B: Reasons for leaving church % Of those who left church because of... **a) Personal issues...**				
...With some feeling that people didn't seem to care about them as a person	18	21	45	16
...Because of some kind of domestic tension	11	23	51	15
...Because they felt they didn't belong to some extent	20	26	40	14
...Because they had some awareness that their questions and observations weren't taken seriously	21	24	38	17

b) Leadership issues...

...Because they didn't get on with the leadership in some way	16	28	41	15
...Because to some extent they didn't like the direction it was going	17	29	38	16

c) Relevance issues...

...Because they found it boring to some extent	25	28	32	15
...Because to some extent they found it irrelevant to their everyday lives	19	27	36	18
...Because they were put off by the sermons	24	23	30	23

d) God issues...

...Because they felt in some way that God had let them down	14	19	44	23

Total (= 100%)	509 respondents

FIGURE 12: Comparison of responses between the denominations

Category	CofE	Bapt	Meth	RC	Othrs
Total people surveyed %	45	15	10	10	20

PART A: Expressed commitment %
Of those who....

	CofE	Bapt	Meth	RC	Othrs
...Went to Sunday School	45	16	12	5	22
...Went to church once a Sunday	44	13	12	13	18
...Went to church more than once a Sunday	39	24	8	5	24
...Were christened, baptized or dedicated as infants	50	11	10	12	17
...Were confirmed	57	5	9	18	11
...Were in leadership within the church	19	27	24	6	24
...Were baptized by immersion in water as a believer	12	50	3	5	30
...Considered themselves a born-again Christian	23	43	4	0	30
...Considered themselves an active committed member of their local church	32	24	17	6	21
Average of above	35	24	11	8	22

PART B: Reasons for leaving church %
Of those who left church because of...
a) Personal issues...

	CofE	Bapt	Meth	RC	Othrs
...With some feeling that people didn't seem to care about them as a person	37	23	10	7	23
...Because of some kind of domestic tension	45	22	6	7	20
...Because they felt they didn't belong to some extent	37	27	12	5	19

...Because they had some awareness that their questions and observations weren't taken seriously	41	24	11	6	18

b) Leadership issues...

...Because they didn't get on with the leadership in some way	47	17	4	9	23
...Because to some extent they didn't like the direction it was going	46	20	10	6	18

c) Relevance issues...

...Because they found it boring to some extent	48	16	7	13	16
...Because to some extent they found it irrelevant to their everyday life	48	14	9	12	17
...Because they were put off by the sermons to some extent	50	17	11	7	15

d) God issues...

...Because they had some feeling that God had let them down	45	17	18	9	11

Total (= 100%)	509 respondents

FIGURE 13: Comparison of responses between the various regions of the UK surveyed

Category	SEE	RofE	RofUK
Total people surveyed %	44	40	16
PART A: Expressed commitment %			
Of those who....			
...Went to Sunday School	45	39	15
...Went to church once a Sunday	47	39	14
...Went to church more than once a Sunday	52	36	12
...Were christened, baptized or dedicated as an infant	47	40	13
...Were confirmed	48	42	10
...Were in leadership in their local church	42	53	5
...Were baptized by immersion in water as believer	55	30	15
...Considered themselves a born-again Christian	58	31	11
...Considered themselves an active committed member of their local church	52	36	12
Average of above	50	38	12
PART B: Reasons for leaving church %			
Of those who left church because of....			
a) Personal issues...			
...With some feeling that people didn't seem to care about them as a person	33	49	18
...Because of some kind of domestic tension	52	39	9
...Because they felt they didn't belong to some extent	48	45	7
...Because they had some awareness that their questions and observations weren't taken seriously	38	56	6

b) Leadership issues...

...Because they didn't get on with the leadership in some way	36	36	28
...Because to some extent they didn't like the direction it was going	40	50	10

c) Relevance issues...

...Because they found it boring to some extent	40	49	11
...Because to some extent they found it irrelevant to their everyday life	44	45	11
...Because they were put off by the sermons to some extent	40	49	11

d) God issues...

...Because they felt in some way that God had let them down	45	47	8

Total (= 100%)	509 respondents

**FIGURE 14: Comparison of responses between surveys
received from church contacts and others**

Category	via	church	random
People surveyed %		27	73

PART A: Expressed commitment %
Of those who....

	via	church	random
...Went to Sunday School		27	73
...Went to church once a Sunday		27	73
...Went to church more than once a Sunday		35	65
...Were christened, baptized or dedicated as an infant		24	76
...Were confirmed		27	73
...Were in leadership within their local church		60	40
...Were baptized by immersion in water as a believer		63	37
...Considered themselves a born-again Christian		51	49
...Considered themselves an active committed member of their local church		44	56
Average of above		40	60

PART B: Reasons for leaving church %
Of those who left church because....
a) Personal issues...

	via	church	random
...With some feeling that people didn't seem to care about them as a person		40	60
...Because of some kind of domestic tension		35	65
...Because they felt they didn't belong to some extent		46	54
...Because they had some awareness that their questions and observations weren't taken seriously		40	60

b) Leadership issues...

...Because they didn't get on with the leadership in some way	36	64
...Because to some extent they didn't like the direction it was going	44	56

c) Relevance issues...

...Because they found it boring to some extent	23	77
...Because to some extent they found it irrelevant to their everyday life	23	77
...Because they were put off by the sermons to some extent	26	74

d) God issues...

...Because they felt in some way that God had let them down	27	73

Total (= 100%)	509 respondents

Bibliography

A wide range of topics has been raised in this book. The following titles may provide more extensive coverage of some of these.

Arnold, Clinton E. *Powers of Darkness*. IVP: Leicester, 1992.

Ashton, Cyril. *Church on the Threshold*. Darton, Longman and Todd: London, 1988.

Bakke, Raymond. *The Urban Christian*. MARC Europe: London, 1987.

Beasley-Murray, Paul. *Dynamic Leadership*. MARC: Eastbourne, 1990.

Beasley-Murray, Paul. *Faith and Festivity*. MARC: Eastbourne, 1991.

Beasley-Murray, Paul. *Pastors Under Pressure*. Kingsway: Eastbourne, 1989.

Boyd, Carolyn. *The Apostle of Hope*. Sovereign World: Chichester, 1991.

Bridge, Donald. *How to Spot a Church Split Before it Happens*. MARC: Eastbourne, 1989.

Brierley, Peter. *'Christian' England*. MARC Europe: London, 1991.

Brierley, Peter. *Vision Building*. Hodder & Stoughton: London, 1989.

Burnett, David. *Clash of Worlds*. MARC: Eastbourne, 1990.

Burton, Jack. *The Gap*. SPCK: London, 1991.

Carey, George. *The Church in the Market Place*. Second Edition. Kingsway: Eastbourne, 1989.

Carr, Wesley. *Say One For Me*. SPCK: London, 1992.

Chalke, Steve. *The Christian Youth Manual*. Revised edition. Kingsway: Eastbourne, 1992.

Cleverly, Charlie. *Church Planting our Future Hope*. Scripture Union: London, 1991.

Coates, Gerald. *An Intelligent Fire*. Kingsway: Eastbourne, 1991.

Coffey, David. *Build That Bridge*. Kingsway: Eastbourne, 1986.

Coffey, Ian (and others). *No Stranger in the City*. IVP: Leicester, 1989.

Cole, Michael (and others). *What is the New Age?* Hodder & Stoughton: London, 1990.

Copley, Derek. *Taking a Lead*. Kingsway: Eastbourne, 1985.

Eddison, John. *What Makes a Leader?* Scripture Union: London, 1974.

English, Donald (Editor). *Ten Praying Churches*. MARC: Eastbourne, 1989.

Facius, Johannes. *God Can Do It—Without Me!* Sovereign World: Chichester, 1990.

Fernando, Ajith. *Reclaiming Friendship*. IVP: Leicester, 1991.

Finney, John. *Finding Faith Today*. British & Foreign Bible Society: Swindon, 1992.

Finney, John. *Understanding Leadership*. Darton, Longman and Todd: London, 1989.

Fletcher, Dr Ben. *Clergy Under Stress*. Mowbray: London, 1990.

Foyle, Marjory F. *Honourably Wounded*. MARC Europe: Bromley, 1987.

Fryling, Alice (Editor). *Disciplemakers' Handbook*. IVP: Leicester, 1990.

Gamble, Robin. *The Irrelevant Church*. Monarch: Eastbourne, 1991.

Gammons, Peter. *Christ's Healing Power Today*. Monarch: Tunbridge Wells, 1992.

Goldsmith, Martin. *What in the World is God Doing?* MARC: Eastbourne, 1991.

Green, Michael. *Evangelism Now and Then*. Darton, Longman and Todd: London, 1992.

Green, Michael. *Evangelism Through the Local Church*. Hodder & Stoughton: London, 1990.

Griffiths, Michael. *Cinderella With Amnesia*. IVP: London, 1975.

Griffiths, Michael. *Get Your Act Together, Cinderella!* IVP: Leicester, 1989.

Griffiths, Michael (Editor). *Ten Sending Churches*. MARC Europe: London, 1985.

Gunstone, John. *Free in Christ*. Darton, Longman and Todd: London, 1989.

Harper, Michael. *That We May Be One*. Hodder & Stoughton: London, 1983.

Harper, Michael. *Let My People Grow*. Second Edition. Hodder & Stoughton: London, 1988.

Hill, Clifford. *Tell My People I Love Them*. Collins: London, 1983.

Horrobin, Peter. *Healing Through Deliverance*. Sovereign World: Chichester, 1991.

Hybels, Bill (and others). *Mastering Contemporary Preaching*. IVP: Leicester, 1991.

King, Philip. *Leadership Explosion*. Hodder & Stoughton: London, 1987.

Kline, Chris. *A Brilliant Deception*. Kingsway: Eastbourne, 1990.

Lawrence, Peter H. *Doing What Comes Supernaturally*. Kingsway: Eastbourne, 1992.

Lewis, C.S. The *Screwtape Letters*. Sixteenth Impression. Collins: London, 1970.

Lukasse, Johan. *Churches with Roots*. MARC: Eastbourne, 1990.

Marshall, Michael. *The Gospel Conspiracy*. Monarch: Tunbridge Wells, 1992.

Marshall, Tom. *Understanding Leadership*. Sovereign World: Chichester, 1991.

Miller, Calvin. *Leadership*. NavPress: Amersham-on-the-Hill, 1987.

Montgomery, Jim. *Dawn 2000: Seven Million Churches To Go*. Highland: Crowborough, 1990.

Moore, Charles (and others). *The Church in Crisis*. Hodder & Stoughton: London, 1986.

Munro, Dr Bill. *Designer Living*. Monarch: Eastbourne, 1991.

Perry, John. *Christian Leadership*. Hodder & Stoughton: London, 1983.

Pogue, Steve L. *The First Year of Your Christian Life*. Scripture Press: Amersham-on-the-Hill, 1990.

Read, Peter. *Unlikely Heroes*. IVP: Leicester, 1990.

Reid, Gavin. *Good News to Share*. Falcon: Eastbourne, 1979.

Robinson, Martin. *A World Apart*. Monarch: Tunbridge Wells, 1992.

Robinson, Martin & Stuart Christine. *Planting Tomorrow's Churches Today*. Monarch: Tunbridge Wells, 1992.

Robison, James. *Winning the Real War*. Kingsway: Eastbourne, 1992.

Rye, James & Nina. *The Survivor's Guide to Church Life*. IVP: Leicester, 1992.

Savage, John S. *The Apathetic and Bored Church Member*. LEAD Consultants: Reynoldsburg, 1976.

Swindoll, Charles R. *Stress Fractures*. Scripture Press: Amersham-on-the-Hill, 1991.

Tinker, Melvin (Editor). *Restoring the Vision*. MARC: Eastbourne, 1990.

Townsend, Dr John. *Hiding from Love*. Scripture Press: Amersham-on-the-Hill, 1992.

Virgo, Terry. *Restoration in the Church*. Kingsway: Eastbourne, 1985.

Wagner, C. Peter (Editor). *Wrestling With Dark Angels*. Monarch: Eastbourne, 1990.

Wagner, C. Peter. *Your Church can Grow*. Regal: Glendale, 1976.

Walker, Tom. *Renew Us by Your Spirit*. Hodder & Stoughton: London, 1982.

Watson, David. *I Believe in the Church*. Hodder & Stoughton: London, 1978.

Wimber, John. *Power Evangelism*. New edition. Hodder & Stoughton: London, 1992.

Wright, Nigel. *Challenge to Change*. Kingsway: Eastbourne, 1991.

Wright, Nigel. *The Fair Face of Evil*. Marshall Pickering: London, 1989.

Wright, Nigel. *The Radical Kingdom*. Kingsway: Eastbourne, 1986.

Wright, H. Norman. *Overcoming Your Hidden Fears*. Scripture Press: Amersham-on-the-Hill, 1990.

Wright, Tom. *New Tasks for a Renewed Church*. Hodder & Stoughton: London, 1992.

Winning Them Back

by Eddie Gibbs

The Church's response to the problem of nominal Christianity

- Can there truly be such a person as a 'nominal' Christian?

- Are such people really pagans masquerading as believers, or self-deceived religious legalists?

- Or do nominal Christians lack spiritual vitality because they are spiritually malnourished?

To address these issues Dr Gibbs undertook a qualitative survey of nominality amongst churches in the English-speaking world. After attempting a working definition of nominality, he surveys biblical insights into the issue, and describes its characteristics and causes. He also assesses the impact of the charismatic renewal and urban lifestyles, and the influences of secularisation and religious pluralism. His important final chapter describes workable strategies for 'winning them back'.

ISBN 1 85424 208 3   £8.99

Monarch
Publications

Reaching and Keeping Teenagers

by Peter Brierley

Each week there are 300 fewer teenagers in church—over 155,000 in the last decade! What can the churches do?

In 1992, with support from many youth organisations including Scripture Union and British Youth for Christ, Peter Brierley undertook a major survey of teenagers and their attitudes toward church, leisure, school and home.

Brierley discovered: 'Teenagers dropping out of the churches are not necessarily doing so because they are dropping out of Christianity. They are dropping out of the adult world into a world of their own'.

He appeals to churches not to judge youth but to accept them and include them as a vital part of church life. 'The father did not criticise the way his prodigal son had spent his money, but welcomed him with love. The churches will need to do the same.'

Peter Brierley is Director of the Christian Research Association and former European Director of MARC Europe. He is Editor of the *UK Christian Handbook* and author of *'Christian' England* and *Priorities, Planning and Paperwork*.

ISBN 1 85424 221 0   £8.99

Monarch Publications

A World Apart
Creating a church for the unchurched: Learning from Willow Creek

Martin Robinson

Like most English speaking cultures, Britain is very largely a nation of the unchurched. The task facing Christians is not merely to propose a set of beliefs, but to change a whole pattern of thinking.

> 'We can only do this,' Dr Robinson argues, 'by recognising that most evangelism is really directed at our own fringe members—and that the hard core of the unchurched remains virtually untouched.'

Dr Robinson draws upon the experience of Willow Creek in Chicago, the fastest-growing Protestant church in North America, to show how it is possible to cross cultural barriers and reach out to those unconnected with the church. He develops specific applications from the Willow Creek model—such as its insight that unbelievers need anonymity, space and time as they adjust—and draws upon initiatives of a similar nature here in Britain to make concrete proposals for reaching the long-term unreached.

The Revd Dr Martin Robinson is the Bible Society's Consultant in Mission and Theology. He has personal experience of church planting in Birmingham. He is co-author with Stuart Christine of *Planting Tomorrow's Churches Today* (Monarch).

ISBN 1 85424 174 5   £7.99

Monarch
Publications

The Irrelevant Church

by Robin Gamble

How can the church discard its middle-class, religious corsetry, and establish itself as a vital and relevant force in working-class communities?

Robin Gamble's passionate indictment of the church in Britain pulls few punches. 'The churches are like a well-known chain store, with branches all over the country, that is sliding towards bankruptcy; either we change or we go bust.'

The Irrelevant Church has three parts. Part I looks at the recent social history of Britain, showing how the rich and powerful, often supported by the churches, have turned against the mass of working people. Part II examines the biblical approach to the poor: 'At the Incarnation Jesus "signed up" to play for the under-privileged. This is not surprising, for they had always been his Father's favourite team'. Part III shows what the churches can do today to redress the balance.

'An exciting challenge in which lie the seeds of hope and growth.'
—The Most Revd George Carey
Archbishop of Canterbury

The Revd Robin Gamble was born and brought up on a council estate in Bradford. He worked as a warehouseman before his conversion to Christ and a subsequent call to the Anglican ministry. He is now vicar of St Augustine's, Bradford.

ISBN 1 85424 163 X   £6.99

Monarch
Publications